The Role of Reading
in Nine Famous Lives

The Role of Reading in Nine Famous Lives

Donald E. Howard

McFarland & Company, Inc., Publishers
Jefferson, North Carolina, and London

LIBRARY OF CONGRESS CATALOGUING-IN-PUBLICATION DATA

Howard, Donald E., 1933–
The role of reading in nine famous lives / Donald E. Howard.
p.   cm.
Includes bibliographical references and index.

ISBN 0-7864-2133-9 (softcover : 50# alkaline paper)

1. Celebrities — Books and reading.   2. Books and reading — History.
3. Celebrities — Biography.
I. Title: Role of reading in 9 famous lives.   II. Title.
Z1039.C45H69   2005   028'.9 — dc22   2005003506

British Library cataloguing data are available

©2005 Donald E. Howard. All rights reserved

*No part of this book may be reproduced or transmitted in any form
or by any means, electronic or mechanical, including photocopying
or recording, or by any information storage and retrieval system,
without permission in writing from the publisher.*

Cover illustration ©2005 PicturesNow

Manufactured in the United States of America

*McFarland & Company, Inc., Publishers
Box 611, Jefferson, North Carolina 28640
www.mcfarlandpub.com*

For

Hannah, Emma, and Levi

With hope that reading will make their lives as exemplary as the individuals they will read about between the covers of this book.

Contents

Introduction 1

Benjamin Franklin 5

Thomas Jefferson 27

Abraham Lincoln 49

Frederick Douglass 71

Susan B. Anthony 91

Booker T. Washington 111

Pearl S. Buck 131

Louis L'Amour 151

Nelson Mandela 171

Bibliography and References 193

Index 197

Introduction

This is a book about the force and power of reading. Herein readers are offered a focused review of the impact of books and reading in the lives of nine famous readers I selected for their outstanding legacies of achievement and contributions to human freedoms and social development. While serving as an educator, with a focus on developmental reading at all levels of the educational spectrum, I came to wonder what the impact of reading could be in a human life. My reading and research led me to select the famous individuals who are profiled in this book as excellent examples of what the power of reading can produce. There are others that could have been included, but those written about here are the personalities that captured my interest and admiration. Their lives and their stories with books and reading deeply affected me. Each in his or her unique way dramatically demonstrated the power of reading in a human life.

Books can be a vital force in molding the lives of those who read. The subjects profiled in this book attest to that force. In the pages that follow you will read about men and women who used reading to develop their lives in such depth and power that they are recognized today as worthy examples of extraordinary human achievement. Awards, honors, and monuments have been bestowed and erected to mark each of them as a high achiever in his or her chosen career. While they each lived different lives in different regions of the world, they all have one thing in common: Each subject used books as a principal aid in the development of his or her exceptional talents. That principal aid, however, did not appear in the lives of these subjects by mere chance. That, too, was a unique event in human history.

As the previous millennium drew to a close, some people began to reflect on the changes that the one-thousand-year period from A.D. 1000 to 2000 had introduced into the world. The discussion often turned to which person had generated the greatest impact on the way we live today. To answer the question, the Arts and Entertainment television network conducted a survey of more than 360 journalists, scholars, and political leaders, asking them to vote for the person who each believed had done the most to shape the world during the millennium just ended. The A & E editorial board reviewed the results and compiled a final list. The person chosen as the one having the most profound impact on the shape of the world as it exists today was Johann Gutenberg (Mitchell and Baird, 1999).

Gutenberg was born in Mainz, Germany, around 1400. The exact year remains unclear. He died in Mainz on February 3, 1468. Our knowledge of Gutenberg is based on rather limited records that shed only skimpy details of his life and work. However, he is credited with an invention that revolutionized the world. That invention was the metal movable type printing press. The limited evidence that remains available suggests the invention occurred around 1449 to 1450 (Hanebutt-Benz, n.d.).

Before Gutenberg's invention, books were hand copied with some limited printing done with wooden letters and equipment that was very slow. The wooden equipment and materials were not durable and quickly wore out. The invention of the metal movable press made possible the printing of hundreds of books at a much more rapid rate than ever before. In addition to the press, Gutenberg invented a new oil-based ink that would adhere to metal so efficiently that it made metal type much more durable for printing. Gutenberg's printing inventions made possible the rapid spread of reading material to a far wider audience. His impact on the world has been so enormous that he was chosen by the A & E poll as the person of the millennium.

Based on the judgment of those polled, no other event influenced human life during the previous 1000 years as much as the invention of the printing press. Rapid printing began providing the opportunity for common people to possess a Bible and their own copies of books. Personal ownership of books permitted reading and drawing of one's own interpretations from the ideas and points of view written by others. Individual interpretations were made, and, collectively, they sparked religious revolutions across the Christian world. The press allowed knowledge and ideas to be passed from one person to another, from generation to generation, without having to rely solely on oral interpretation by those few who claimed to possess that skill to the exclusion of others. The printing boom that followed the Guttenberg invention paved the way for schools and the media industry that we know today.

The social, informational, and technological effects of the Gutenberg invention have shaped nearly every aspect of living today. The public wrested the control of literature from the closed circles of the educated, the wealthy, and the church and moved it to a far broader audience. A large reading public sprang up. Within three decades of Gutenberg's invention, mass printing spread across Europe, where it became one of the principal means by which knowledge was transmitted from one culture to another. In time the printed book became a means of spreading knowledge and new ideas about governments that led to political revolutions, especially during the eighteenth century.

By 1499 printing had become established in more than 250 cities across Europe (De La Mare, 1997). The technology to print books in greater volume produced a host of writers, such as Shakespeare, Bunyan, and Dryden, who are still widely read. In the seventeenth century a diverse range of books appeared, such as romance novels, plays produced for a reading audience, farming books, and, with the introduction and spread of the horse-drawn carriage, travel books became popular. While the percentage of the public that could read remained small in the centuries immediately following Guttenberg's invention, reading was spreading. In 1639 the first American press was set up. In 1724 Benjamin Franklin traveled to London to acquire more knowledge and up-to-date equipment to use in his own shop in the rapidly growing printing trade.

The spread of printing around the world spawned an interest in reading, and books created new business and economic activity. The growth of the railway network across the world created railway bookstalls where passengers could buy books to read while they traveled by train. Daily and weekly newspapers became commonplace across the urban and rural landscapes of the world.

Today, virtually no aspect of modern living is free of influence from Gutenberg's invention. But with all the change that printing generated, perhaps its greatest influence has been the freedom made possible for everyone to learn to read and have open access to the wealth of human knowledge stored in books around the world. That is the subject of this book.

My ambition is to impress on each reader the remarkable influence that wide reading can exert on human development. The exceptional range of riches and varieties of experience that can be discovered through reading is lived and relived in the lives of the subjects profiled in this book. After years of study and reflection on the power of reading, I believe that reading widely in the books and the literature of the world can enrich a person's life beyond any other single activity in which one can engage. Remove books from the lives of the subjects presented in this volume and each would have been a very different personality.

In this book you will read about famous people who lived life courageously, fruitfully and intelligently. You will see how books and reading molded their lives and helped them become the acclaimed individuals in history that are known to the world. As you read, you will see how each subject used books to build the knowledge and fortitude to face the world with courage and confidence. Each of our subjects was a unique individual with a unique background, unique obstacles to overcome along life's journey, and unique opportunities, largely created through individual initiative.

In each of the nine chapters that follow, one life is briefly sketched and described with a focus on the role of reading in that person's life. Attention is given to who each person was and what each one did. Included are their major achievements and the roads they traveled to achieve their goals. While their lives and careers differed significantly in many ways, they are all interesting and enriching lives for us to write and read about. The common thread in each of their stories is that books and reading were central to their lives. And each, in his or her way, contributed to expanding human freedoms and compassion and bestowed upon the world stage an honorable legacy.

The nine subjects presented will appear in the chronological order of their births, beginning with the first born. Their life stories dramatize the power of reading for all of us today, especially for young people, their parents, and their teachers. I believe that teaching and training our citizens to be good readers is probably the best guarantee of a free and secure future for all of us. For evidence, we need look no further than the life and work of the subjects presented here.

Benjamin Franklin

A Brief Biography

Benjamin Franklin was born in 1706 in Boston, Massachusetts, into a family of relatively poor shopkeepers and craftsmen. Through personal initiative, independence of mind, and devoted self-development, he became the prototype citizen for a young nation soon to fight for its independence from British rule. Phillips Russell, a Franklin biographer, called Benjamin "the first civilized American" (Russell, 1926). A. B. Tourtellot, another biographer, called him "the first genius born in the New World" (Tourtellot, 1977, p. xviii).

From birth to his death, Franklin created and lived a life of human achievement and public service that scores of men and women have long tried to model. Esteemed by kings and peasants alike, his fame spread virtually the world over. Wherever he lived, wherever he traveled, people used any means they could contrive to gain his counsel and his company. His friends and acquaintances numbered in the hundreds and encompassed people from all walks of life.

In a letter written to Franklin in 1789, about one year before he died, George Washington said, "If to be venerated for benevolence, if to be admired for talents, if to be esteemed for patriotism, if to be beloved for philanthropy, can gratify the human mind, you must have the pleasing consolation to know that you have not lived in vain" (Russell, 1926, p. 24). Franklin's achievements were many, and his name was honored far and wide. At the end of his life, he had traveled many roads and made many contributions to the world in which he had lived. However, he began life in very modest circumstances.

Benjamin was born the youngest son of eighteen children produced by his father and his successive two wives. Two daughters were born after Benjamin. As a young boy, he sat at the dinner table and listened to talk about current issues by his family along with invited neighbors and friends who were selected so as to provide interest in imaginative and useful topics. He grew up within easy walking distance of the busiest shipping harbor in the American colonies. Benjamin liked to walk along the Boston harbor surveying the ships and men that docked from all the major ports of the world. From early in life he harbored a yearning to go to sea. A thirst for travel and adventure grew even more appealing through a study of the world maps that covered the walls of his father's home office. Everything around him suggested a life at sea. In addition to the ships that docked at Boston, the harbor was a major shipbuilding site. An average of thirty-three new ships per year were launched not far from young Benjamin's home (Tourtellot, 1977).

At the age of ten young Franklin began assisting his father in the family's tallow-chandlery business. He worked there for two years before his father decided that Benjamin should learn the printing trade. The father apprenticed Benjamin to the boy's older brother, James, who operated his own printing shop. The two brothers did not get on very well together, but Benjamin stuck it out while waiting for the day he could go into the world on his own. After five years in his brother's shop, at the age of seventeen, Benjamin left Boston to look for work in New York City.

Upon reaching New York Franklin began walking the streets looking for work. After a fruitless search, he learned from a printer he met that work in the printing trade could be found in Philadelphia. Traveling alone, Benjamin made his way to the city that had been suggested. Upon reaching Philadelphia he soon found work in Keimer's Print Shop. The apprentice from Boston worked hard for Keimer, gained a good reputation as a craftsman, and met many influential people in the course of his work. Being a sociable person, he made friends easily in the city he had chosen to be his new home.

One day in Philadelphia, Franklin met the governor of Pennsylvania. As the young printer and government leader got to know each other, the governor took an interest in young Franklin's potential as a future businessman. He offered to set Benjamin up in the printing trade and suggested that Franklin go to London and purchase the equipment that would be needed to get started. Benjamin accepted the offer and set out for London. Upon arriving there, he learned that the governor had not sent the money promised for the purchase of equipment. Benjamin sadly discovered that the governor could not be trusted.

Nearly out of money in a strange city, Franklin looked for work. He eventually found a job with Palmer's Printing House, where he worked for nearly a year. Later he changed employment by moving to a much larger printing house, named Watt's, where he worked until he left London to return to Philadelphia.

While in London Franklin made many friends and traveled widely. The opportunity to work in London's printing industry gave him firsthand knowledge and experience with the most innovative and up-to-date equipment available at the time.

In 1726 Franklin returned to his home in Philadelphia and found work in the printing trade in the shop of a friend. When his friend became gravely ill and passed away, Benjamin found work with his previous employer at Keimer's Print Shop. Keimer soon recognized that his employee had acquired some important skills while in London and soon put Benjamin in charge of the print shop while Keimer focused his time on other businesses he had created. Under Franklin's management, the shop increased both its volume and quality of work. He hired and trained additional employees required in the rapidly expanding volume of trade. In a relatively brief time, Keimer grew envious of Franklin's success and growing influence and began to treat the shop manager with an authoritarian attitude. Benjamin decided he could run a business of his own and left Keimer.

At the age of twenty-two Franklin and a young man he had trained in the printing craft opened their own print shop as equal partners. With the experience Franklin had gained in the printing craft, with his thorough knowledge of the colonies and his contacts in London, he had become a man of influence in Philadelphia's business community. Within a short time the Franklin and Meredith shop became a powerful competitor to Keimer. Much of the work Franklin had been doing at the Keimer shop for government agencies and private firms followed him to his own shop. As his reputation for creative and quality work grew, his business expanded dramatically.

Having become successful in business, Franklin next wanted a wife and family. On September 1, 1730, he took as his wife Deborah Read, a girl he had courted before he went to England. She had married while he was away, but her husband had disappeared by the time Franklin returned to America. By his own account, Deborah proved to be a good and faithful partner who assisted him in attending his business (Franklin, 1793). Successful both in life and in business, the couple eventually became mildly wealthy.

In 1730 or early 1731, the date is unclear, Franklin became the father of an infant son that he named William. The circumstances surrounding the birth of William are unclear and mysterious. The mother of the infant boy was never publicly identified. Some have speculated that she was a servant girl who worked in the Franklin home. Others believed the mother may have been Deborah Read, since the child was born at or near the time she took the name of Franklin (Van Doren, 1938). Regardless of the mother's identity, Benjamin took the boy into his home and reared him as his son to adulthood. Deborah and Benjamin produced two children after William; one, a boy born on October 20, 1732, died at the age of four; a girl named Sarah, born on August 31, 1743, survived her father by several years.

Married and settled into a satisfactory domestic life, Benjamin expanded his business world into that of a major entrepreneur. In time he created print shop partnerships with people in other regions of the colonies. Business ventures into general merchandising, newspaper and almanac publications, and printing for the government were added to his already successful print shop operation.

By the age of forty, Franklin had become a wealthy man for his time and place. He gradually began to divest himself of business obligations and assumed many of the trappings of a man of leisure. Other interests began to occupy his time and energy. Perhaps foretelling the course his future would take, Benjamin began a study of foreign languages, learning French, Spanish, and Italian. At the same time he became deeply involved in the political affairs of his colony. From that time until the end of his life, he became a devoted public servant in service to his colony and his country. During the arduous process of the Revolutionary War for independence from England, he played a huge role in the creation of a new nation that would unite all the American colonies under one constitutional government.

Reading in Early Life

Benjamin Franklin was born into a mentally stimulating environment. He had the good fortune to grow up in an age of intellectual questioning and discovery into the principles that characterize human existence (Russell, 1926). In addition, his father, Josiah Franklin, came to America from England in 1683, bringing with him a tradition of learning and of purposeful work. That tradition was passed on to his children. Speaking of his father, Benjamin once wrote, "He turned our attention to what was good, just and prudent in the conduct of life" (Franklin, 1793, ch. 1, p. 6). The father took time to teach and create curiosity and interest in his son Benjamin. On walks around Boston the son was tutored on how to observe and learn from the activity of the environment: how joiners, bricklayers, turners, and other artisans performed their work.

There were many artisans to observe in the Boston of young Franklin's day. As early as 1650 a chronicler of the trades in New England had identified as many as thirty in which men earned their livelihoods (Tourtellot, 1977, p. 201). The walks with his father stimulated young Benjamin's interest in learning about hand tools and how to use them to make useful appliances and objects. Early in life he learned to use his intellect to creative purpose. An early example is his discovery that he could use the power of the wind blowing against his kite to draw himself across a pond of water.

The Franklin family practiced a tradition of reading and association with books. Young Benjamin inherited that tradition, and during the course of his life he advanced it far beyond the reading depth of his ancestors. Benjamin once wrote that he could not remember when he could not read (Franklin, 1793). From as far back as he could recall he had been an avid reader, hungry for knowledge. His early reading was done principally in religious books from his father's small library. His father expected his son to train for the ministry; therefore, religious reading was encouraged. But the young reader soon grew tired of religious material and began to look for books that offered a greater variety in subject matter. Years later he wrote that he wished he had been able to gain access to more substantive books in his youth (Franklin 1793).

While still quite young, Benjamin began to build his own personal library. He later wrote, "From a child I was fond of reading, and all the little money that came into my hands was ever laid out in books" (Franklin, 1793, ch. 1, p. 7). The first book purchased was John Bunyan's *Pilgrim's Progress*. "Pleased with *Pilgrim's Progress*, my first collection was of John Bunyan's works in separate little volumes" (Franklin, 1793, ch. 1, p. 7). In that book Benjamin met the idea of progress, the notion that people could progress in life, could move beyond the point and station of their birth. The idea must have taken root with the young Bostonian, for his life represents growth and progress as much or more than any other person that might be named.

After reading all the Bunyan books he could purchase, Franklin sold those to buy Burton's Historical Collections of chapman's books, forty to fifty in number, that were cheaply priced. The chapman's books opened to the young reader an expansive view of the English-speaking world that was new to his experience. That view extended his vision of life far beyond the shores of Boston and the puritanical atmosphere that so enveloped the environment of his boyhood. Soon afterward came Plutarch's *Lives*. In Plutarch Franklin learned about great achievements by real people in the societies of the distant past. What he gleaned from reading became models from which he could shape his own destiny, for he truly became a self-taught man. Years later he wrote that the time he spent reading those works resulted in time "spent to great advantage" (Franklin, 1793, ch. 1, p. 7).

One life that made a profound impression on young Franklin was that of Pericles of Greece. As he read through that famous life of ancient days, Benjamin discovered an ideal model unfolding as he read through the daily work and achievements of the man. A life lived as Pericles had lived demonstrated to him "that every man, if he chooses, has a natural power to turn himself upon all occasions, and to change and shift with the greatest ease to what he himself shall judge desirable" (Tourtellot, 1977, p. 181). As Benjamin grew toward manhood, he began to make definitive choices regarding the person he wanted to become and the life he wanted to live.

Living near the sea gave Franklin easy exposure to water. He learned early to enjoy water activities and he became an excellent swimmer. The frequent excursions into water, in which he delighted, developed his arm and shoulder muscles to the point that he eventually grew into a physically strong man. To enhance his swimming skills, he found and read a book by Thevenot titled *The Art of Swimming*. The book introduced Benjamin to water acrobatics, many of which he learned to perform for his friends. Later, when he traveled to London for the first time, his swimming stamina and acrobatics made a deep impression on new friends he made while there. Swimming was just one of so many endeavors in which Franklin used reading to enhance his performance.

A book that was to have a profound impact on Franklin's life was Daniel Defoe's *Essays upon Several Projects*. Writing about London, Defoe proposed that the best way for people to serve God and excel in life was through equitable and decent behavior in social interactions with others through useful projects. As he read the book, Benjamin could see the application of many of Defoe's ideas to the community of Boston. The book opened his mind to a world of projects for improving everyday living. There were ideas on creating banks and banking, insurance, mutual aid programs that promoted joint self-help activities, and academies to train and develop the talents of both men and women. Many of the ideas Benjamin gleaned from that book he would later help to implement in America over the course of his long life.

A book that further sharpened Franklin's focus for his own life was *Essays upon the Good That Is to Be Devised and Designed by Those Who Desire to Answer the Great End of Life, and to Do Good While They Live* authored by Cotton Mather. Burdened with an obviously lengthy title, the book ultimately came to be titled *Essays to Do Good*. In the book Franklin read how the wisdom of even a poor man could initiate an idea that might save a city or even serve a nation. Perhaps seeing himself in that role, Benjamin would later serve his community and nation admirably well. Virtually all that he did in life was somehow directed to doing good to others. Late in his life, in a letter to Mather's son, Franklin wrote that the essays, ones he had read while still a boy, had given him such a "turn of thinking as to have an influence on my conduct through life" (Russell, 1926, p. 15).

Not many years after reading Mather's book, Franklin read John Locke's essay titled *Upon the Human Understanding* and *The Art of Thinking* by Messieurs of the Port Royal, a group of French writers and teachers. Those volumes appealed to Benjamin's sense of independent thinking, a trait that had already begun to emerge in his personality. Two essays by Shaftesbury, *Inquiry Concerning Virtue* and *Essay on the Freedom of Wit and Humor*, were writings that also moved Franklin's increasingly independent thinking further away from the religious books and doctrines that were so pervasive in his home and community. To enhance his language development, he also read *Essays Toward a Practical English Grammar, Describing the Genius and Nature of the English Tongue* by James Greenwood. With each book and essay Benjamin read, we are able to follow his interest as it grew and expanded. We can easily see that he had put himself on a mission to use reading to mold himself into the man that he wanted to become.

When Franklin attended the writing and arithmetic school in Boston while still a young boy, he performed poorly in arithmetic because he did not like the subject. Later, when he was an apprentice in his brother's print shop, he realized that to do well in life, especially in business and financial affairs, he would need to acquire numerical skills. Having already failed the subject under the instruction of a teacher, he decided to learn it on his own. To aid in his self-education in arithmetic, he read Cocker's *Book of Arithmetick*. That book in turn helped him to understand books on navigation that he then read. Among the selections included were *An Epitome of the Art of Navigation* by John Sellers and *The Mariner's Magazine* by Samuel Sturmy.

At the age of twelve, Benjamin became an apprentice in his brother's print shop. Three years later the brother began publishing a newspaper, the *New England Courant*. From the start, the paper attracted a good audience of readers. As an assistant in the print shop, Benjamin had the privilege of reading and absorbing the ideas and knowledge submitted by others to be printed in the paper. In time he decided he wanted to write some articles himself but felt that his brother would not print what he submitted. He, therefore, began writing essays for publication under the pseudonym "Silence Dogood." The essays were left under the door of the print shop at night, thereby concealing the identity of the real author.

The first article submitted by Silence Dogood appeared in 1722 and immediately attracted much interest from its readers (Franklin, 1793, ch. 2, p. 1–2). Ever alert to see what attention his first article would attract, Benjamin overheard his brother and other contributors discussing the article that Silence Dogood had authored. The discussion praised the article and centered on who the true author might be. As Benjamin secretly listened in on the discussion, he was pleased to hear the names of several men of good character and learning in the community suggested as the likely author. That positive reception of his first product brought the young author much joy and confidence in his writing skills.

In several Silence Dogood articles that were published in his brother's newspaper, Benjamin focused primarily on projects and issues that he believed would improve the lives of common people. For example, he called for programs to help indigent widows, of which there were many in the Boston of that day. In many ways, Benjamin used his articles to fulfill a vow he had made at an early age, namely to "do good to others" (Franklin, 1793). At the young age of sixteen, he had found an excellent medium through which he would work toward that goal.

Franklin's appetite for reading and intellectual discussion with his friends and acquaintances continued to grow with time. To further his development while working as a printer's apprentice, he read as many books as he could find available. One volume was *Logic: Or the Art of Thinking* by Antoine Arnauld and Pierre Nickole, two French lay theologians. By the time he read that book, his views on religion were well established, but he sought to improve his skill in expressing and defending his views. Another volume read was Xenophon's *Memorable Things of Socrates*, in which he found that the Socratic method of debate greatly increased his ability to influence the course of a discussion without the argumentative style that was so widely practiced. He relied on that method for the remainder of his distinguished career, as it won for him enormous respect among his colleagues both in America and abroad. Among the thousands of notable figures in world literature about whom he read, Socrates became one of his heroes (Russell, 1926).

A book that made an enormous impact on young Benjamin was a multiple-volume publication in London by Addison and Steele titled *The Spectator*. Totally by chance, he came across the third volume of the series and found himself thoroughly delighted with what he read, so much so that he read it many times. The writing he judged to be among the best he had read, and he wished that he could some day write as well. The authors used a graceful writing style and an excellent vocabulary. But even more appealing was the content. Benjamin read about people who were free to go about their daily lives without the restraints of religious dogma, confusing moral dilemmas, or the oppressive human gossip by so many against others, a common practice in the Puritan Boston of his youth.

The eighty-one essays in *The Spectator* treated subjects of universal interest such as moral virtue, jealousy, ambition, laughter, seduction, and flattery. Franklin's vision of such a world would be one in which he could live very happily. So carried away was he with what he read that, when money and opportunity permitted, he bought all the volumes of the series.

One of Benjamin's duties at the print shop was to call on bookshops and book agents. He discovered that he could borrow books he had never read from their shelves and stock rooms so long as he returned them promptly and clean. When his honesty and trustworthiness had been firmly established, many books were borrowed and read. His best time for reading so many books was at night, before and after daily work, and on Sunday, when he could manage to skip going to church. Skipping church he accomplished by pretending he had work that must be completed at the shop, but what he actually did was to hide out where he could read all day without bother from anyone.

Forever creative in finding ways to secure books to feed his reading passion, Benjamin came up with a most original scheme for acquiring money with which to buy books. As an apprentice to his brother, the shop owner was responsible for furnishing meals for Benjamin. The brother did not want to cook, so he arranged with a boarding house to prepare meals for both. Among the many books read during this time, Benjamin came across one titled *The Way to Health, Long Life and Happiness, or a Discourse of Temperance* by Thomas Tryon, a book that essentially promoted vegetarianism.

For a short time after reading the book, Benjamin was drawn to the practice of eating no meat and cooked up a scheme where he could use vegetarianism to realize a little money. He offered a deal to his brother stipulating that, if the brother would give him just half the money that he paid for Benjamin's meals, Benjamin would furnish his own meals. That was an offer the brother couldn't refuse. Benjamin received his money, ate raisins, sandwiches, along with other meatless and cheaper foods, and used the money he saved to buy books. While other shop workers were out for lunch, Benjamin ate what he had brought to the shop and spent the lunch hour reading. In time, he grew tired of eating nothing but fruits and vegetables and returned to a more balanced diet.

At the print shop Benjamin often made friends that would open access to books he had not previously read. Matthew Adams was a contributor to the James Franklin newspaper and called often at the shop. Benjamin developed a friendship with the contributor, who returned his friendship by loaning the young apprentice books from his personal library. In addition to that source, Benjamin developed friendships with many of the apprentices who worked in bookshops in and around Boston. His new friends would smuggle books out at night after the shops closed and let him keep them for the night, to be returned before the shops opened the next morning. In order to get borrowed books back on time, he often sat up reading the greater part of the night (Tourtellot, 1977).

In addition to books acquired through friendships, Benjamin had access to all the books printed and those offered for sale in his brother's shop. At one point, the shop listed thirty-eight works that included a broad range of subjects. Among those listed were titles that ranged from a twenty-book history of the ancient Jewish people to imports from London such as *The Ladies Pacquet* and *The Ladies Calling* (Tourtellot, 1977).

Two years after starting the *New England Courant*, James Franklin found himself in trouble with the Puritan-minded leaders of the community. Some of the articles he had published offended their ideals and beliefs. The issue finally reached such an emotional high that James was banned from further publications by the governing body of the town. He was forced to turn control, but not the ownership of the paper, over to Benjamin, who, at the age of seventeen, became the publisher of a newspaper. The first edition to appear under Benjamin's name was dated February 11, 1723 (Tourtellot, 1977).

Upon becoming the official publisher, Franklin turned his inventive mind and imagination to the task of producing a successful and progressive paper. From his pen came interesting stories and human intrigues that led readers to purchase his paper in greater numbers. Brother James had difficulty accepting Benjamin's success. The more James saw, the more envious he grew. James began to intervene in the publication of the paper. He tried to tell Benjamin what to do and how to do it. When the younger Franklin refused to bow to his brother's demands, the older attempted to physically bring the younger in line. Finally, James was allowed by officials to resume publication under his name. The disputes between the brothers continued, however. Finally, Benjamin had enough and quit the paper. In need of money to get started in a career on his own, he sold enough of his book collection to buy a ship's passage to New York with hope that he could find work in the printer's trade there. However, he would have to travel to Philadelphia before he could find work.

On the trip from Boston to Philadelphia, Benjamin traveled most of the way by boat. After thirty hours on water without food or anything to drink except a bottle of filthy rum, the voyage ended in a storm near Philadelphia. In the evening he became very feverish and went to bed. Having read somewhere that drinking lots of cold water was good for a fever, he consumed much water that evening. During the night his body perspired profusely. But there was good news the next morning. His fever was gone. Reading had been instrumental in helping him to combat a pesky fever.

In Philadelphia, Franklin found work in Keimer's Print Shop. When he had free time, he continued to read widely and sought others who also enjoyed books. Friendships were developed with three young men near his age. They all enjoyed books. A favorite recreation for the group of four was to stroll through the woods on Sunday and read aloud to each other from favorite books, discuss their meanings, and talk about their personal ambitions in life. The weekly schedule at the print shop also accommodated Benjamin's reading passion. The owner did not open on Saturday and Sunday, thus, as Benjamin later wrote, "I had two days for reading" (Franklin, 1793, ch. 6, p. 3).

In 1724 Franklin returned to Boston for a visit and to collect some books and personal items he had left behind. On his way back to Philadelphia, the governor of New York heard about Franklin and his books from the captain of the sloop on which he traveled. The governor sent word for Benjamin to come for a visit. When the two met, the governor showed the visitor his large library. They then spent some time talking about books and favorite authors they both enjoyed.

Back in Philadelphia, the governor of Pennsylvania took an interest in young Franklin's potential as a businessman in the printing trade. He offered to financially sponsor Benjamin in a business if he would go to London to purchase the necessary printing equipment. Benjamin agreed and soon set sail across the Atlantic. Upon arriving in London, he learned that the governor had no credit line there, and no money arrived to cover the purchases. The governor's promise had been nothing more than a cruel hoax played on an unsuspecting young man. Much too late, Benjamin learned from people who knew the governor that he was never to be trusted.

In a strange city and nearly broke, Franklin began looking for work. After finding employment in a print ship, he moved into a flat next to a bookshop in a section called Little Britain. Benjamin and the shop owner, Mr. Wilcox, soon became friends. In order to feed his still ravenous appetite for reading, Benjamin made an arrangement with Wilcox that permitted him to borrow any book he wanted to read and return it when finished. The arrangement delighted the avid reader from America, and that opportunity remained a fond memory for years afterward. In his autobiography he recalled that he spent about eighteen months in London, where he worked hard at the printing craft, enjoyed some plays and, he wrote, "I had read considerably" (Franklin 1793, ch. 5, p. 8).

On the return voyage, Franklin rose early each morning and read for an hour or two before joining his shipmates for talk and social activities, mostly games. On board Benjamin kept a diary in which he recorded stories and observations that attracted his interest. One story he noted was about a practice he learned about while in England. There existed a dungeon into which the queen's soldiers were often thrown for the most trifling offences. In his reading of history, Benjamin had learned that the great military leaders, Alexander and Caesar, had received more faithful service from their soldiers by winning their love and respect. The story established for Benjamin an important principle for the conduct of his life. He vowed to be loved and respected by his fellow man.

Franklin's diary also included entries on natural observations and scientific investigations in which he invested a considerable amount of time. One investigation involved the capture of an infant crab that was kept in a glass tube to study its protective shell, comparing its likenesses and differences to that of silkworms and butterflies. Benjamin studied and recorded observations of ocean currents and temperatures while crossing the Atlantic. By the time he was again on American soil, his diary bore a host of interesting entries.

One important diary entry set forth guidelines by which he would strive to conduct his life from that time forward: "To endeavor to speak the truth in every instance, to give nobody expectations that are not likely to be answered, but aim at sincerity in every word and action; the most amiable excellence in a rational being" (Van Doren, 1938, p. 69). In effect, the Boston native was still evolving his design to "do good to others."

READING DURING ENTREPRENEURIAL LIFE

When Franklin was once again settled in America, he devoted himself to an agreeable family life and success in his own business. For the next twenty years, he and his wife worked together to build a successful print, publishing, and general retail business. While his hectic business required much of his time, he did not completely remove himself from reading. The search for a comfortable spiritualism continued to be an interest, a point of view that he could live with in harmony. Scores of books and materials that included pamphlets and essays were read and studied. The materials covered a variety of cultural views on the nature of religion in the human experience. Among many sources read were Ray's *Wisdom of God in the Creation*, Blackmore's *Creation*, and Cambray's *Demonstration on the Being of a God*.

At the age of twenty-three Franklin became the publisher of his own newspaper. The name *Philadelphia Gazette* was chosen, and the first edition was published on October 2, 1729 (Van Doren, 1938). In 1732 he launched the publication of his famous *Poor Richard's Almanac* under the fictional name of "Richard Saunders." The almanac was designed to instruct the average citizen who generally did not engage in educational or leisure reading. Benjamin hoped the publication would lift the common citizen with knowledge and guidance useful in everyday issues and decisions. An extra effort was made to produce a booklet with funny stories, sayings, and proverbs that would be entertaining and enjoyable to its readers. Benjamin wanted to get people to read. He believed that those who did little reading were mentally limp and inept, suggesting one of the almanac's proverbs: "An empty bag cannot stand upright" (Van Doren, 1938, p. 112). The almanac proved to be so successful that its publisher and author reaped a large economic return on the venture.

Franklin's passion for reading could, at times, create inner conflict in his daily life. After becoming sole owner of his newspaper, he determined to be a man of industry and respect. Conscious of the degree to which public confidence in a publisher and editor is important to the success of a newspaper, Franklin worked hard and practiced those daily human habits of conduct that win esteem from others. Most of the leisure activities he had enjoyed while growing up were cast aside. No activity that could be judged by others as wasted time or exercise of poor judgment would he be guilty of indulging. However, the one passion he found impossible to drop was reading.

Many people at that time could not read, and many of those that did read looked upon the newspaper as the only reading that merited one's time. Additional time spent with books was thought to be a sign of laziness and poor application of useful time. In trying to earn the highest respect for his industry among the citizens of Philadelphia, Benjamin tried to accept that mindset for himself. But he often failed. He tried to avoid all diversions that others considered to be useless except for an occasional book that "sometimes debauched me from my work" (Franklin, 1793, ch. 7, p. 7). Books had always been an important part of his life and, as Van Doren wrote, "There were always books in his inner life, books in his business, books in his friendships" (Van Doren, 1938, p. 104).

To further enrich his intellectual interest and desire to "do good to others," Franklin created a group that he called the "Junto Club." The club was comprised of a group of young men that met on Friday evenings to discuss issues of morals, politics, or natural philosophy. In addition, once each three months, each member would write and read to the group an original essay he had written on a topic of his own choosing. The club proved to be an overwhelming success and lasted for almost forty years. During its existence, the Junto Club educated its members, taught them tolerance, and significantly raised their level of conversation. It achieved what Franklin had worked so hard to become himself. It made of them civilized men.

During the next several years Franklin expanded his business world into that of a major entrepreneur. He created print shop partnerships with people in other regions of the colonies. After a period of successful operation, the partner would be allowed to buy Benjamin out and become sole owner. That arrangement proved to be highly profitable for Benjamin and the partners. Franklin would then invest his money into assets that produced financial security for himself and his family, principally in land. By the time Franklin had reached his early forties, he had become sufficiently wealthy to withdraw from the business world and pursue his interest in inventing and public service.

READING IN POLITICAL LIFE

With more time to devote to the welfare of his colony, Franklin grew increasingly active in public affairs in Pennsylvania. He was elected to his first political office, that of clerk of the Pennsylvania General Assembly. A member of the assembly had vigorously opposed his appointment to that office. Drawing on his early code for conducting his life, wherein he would "do good to others" and make them like him, Franklin devised a plan to win the assembly member over.

Franklin learned that the man owned a certain rare book that he was proud to possess. Benjamin wrote to the member with a gracious note requesting the privilege of borrowing the book for reading. The man replied and sent the book promptly. Within a week Benjamin returned the book with a note profusely thanking the owner for such a kind gesture on his part. The assemblyman then sought Benjamin out and spoke to him, a thing he had never done before. The two became great friends and remained so until death cast them apart. That experience taught Franklin an important lesson for conduct in human affairs: "He that has once done you a kindness will be more ready to do you another, than he whom you yourself have obliged" (Franklin, 1793, ch. 9, p. 7). In that small maneuver, Franklin displayed an art of politics that he would use to great advantage in serving his people through the colonial revolution and its aftermath.

As Franklin's prestige in public service grew, he found many projects to present to the people of Philadelphia. He was instrumental in creating the first municipal police force that was paid for through a form of local taxation. He initiated the formation of the first volunteer fire department. In 1743 he drew up a proposal to launch an academy for educating the youth of the city. After much work the academy was finally opened in 1751 with Franklin as its president. The academy later became the University of Pennsylvania.

In 1744 Franklin initiated the formation of the American Philosophical Society and also became Pennsylvania's deputy postmaster-general. In forming the Philosophical Society, Benjamin wanted to bring together men of intelligence and creativity, original thinkers who could pool their knowledge for the good of everyone. He was interested in promoting new ideas and discoveries in chemistry or new methods in improving the breed of animals, any ideas that appeared to be helpful in raising the level of living for all people. In most of the projects that he initiated, Franklin did not want the credit to accrue to him personally. His interest was in initiating ideas with others. When enough interest had been generated that a person or a group would begin implementation, Benjamin would back away and let others take the lead and the credit.

With his newly found leisure, Franklin found much time to read and study subjects in which his curious mind craved more learning. His reading often led him to initiate new projects and experiments that could lift the level of living for all. A book titled *Boyle's Lectures* was a compilation of a hodgepodge of topics, some on simple experiments in the natural environment and with common household phenomena. Those ideas often generated new ideas in Benjamin. Such an idea came to him one day as he sat in front of his fireplace. The result was the creation of the Franklin wood-burning stove.

Franklin constructed his new stove from cast iron. In contrast to a standard fireplace, the stove was placed away from the fireplace recess with a flue extending into the chimney. That placement allowed the heat produced to circulate within the room rather than escape up the chimney. The new concept conserved far more heat from a wood fire than the conventional fireplaces that were in common usage in most colonial homes. Benjamin was offered a patent for his stove design but rejected it in the belief that "we enjoy great advantages from the inventions of others" and, therefore, we should be happy when we can serve others by the invention of a useful device (Franklin, 1793, ch. 10, p. 10). The stove became a big success and is still copied in different designs even today.

The inventions for which Franklin is best known include clocks, the wood stove, lightening rods, some astronomical instruments, eyeglasses, a chair that could be converted into a ladder, a clothes-pressing machine, laboratory equipment, and a musical instrument called an "armonica." For the most part, he never applied for a patent for his inventions. His utmost desire was that others have free use of any idea for which he was responsible if that idea could improve life for others. That was all a part of his ongoing plan to "do good to others." Other inventors often adopted his ideas, altered them slightly, and secured their own patents. But he did not mind. So long as people were benefiting in some way from his work, he was happy.

For a time Franklin's interest was focused on learning more about electricity. His utmost desire was to find a way to make electrical charges useful to humanity. During the six-year period from 1746 to 1752, he made scientific discoveries in electricity that lead to many useful applications (Van Doren, 1938). However, his experiments did not always work as he had anticipated. On at least two occasions, he was knocked stone cold by powerful electrical charges. Perhaps his most famous experiment was that with the kite. By flying a silk kite into an electrical storm, he proved that the lightning produced by a thunderstorm held the same characteristics as electricity. He then proved that iron rods could be erected so as to protect buildings from the hazards of the electrical charges from the sky. These discoveries were written up by Benjamin and were widely reported. His name became famous in America and Europe, and his writings were translated into French, German, and Italian.

Unable to let a need go unmet, Franklin designed streetlights that were installed in Philadelphia. His continuing search for ways to make life better led him to conduct experiments in farming that resulted in improved crop production. In all the improvements to daily life that he helped to introduce, he felt that he was achieving the rule for living that he had adopted early in his life, namely, that he would work hard to "do good to others." His sense of "good to people" was not viewed as one or two big creations that gained great attention and publicity but, rather, lay in the "little advantages that occur every day" (Franklin, 1793, ch. 11, p. 9).

Franklin performed scores of good deeds in Philadelphia. His name garnered respect near and far. His life became so identified with "doing good to others" that any proposal for public works that he had not publicly endorsed accrued little support. Such was the case with the first hospital to be created in Philadelphia. Dr. Thomas Bond had tried to get support to establish a hospital for the care of a large number of citizens that were in need of professional treatment. When he approached people for support for the idea he was usually asked if he had consulted Benjamin Franklin. They wanted to know what Franklin thought. When Dr. Bond responded that he had not discussed the idea with Franklin, little interest was shown.

Dr. Bond decided that he would have to consult with Franklin about his idea for a hospital. In discussing the idea he conveyed to Benjamin that he was finding it virtually impossible to carry through a public project without his endorsement. Franklin not only endorsed the idea, but he helped in the design and solicitation of support from many others by promoting the project. In his autobiography, Franklin dismissed all the credit that had accrued to him for the creation of the hospital, simply noting that the credit belonged to Dr. Bond (Franklin, 1793).

In 1764 Franklin returned for the third time to London. While there he read *Elements of Criticism* by Lord Kames. After completing the book, Benjamin stated that he wished the author had "examined more fully the subject of music," a subject that Franklin enjoyed and on which he offered some original ideas (Van Doren, 1938, p. 325). Books were still an integral part of Benjamin's life while he lived in London. When he moved into another home, he wrote to his son telling him of his move. In addition, he noted that much time had been required in sorting his papers and placing his books in proper order after the move. He was, he wrote, amazed at the number of books he had accumulated in London, in view of the fact that he had brought none with him from America (Van Doren, 1938, p. 412). But, he had collected many books since leaving America, not just in England but in Germany, Holland, and France, books he believed would be useful to America upon his return.

In 1776 Franklin was selected by the Continental Congress to represent the colonies in France in a quest to bring French support to the side of the colonies in their war with England. At the age of seventy-two, he left his home and sailed to Paris. While there his work with the French government on behalf of the colonies was crucial to the victory of the colonies over the British. Among the many services he performed for his government, he was instrumental in negotiating badly needed money and loans that ultimately totaled 26 million francs (Russell, 1926).

Franklin's name was already well known to the French people upon his arrival in Paris. The reputation he had built as a scientist, inventor, publisher, humanitarian, and public servant had already endeared him to the French people. Nothing he did while there diminished his appeal. French people so adored the distinguished citizen from the colonies that pictures and busts of his head and shoulders were visible throughout the nation. His image became so prolific that he wrote to his daughter suggesting the French had made so many portraits and medallions of her father's face that his image was as well known there "as that of the moon…. Some [images] to be set in the lids of snuffboxes and some so small as to be worn in rings, and the numbers sold are incredible" (Van Doren, 1938, p. 571).

In 1785, Franklin turned his work in France over to Thomas Jefferson and returned to his home in Philadelphia. He had been in that country for about nine years and had reached the age of seventy-eight. While there, he had won French support for the war against British rule and had been a chief negotiator for a peace treaty with England that gave the colonies unconditional freedom. The workload had been heavy, and he longed for some free time to indulge his interest in science and more time for reading.

Franklin remained a lover of books throughout his long life. In a 1750 letter to his mother he related how he spent his leisure time, now that he was free of managing his several businesses. Among the hobbies and interest he enjoyed, he wrote that, "I read a great deal" (Van Doren, 1938, p. 198). Always an avid reader, he lost no opportunity to encourage others to read and learn. One such occasion occurred in 1778 when a new town in Massachusetts adopted the name Franklin. The town leaders wrote Benjamin a letter asking if he would be willing to contribute a bell to his new namesake. He responded to the request, but instead of a bell, he contributed books for a library to be used by all the citizens for the uplifting of their social discourse. He wrote, "Sense being preferable to sound" (Van Doren, 1938, p. 741), books would serve the people better than a bell.

In 1788, two years before his death, a member of the French National Assembly visited Franklin at his home in Philadelphia. The Frenchman later told about that visit by writing, in part, "I have just been to see him and enjoyed his conversation in the midst of his books, which he still calls his best friends" (Russell, 1926, p. 316). Books were central and dominant in his home. Franklin's library has been described as "a very large chamber and high-studded. The walls are covered with bookshelves filled with books; besides there are four large alcoves, extending two-thirds of the length of the chamber, filled in the same manner ... the largest and by far the best private library in America" (Van Doren, 1938, p. 750).

In his final days, when pain did not wrack his body, Franklin spent his time in conversation with friends, in writing, and with his books. He often enjoyed sitting in his tub during long hot baths with a book propped on a vamp over the lower half of the tub, while he sat and read. When he was too weak or ill to read for himself, a friend read to him. One of the books read was Johnson's *Lives of the Poets*. One selection from the volume was the life of Watts, a favorite author of Franklin (Russell, 1926, p. 319). After the reading, he recited several of Watts' poems and talked about the meaning and beauty of the verse that came through to him. To the very end, books and reading remained Benjamin's great passion.

THE IMPACT OF READING

Without books and good reading skills, Benjamin Franklin might well have followed in the footsteps of his father in the tallow shop. The young boy was not particularly attracted to formal schooling but was strongly attracted to learning. He might have spent his life engaged in one of the many trades that were active in his community, or he could have followed an early interest to go to sea, as did an older brother. That was not a good option, however, in that the brother was lost at sea, and the father was dead set against another taking such a risk with his life. But all of that is mere speculation. Benjamin did learn to read and used that skill to make of himself one of the most important figures in American history.

The hundreds of books that Franklin read during his boyhood extended his intellectual reach well beyond the provincial world of his Boston home and community. Early in life he recognized that the world was big and highly interesting to a curious mind. Out there were people who explored new ideas and places that he was drawn to learn more about. Through reading he discovered the lives of great and superior men, men who possessed elegance, wit, poise, and sensitivity.

Plutarch's *Parallel Lives of the Noble Greeks and Romans* comprised a collection of forty-six biographies that introduced Franklin to many great men that lived well before the recorded history of England began. From those lives he was able to select the traits and characteristics he judged to be most noble and worth emulating. Benjamin made many of those traits a part of his own personality.

Franklin grew up in a home that was deeply steeped in religious belief and practice. Although his father accepted certain nonreligious activities, like work and social intercourse with the people in his community as a necessary part of daily living, his life was regulated by religious observance. As an attentive father, he tried to convey his beliefs to his children. But by the age of fifteen, Benjamin had learned enough through reading that he could not accept the same doctrines subscribed to by his father. Reading led him to a different point of view. As he read and listened to various points of religion debated and questioned, he found himself questioning also. As he later wrote, "I began to doubt of Revelation itself" (Franklin, 1793, ch. 6, p. 5). Benjamin did believe in a God and subscribed to certain prayers and religious observance throughout his life, but not the Puritan doctrines of his boyhood. In the end his reading led him to the belief that "the most acceptable service of God is doing good to man" (Franklin, 1793, ch. 9, p. 2).

Up to the age of sixteen, Franklin was still a captive in his environment. By law he was still subjugated to his parents, he worked as an apprentice to his brother who controlled his life, and the people in his environment controlled the ideas and beliefs to which he was expected to adhere. But having been an avid reader, he had been able to develop his own ideals and values, ones that did not always conform to the culture in which he lived. Benjamin began to share his ideals with an audience when he secretly wrote articles that were published in his brother's newspaper under the pseudonym "Silence Dogood." When his articles proved to be well liked by the readers of the paper, his desire to express himself freely grew even stronger. At the age of seventeen he left Boston and ventured into a wider world where he could better live the life of a free person with a curious mind.

The thirst for books that Franklin exhibited as a small boy led his father to apprentice him in the printing trade. That training would later become his avenue to wealth and distinction in America and Europe. Drawing on his training and the extensive knowledge he had acquired from books, Benjamin built a publishing and printing business that became hugely successful. His newspaper and almanac were used to educate and elevate the lives of ordinary people who needed someone like Franklin to provide them with inspiration and leadership. It became another way for him to "do good to others."

In starting a newspaper in Philadelphia, Franklin believed he had achieved the knowledge and skills necessary to guide and direct a quality news journal. When he became the sole owner of the *Pennsylvania Gazette*, he defined the qualities he thought a good newspaper publisher should possess. Among the traits he named were an extensive acquaintance with languages, a great easiness with writing, a good knowledge of war by land and sea, a thorough acquaintance with geography and the history of the time, manners, and a knowledge of customs of all nations. Through his reading Franklin had acquired those assets and more (Van Doren, 1938, p. 99).

The small tradesmen and farmers who read his publications learned from Franklin how to work hard and save their money so that they might become proprietors of their own farms and businesses, just as Franklin had done. Through his proverbs, verses, and simple stories that he had gleaned from his reading, some modified and others created, Benjamin conveyed a simple and honest attitude toward living a resourceful life. For people who had been held in economic bondage to others for the entirety of their lives, his advice was deeply appreciated. Franklin's philosophy of self-reliance and resourcefulness was eagerly accepted by a mercantile class in France, where his almanac was translated, that had grown tired of restrictions and limitations placed on their lives by monarchs and the aristocracy. They were weary of the heavy taxes and burdens placed on private enterprise (Russell, 1926).

After Franklin gave up most of his private business activity he became increasingly involved in political and governmental affairs. His extensive knowledge of people, nations, and governments quickly earned him the respect of those with whom he interacted. In representing his city, colony and nation, he proved to be skillful and highly regarded in representing the interest of his people. Russell expressed the view that Franklin's "mental agility, adroitness, and subtlety, added to his wide reading and observation of human nature, made him, when aroused, a sinuous and doughty opponent" (Russell, 1926, p. 277).

Franklin wrote that he could not remember ever being unable to read (Franklin, 1793, ch. 1, p. 4). That reading was the biggest influence in molding him into the man he became there can be little doubt. Tourtellot said of him, "The chief force in shaping the latent genius in Franklin was his insatiable appetite for books" (Tourtellot, 1977, p. 165). Books were the principal influence in his boyhood years. Reading turned him from the Puritanism of his youth to the enlightenment that he was to represent to the world in adulthood.

From Daniel Defoe's *An Essay upon Projects* Franklin collected many ideas for the improvement of living that he helped to implement in his community. Those, along with many others, he wrote about and supported through his newspaper and almanac. One of Defoe's most progressive projects for his day was that of educating women. In his book he proposed the prompt establishment of academies to educate young women. Upon reading this proposal, Benjamin promptly accepted it as a good and worthy project. He became a strong proponent of educational programs for women that would be equal to those for men.

Franklin's many projects were strongly influenced, as was his life, by the Cotton Mather book titled *Essays to Do Good*. After reading the book, Franklin constantly looked for ways to improve the conditions of human living whenever and wherever he could. The book continued to be a strong influence throughout his life. He wrote that he had always set a great value on doing good, and if he had been successful, "the public owes the advantage of it to that book" (Russell, 1926, p. 15).

HONORS AND MONUMENTS

During his long life, Benjamin Franklin was the recipient of numerous prestigious honors. Long after his death memorials dedicated to his life continue to be created. The most impressive, perhaps, is one of the most recent. That is the Benjamin Franklin National Memorial.

The memorial is located in the rotunda of The Franklin Institute Science Museum in Philadelphia, Pennsylvania. The place of honor inside the museum is Memorial Hall where a twenty-foot tall marble statue of Franklin is on display. The massive statue weighs thirty tons and sits on a ninety-two ton pedestal of white Seravezza marble. Memorial Hall also houses many of Franklin's original possessions, including his composing table and several of his original publications. The national memorial hosts a range of activities designed to perpetuate the legacy of Franklin, including the study of problems that face humanity, just as did Franklin during his life. Admission to the National Memorial is free (Memorial, 1976).

Thomas Jefferson

A Brief Biography

Thomas Jefferson served as the third president of the United States. Born at Shadwell in Albermarle County, Virginia, on April 13, 1743, he was not given a middle name. His family lineage was Welsh, Scotch, and Irish. Jefferson claimed no specific religious affiliation, although he did acknowledge a personal spirituality and the existence of a Supreme Being.

The strongest influence in Jefferson's early boyhood was his father, Peter. When Thomas was five years of age his father placed him in an English school and then in a Latin school at age nine. Young Thomas remained in the Latin school until his father's death at age forty-nine in 1757. Thomas was only fourteen at the time.

Upon his father's death, Thomas inherited the family estate at Shadwell and about 1,000 acres of land. He continued to make his home there with his family on weekends, but his weekdays were spent away in a small classical academy at the home of Reverend James Maury, a school his dying father had requested he attend.

After two years at the Maury school, Thomas, now seventeen years of age, enrolled as a student at the College of William and Mary in Williamsburg, Virginia. He remained there until April 1762, when he left to study law under George Wythe, a highly regarded attorney in Williamsburg. Thomas studied law for five years, after which he was admitted to the Virginia bar in April 1767.

When his legal career settled into stable and profitable work, Jefferson's thoughts turned to building a home of his own. On the Shadwell estate that he had inherited was a small mountain. He had been there often during his boyhood days, thinking that, if someday he would own that mountain, he would build his home there. In 1769 he began building the home of his dreams on the mountain, starting with a small cottage that would later become a part of the larger home he had planned. Thomas named his home Monticello, meaning "little mountain" in Italian. As fate would have it, in 1770, the family home at Shadwell was destroyed by fire. Although his new home at Monticello was far from finished, he moved into the small cottage that was, by then, nearly complete.

With his legal career progressing well, Jefferson's thoughts also turned to politics. In 1769, he was elected to represent his home district in the Virginia House of Burgesses. He would be reelected annually six times to the seat, serving until 1775. During the course of his tenure in the house, Jefferson became involved in a developing controversy between the American colonies and the king's royal government in England. As subjects of England, American colonial citizens were growing restless and impatient with their inability to get the mother country to address their needs. The question that the colonial governments kept debating was, what should be done if the king refused to address their grievances?

To bring some focus to the debate, Jefferson prepared a document outlining the position he believed the Virginia representatives should adopt with regard to England's treatment of the colonies. Due to illness, Jefferson was unable to attend the convention of delegates in Williamsburg when his document would be presented. However, his paper was presented in his absence. Later titled "A Summary View of the Rights of British America," the position outlined by Jefferson proved to be too radical by a majority of the delegates. The document, therefore, received no official action by the convention.

The next big step in Jefferson's public service career came when he was elected by the House of Burgesses to attend the Second Continental Congress that met in Philadelphia in June 1775. While serving as a member of that congress, he was appointed to serve on a five-man committee to prepare a paper in which the colonies would declare their independence from the rule of England. The other four members of the committee asked Thomas to write a first draft of a declaration. When his draft was presented to the committee and the congress, it went through some alteration, but the document that was adopted on July 4, 1776, by the congress remained in spirit and essential content the one Jefferson had written. The delegate from Monticello signed the Declaration of Independence on August 2, 1776. He and John Adams were the only two signers to ever hold the office of president of the United States.

In January 1779, Jefferson was elected governor of Virginia. During his first term, he was instrumental in moving Virginia's state capital from Williamsburg to Richmond. In 1779, he wrote and made available to the Virginia legislature a statute that would legally separate church and state and guarantee religious freedom in Virginia. Known as the Statute of Virginia for Religious Freedom, it stipulated that each individual has an inherent, natural right to intellectual and religious independence. The statute failed to gain acceptance at the time, in large measure due to its sharp departure from mainstream thinking in Virginia. But it did not disappear from debate and discussion among those who agreed with Jefferson. The statute was kicked around and discussed until it was finally passed, with a few modifications, into Virginia law in 1786.

In May 1784, Jefferson was elected to represent the United States as a commissioner in France. He would be working with Benjamin Franklin and John Adams to negotiate treaties, create trade agreements, and establish peaceful relations with European nations. In 1785, while still in France, he was made United States minister to France. During the same year, the only book he ever had published was privately printed in Paris. The book was publicly published in London in 1787, and an American edition was published in 1788. Titled *Notes on the State of Virginia*, the book is more commonly known today as *Notes on Virginia*. The content of the work is a compilation of the natural beauty, flora and fauna, waterways, and unusual landmarks and topographical features that Jefferson had noted while traveling and doing survey work around the Virginia colony. Chief among his discoveries was a limestone rock bridge that came to be known as Natural Bridge. Jefferson thought the rock formation to be such a natural wonder that he soon purchased the property (Jefferson, 1944).

When George Washington became the first president of the United States in 1789, he selected Thomas Jefferson to be his first secretary of state. He accepted and remained in the post until December 1793 when he resigned. In 1797 he was elected vice-president of the United States to serve with President John Adams. As political parties began to form in the young nation, Jefferson and Adams found themselves the de facto leaders of the two separate principal parties; Adams with the Federalist and Jefferson with the Republican Party. The political pressures of their separate constituencies and differences in their own evolving political ideals slowly drove the two long-time friends further and further apart politically.

In the presidential election of 1800, Adams and Jefferson both ran for president under the banner of their respective parties. When the votes were tallied, Jefferson was declared the winner. He served the nation as its third president for the next eight years. During his two terms in office, his two most notable achievements were the Louisiana Purchase from France, an acquisition that more than doubled the territorial size of the United States, and the creation, with congressional approval, of the Lewis and Clark expedition that explored and created maps of the Louisiana Territory all the way to the Pacific Ocean. While on the expedition, the two explorers sent back to Jefferson many samples of plant and animal life, some of which are still on display at his Monticello home.

After eight years in the White House, Jefferson returned to his home at Monticello. He never served in public office again. In retirement he had one final dream to fulfill, one of three that in the end, would be most dear to his heart. That dream was to create a premier educational institution for young southern adults. In 1819, such a school was chartered by the state of Virginia. Jefferson began and remained the driving force behind the school. He designed the buildings, supervised their construction, spelled out the curriculum, and selected the faculty. The University of Virginia opened for study in March 1825 with forty students.

Thomas Jefferson died on American Independence Day, July 4, 1826, a day that he had been so instrumental in bringing to the young American nation. Before his death he had requested to his oldest grandson to have engraved on his gravestone the three lifetime achievements for which he held the greatest pride: author of the Declaration of American Independence, author of the Statute of Virginia for Religious Freedom, and father of the University of Virginia. That is what visitors to his Monticello gravesite will see today.

READING IN EARLY LIFE

Thomas Jefferson's father kept a small library in his home at Shadwell. Young Thomas frequently observed his father reading books and poring over maps of the lands he had helped to survey and map. It has been written that Thomas had read all the books in his father's library by the time he entered school at age five (Randall, 1993). Among the books young Thomas read, according to family legend, were the Bible, Rapin's *History of England*, and *The Spectator*.

When he was placed in a Latin school, Thomas found a larger library open to his reading interests. There is some evidence that he also began building a library of his own during this period (Wilson, 1996). His father's records show expenditures for books for his son. At his father's death in 1757, Thomas inherited Peter's library of about forty volumes.

When young Jefferson moved to the classical school taught by the Reverend James Maury, he gained access to a library of two- to three-hundred volumes. While there, he was an eager learner. He listened and paid heed to the advice Reverend Maury gave to his own son about reading and learning: observe closely what you read and digest well; observe and note any remarkable beauties of diction; observe closely how the author leads to the accomplishment of his objective (Randall, 1993).

By all accounts available to us today, the evidence is strong that Jefferson became an avid reader very early in life, probably before the age of five. Reading became for him a leisure activity. While still just a young boy, he and his friend, Dabney Carr, would take some books and go to a wooded mountainside near their homes to read and study beneath the shade of a favorite oak tree.

Sometime during his early youth, Thomas started keeping a record of his reading in what he called "commonplace books." His early recordings show that he read classical writers such as Horace, Cicero, Ovid, Virgil, Pope, Milton, and Shakespeare. From his reading he copied into his books passages on honor, morality, and philosophical issues that perked his interest and that helped him to build a mental framework for the nature of life and living. Some passages dealt with aspects of death. Others were concerned with issues associated with rebellion and defiance, perhaps early guidelines for the role he would one day play in the colonial revolution against England. The volume of his reading indicates that he virtually always had a book in his hand.

Upon entering the College of William and Mary in 1760, Jefferson had access to a substantial institutional library that enriched his growing appetite for reading. In Williamsburg he also gained easy access to a commercial bookshop, which aided his efforts in building his own library. In college he became a student and friend of Dr. William Small, a professor that had come to Williamsburg from Scotland. Dr. Small greatly expanded Jefferson's knowledge in mathematics, science, ethics, rhetoric, and literature.

While the delights and charms of the capital of the Virginia colony provided exhilarating experiences for the young man from Virginia's western wilderness, Thomas did not allow the elevated social intercourse to pull him away from his pursuit of knowledge. By all accounts his application to reading and study remained intense. Reports from the period indicate that, even while he was on vacation from school, he devoted three-fourths of his time to his books (Malone, 1948, p. 56). Included in his library were books by John Locke in which Locke discussed his theories and beliefs on acquiring a well-grounded education. One component had to do with a study of law. Locke had written that any one supposing himself to be an English gentleman should not remain ignorant about the laws of his country (Randall, 1993). Locke's writing must have made an impact on young Thomas, for he became an intense student of law.

After two years in college, Jefferson left to study law under George Wythe. During a five-year period of legal study, he read his way through scores of law books. During the time he also devoted a considerable amount of time and money to building his personal library. Surviving records show that during the years of 1764 and 1765, Jefferson purchased fifty-six volumes (Wilson, 1996). A large number of those books were on law and history. By his own admission, he was fond of readings in the history of the world (Wilson, 1996). Some histories purchased at this time include books on the histories of the French civil war, England, Scotland, and the discovery and settlement of Virginia. In poetry he purchased works by John Milton, Edward Young, and William Shenstone. Most of these books were read, extracted, and paraphrased in his commonplace books.

By the time he had reached the age of nineteen, reading and study dominated Jefferson's interest and time. In a letter to a friend, he wrote that the generations before him had said that one must read to gain knowledge. By gaining knowledge one could be happy and admired. That advice, said Thomas, "may be worth following" (Jefferson, 1972, p. 354). In addition to law and history, other areas of reading that held his interest include religion, agriculture, medicine, classical literature, landscape gardening, and philosophy. Thomas also enjoyed books on the beauties and glory of rural life, with which he could so easily identify. In addition, he enjoyed seeing and reading plays, many of which were extracted in his commonplace books. During the mid–1760s, books on the theory and philosophy of natural rights in society became important reading material.

During the time he spent in Virginia's colonial capitol, Jefferson circulated in the society of Virginia's most prominent citizens. His acquaintances included royal governor Fauquier, George Wythe, and many important colonial political leaders. He also had occasion to stand at the door of the House of Burgesses and listen to his friend Patrick Henry speak before Virginia's legislative body. He later wrote that Henry was "the greatest orator that ever lived" (Malone, 1981, p. 225). The opportunity to enjoy the company of prominent political leaders and observe politicians at work added to his vast political reading and built in Jefferson a desire to become a part of that interesting arena of human activity.

READING DURING COLONIAL POLITICS

In 1769 Jefferson achieved his first election to public office in becoming a member of the Virginia House of Burgesses. During the same year he made a purchase of thirteen books from London (Wilson, 1996). The range of topics included books on legislation and government and the history and workings of Parliament. The purchase also included several books on political theory, including works by Montesquieu, Burlamaqui, and Locke. These works, along with others on political thinking, had a profound influence on Jefferson's political beliefs and ideals and demonstrated the channel of interest his mind was following at the time.

In the fall of 1765, Jefferson's beloved older sister, Jane, died at the age of twenty-eight. To help relieve the grief that hovered over his life, he sought solace in devotion to his books and his work. After five years of study in the law, he became an attorney under the mentorship of George Wythe in 1767. For the next eight years, he practiced law, working with a total of 939 cases (Malone, 1948). He also continued to serve in the House of Burgesses until 1775. When not involved in his work and public service to his colony, Thomas continued to read and seek knowledge in whatever subjects piqued his interest. His desire to expand his sphere of learning remained insatiable.

During the decade of the 1760s, it is clear that Jefferson read widely in many books covering a wide range of subjects. From the time he was a boy and found pleasure in books, he never had to search for a way to use idle time wisely. The long hours he spent with books continued to expand his mind and concepts about life, society, government, religion, human freedoms, and rights. He acquired a solid foundation of learning that lifted him above most others of his time and place. He became an accomplished mathematician as well as a finished scholar in the Greek, Latin, French, Spanish, and Italian languages. His ability to read in so many languages opened to him the opportunity to read and learn from much of the recorded knowledge present in the world of his day. The range of knowledge he acquired has prompted some to refer to him as a "walking encyclopedia."

As the problems between the colonies and England increased, Jefferson read more intently about the history and foundations of politics. That reading would position him to play a leading role in the fight for American independence from England. As an estate owner and farmer, he also read widely from books, ancient and current, on farming methods and scientific applications. While he never developed into a highly successful farmer, his readings in architecture did produce good results. He became a skilled designer and builder of numerous structures that are still admired in this century. His model and master for architectural inspiration was the great Italian designer Andrea Palladio. Palladio's classic work *The Four Books of Architecture* was read and studied by Jefferson and served as his guide for design inspiration. The influence of reading during the decade would contribute to remarkable achievements by the man from Monticello.

The burning of the family home at Shadwell destroyed all of Jefferson's papers and almost all of his books. He had been a serious book collector for at least ten years and had begun building his own library much earlier. The loss included the books he had inherited from his father, the ones his father had bought for him, and the large quantity Thomas had purchased during the decade of the sixties. When told that his home had burned, his first question addressed the fate of his books. The messenger reported that they were lost, but "we saved your fiddle" (Malone, 1948, p. 126).

The size of the library that was lost can only be estimated from records and the value of two hundred pounds sterling that Jefferson placed upon his loss. Professional estimates place the number lost at between three and four hundred volumes (Wilson, 1996). For a young man of twenty-six years, at that time, he had owned a large library.

After the fire, Jefferson moved into a small cottage that would become a part of his new home at Monticello. It seems reasonably clear from his writings and records that his plan for a permanent home on the little mountain included plans for a comprehensive new library. He began almost immediately to acquire a new collection of books. According to records he kept, by August 1773 he had accumulated a total of 1,256 volumes at Monticello (Wilson, 1996). This total did not include some volumes of music or books he still owned that were in Williamsburg. In the three and a half years since his first library had burned, he had collected another library three to four times the size of the one lost to fire.

The voracious reader acquired books from any and all sources. Many were ordered from abroad. Two entire collections Jefferson purchased from two prominent Virginians, Peyton Randolph and Richard Bland. Both of those collections contained important records of early Virginia history, a history Jefferson greatly valued. Known to be a serious book collector and an avid reader, books also came to him through the deaths of relatives and friends. Two that are noteworthy were his father-in-law, John Wayles, and his close friend, Dabney Carr.

As he moved through the days of his life, books and reading became ever more important to Thomas Jefferson. Upon the death of his father-in-law in 1773, his wife inherited land and property that doubled his wealth. The improved financial position permitted him to slowly give up his law practice and devote more time to reading and politics. The philosophies and structures of government became increasingly important in his quest for knowledge. He read and copied passages into his commonplace books from the early histories of the governments of Europe. He read deeply about various forms of governmental designs and structures. Law and history were studied as far back as the Norman conquest of England in the year 1066. It seemed the more he learned, the more he wanted to know. All the while he still served in a variety of public positions in service to his people. At times he grew weary of public service and longed for a return to private life where he could spend more time with his books and his family. In 1788, just a year before returning home from France, he wrote to a friend that he longed to be in a modest cottage with his books, family, and a few old friends, "dining on simple bacon and letting the world roll on as it liked, than to occupy the most splendid post, which any human power can give" (Jefferson, 1944, p. 443). But his deep sense of public duty would make that choice difficult time and again.

The growing divide between the Virginia colony and England opened the door for Jefferson to acquire a large number of books. He purchased many from the collections of a William and Mary College president and two faculty members. When hostilities seemed to threaten those that remained loyal to the English king, many fled to England. Jefferson was able to buy books from many of their collections. When the rector of Bruton's Parish in Williamsburg fled to England, Jefferson wrote his friend John Page, asking him to purchase two books that he recalled were in the parson's library. One was Pelloutier's two-volume *Histoire des Celtes* and Payne's eight-volume *Observations on Gardening*. He was even able to acquire some books from the collection of the fleeing royal governor of Virginia, Lord Dunmore.

While making trips to and from Philadelphia as a member of the Continental Congress, Jefferson had access to good bookstores. His memorandum books show many purchases during his time spent in the cultural center of the colonies. By the time he sailed for France as an American commissioner in 1784, his records indicate that he had amassed a book collection of about 2,640 volumes (Wilson, 1996). However, his book collecting had only just begun. In France he was to shop for books with a passion equal to that of a gold mine prospector believing he was on the brink of finding the mother lode.

While he lived in France, Jefferson spent every free afternoon roving through the bookstores of Paris, handling every book he found, and buying those that related in some way to America. In addition to the Paris shops, he maintained standing orders with book markets in the principal cities of Europe for books about America that were unavailable in Paris. In addition to building his own collection, he purchased books that were requested by friends and acquaintances back home. According to Douglas L. Wilson, an author who has studied Jefferson's books and reading interest in depth, during the five years Jefferson spent in Paris, he added approximately 2,000 volumes to his personal library (Wilson, 1996). Wilson estimates that the 2,640 books owned when Jefferson sailed for France, plus the 2,000 he bought while in France, in addition to those bought at other times and places while he was traveling, increased Jefferson's library to about 5,000 volumes by the time he returned to the United States in 1789.

READING DURING SERVICE TO A NEW NATION

In 1789 George Washington took office as the first president of the United States under a new constitutional government for the young nation. Washington wrote to Jefferson requesting that he accept the position of secretary of state. His sense of duty overriding his desire to spend more time with his books and family, Jefferson accepted the call. But his longing for family and books never waned. In letters to the president, he often stated his desire to return to the enjoyment of his family, his farm, and "my books." In a 1793 letter to his friend and political colleague James Madison, he expressed again his desire to leave public office. He wished to return to family, farm, neighbors, "and my books" (Jefferson, 1944, p. 523). However, his public offices did not entirely separate him from books and book collecting.

For the next several years while holding important national offices, Jefferson's library continued to expand dramatically. While his fame as the author of the Declaration of Independence and as a public servant continued to grow, many books came to him from authors who sent him personal copies of their work. Upon the death of his close friend and mentor George Wythe in 1806, he inherited Wythe's extensive library. While serving in public office in New York, Philadelphia, and Washington, he continued his book collecting. By these means his already large library continued to expand. But Jefferson was not just a book collector. He was a reader who used books to build a vast storehouse of knowledge.

Everyone who knew Jefferson at all knew of his love for and need of books in his life. A French visitor to Monticello in 1782 who viewed Jefferson's family, farm, and his library, stated that, "it seemed as if from his youth, he had placed his mind, as he had done his house, on an elevated situation, from which he might contemplate the universe" (Malone, 1948, p. 391).

When writing to relatives, friends, and acquaintances, Jefferson often spoke about reading and its importance in his life. His message to an aspiring young law student in 1790 advised the young man to read and learn thoroughly and not to be satisfied with just getting by. Based on his experience, the power of knowledge could lift one above those with whom he must compete. To the young man, he wrote, "It is the superiority of knowledge which can alone lift you above the heads of your competitors, and ensure you success" (Jefferson, 1944, p. 499).

The extensive early education and reading that Jefferson's father had arranged for his son brought Thomas exceptional joy during the mature years of his reading life. The ability to read in many languages put him in an elite group to which few Virginians could claim entitlement. In 1800 in a letter to an acquaintance, Jefferson wrote, "to read the Latin and Greek authors in their original, is a sublime luxury.... I enjoy Homer in his own language infinitely beyond Pope's translation of him, and both beyond the dull narrative of the same events by Dares Phrygius" (Jefferson, 1944, p. 554). The lofty level that Jefferson had achieved in the world of knowledge produced a sense of certainty in his ideals that sometimes separated him from those with whom he worked.

He addressed that circumstance in a letter to Mrs. John Adams in 1804. Her husband and Jefferson had developed some well-publicized political differences after having been friends and colleagues throughout the turmoil of the American Revolution. As Jefferson saw it, they had each lived in different regions of the colonies, each having different economic interests and social issues to address. Both men were avid readers that had been influenced in different ways by what they read and experienced. To Mrs. Adams he wrote, "The different conclusions we had drawn from our political reading and reflections were not permitted to lessen personal esteem — each party being conscious they were the result of an honest conviction in the other" (Randolph, 1978, p. 306). However, their friendship had diminished when they came under the persuasion and influence of separate political parties under the new constitutional government. But, Jefferson's plea was that political differences should not lessen the personal esteem they had held for each other over the long years they worked together to recast the colonies into a free and independent nation.

During the eight years Jefferson served as the nation's president, he continued to read as much as a demanding schedule would permit. In 1804 he received from an acquaintance two volumes on political economy. After skimming some chapters he wrote the author saying that he found the content interesting and anticipated reading the complete work with much pleasure.

Writing and reading letters held an important place in Jefferson's life. In a letter to his young granddaughter, Cornelia Randolph, he wrote in 1808 how pleased he was to have received from her a letter written in her own hand, proving she had learned to write. He liked knowing that she could write because it is to writing "that we are indebted for all our reading; because it must be written before we can read it" (Randolph, 1978, p. 320). In the same letter Jefferson took advantage of an opportunity to promote reading in the life of the granddaughter. He wrote, "To this [writing] we are indebted for the *Iliad*, the *Aeneid*, the *Columbiad*, "Henriad," "Dunciad," and now, for the most glorious poem of all, the "Terrapiniad," which I now inclose [sic] you" (Randolph, p. 320). In listing several important works that he had read, he shared a little of his own reading life with his granddaughter.

Because he was away from home serving his nation so much, the only way Jefferson could keep in close touch with his family was through the exchange of letters. The loneliness he so often felt made letters from home all the more important. His eagerness to receive letters from his daughters and sons-in-law is stated over and over again in his correspondence. At times his letters could be tinged with a tone of subtle irritation if he felt they were failing to write as often as they should. In a letter written to his youngest daughter, Maria, on July 31, 1791, when he was living in Philadelphia serving as secretary of state, he admonishes Maria for failing to write as often as he had asked of her, complaining that he had not received a word from her in nine weeks. He stated, "Those which you ought to have written on June 19 and July 10 would have reached me before this if they had been written" (Randolph, 1978, p. 204). The day did finally arrive, however, when he could see his family daily and not have to depend on the reading of letters to know what they were doing.

READING IN RETIREMENT

After serving his country as president for eight years, Jefferson left public life for good on March 4, 1809. Comfortably settled on his mountaintop at Monticello, he again indulged his passion for reading, family, and his farms. In a letter to a friend written within the first year of his return to Monticello, he told about his life in retirement and how he passed the days. Between breakfast and dinner he spent in his farm shops or in his garden or on horseback directing the farm work. From dinner to dark was given to social interaction with family and friends. From dark to bedtime he devoted to reading (Randolph, 1978). One of his granddaughters found that Jefferson's retirement at Monticello was an easy transition for the longtime public servant. She wrote to an acquaintance saying, "With regard to the tastes and wishes which he carried with him into the country, his love of reading alone would have made leisure and retirement delightful to him" (Randolph, 1978, p. 340). Reflecting a similar assessment of his contentment, Jefferson wrote to an acquaintance in 1810, not long after his retirement, stating, "I am retired to Monticello, where, in the bosom of my family, and surrounded by my books, I enjoy a repose to which I have been long a stranger" (Jefferson, 1944, p. 602).

In retirement the former president continued to read the works of the great writers. His ability to read in many languages gave him a broad range of choice in what he read. Works by Homer, Virgil, Dante, Corneille, Cervantes, Shakespeare, and Milton were among the books read. Included were many of the great Athenian tragedies that he enjoyed to the end of his days. The year before his death he read through the works of Aeschylus, Sophocles, and Euripides. Jefferson still enjoyed reading history, having a great fascination for the ancients, much of it read in Greek and Latin. To a friend he wrote that he had grown tired of practical politics and was "happier while reading the history of ancient than of modern times" (Jefferson, 1944, p. 626). He still read some current news and reviews, but on a far more limited scope than when in public office.

If possible, Jefferson's passion for reading increased with time. In a letter to John Adams in 1812, he reported that he spent little time thinking about politics and "I have given up newspapers in exchange for Tacitus and Thucydides, for Newton and Euclid, and I find myself much the happier" (Jefferson, 1944, p. 617).

Jefferson's reputation as an avid reader and learned man grew to such heights that authors far and wide sent him copies of their books. In 1814 he received a copy of *Second Thoughts on Instinctive Impulses* by Thomas Law. He took the book with him to Poplar Forest, his retreat in Bedford County. After completing the book, he wrote the author saying, "I brought it with me and read it with great satisfaction, and with the more as it contained exactly my own creed on the foundation of morality in man" (Jefferson, 1944, p. 636). In 1816 another book reached Monticello, a work by John Taylor titled *Inquiry into the Principles of Our Government*. Jefferson scanned most of the book and read some parts in depth. So pleased was he that a letter went out to Mr. Taylor saying, in part, "I see in it much matter for profound reflection; much which should confirm our adhesion, in practice, to the good principles of our Constitution, and fix our attention on what is yet to be made good" (Jefferson, 1944, p. 669).

Intrusions and obligations that pulled the former president away from reading were an annoyance. In a letter to a friend in 1816 Jefferson complained of the time required to answer the letters he received daily from friends, acquaintances, former colleagues, and persons unknown to him who wanted his views on a particular subject. His sense of social courtesy required that he answer all letters, but the time consumed in doing so "keeps me at the drudgery of the writing-table all the prime hours of the day, leaving for the gratification of my appetite for reading, only what I can steal from the hours of sleep" (Jefferson, 1944. p. 660). In one single year he received 1,267 letters, some of which required extensive research on his part to answer properly (Jefferson, 1944, p. 380). In another letter to John Adams in 1822, Jefferson talked of growing old and approaching death. He confessed that walking now tired him, and he could only walk as far as his garden, and even that produced considerable fatigue. "But," he admitted, "reading is my delight" (Jefferson, 1944, p. 379).

Jefferson's years in retirement provided time for him to delve with passion into the vast library he had been building since the loss of his first book collection in the fire at Shadwell in 1770. By 1815 his second book collection had grown to approximately 6,700 volumes (Wilson, 1996). The avid reader and long-time public servant had portrayed every indication of planning his life in retirement in such a way that he could spend his golden years in the luxury of his farms, family, and books. As already noted previously, his letters often made reference to that expectation. However, everything in Jefferson's life was not secure and stable. A depressing gloom shadowed the background of his anticipated joy.

For years Jefferson's financial condition had been growing bothersome. Not long into retirement, that condition grew to be much more serious. Weak farm prices, poor crop production due to drought, embargoes by the British that reduced exports of American produce, financial aid to friends who could not repay loans, and living beyond his means while incurring more debt with the hope that circumstances would soon improve all contributed to Jefferson's evolving financial crisis. What could he do? He owned lots of land, but prices were so much below what they had been that selling farmland might not remove his economic woes. What assets did he own that held good value? Upon study and reflection, his extensive library seemed to be one of his best, if not the best, assets. Unanticipated events surrounding the government and the nation's capital would soon directly affect Jefferson and his library.

In 1812 the United States found itself again at war with the British, a war that dragged on until 1815. Grievances and unresolved issues had lingered from the Revolutionary War, despite numerous attempts by the American government to settle differences with the king's representatives. One event that occurred in the 1812 war would come to have a direct bearing on Jefferson's financial crisis.

In a raid on the nation's capital in 1814, the British sacked and destroyed many government buildings, including the Capitol. Lost in the destruction was the congressional library. A collection of books for the use of senators and representatives had been initiated in 1800 during Adams's administration at about the time the national government moved from Philadelphia to its permanent home in Washington. When Jefferson became president in 1801, he began to build the library into a more extensive collection. By the time the library was destroyed, the size of the collection had grown to approximately 3,000 volumes.

Upon learning of the loss of the congressional collection, Jefferson wrote to a congressional friend offering to sell his complete Monticello library as a replacement for the one destroyed by the British, at whatever price Congress should assess as its value. In making the offer, Jefferson at first estimated the size of his collection to be somewhere between 9,000 and 10,000 volumes. Later counts by Jefferson and others would reduce that number considerably (Wilson, 1996).

In the offer to sell his books to Congress, Jefferson stipulated that it should take all or none. His rationale appears to have been a vision he held that the Library of Congress should, in due time, become a depository for the depth and breadth of human knowledge. Jefferson believed he had assembled the best library then in the country, and it would, as it existed with all its volumes, constitute an excellent beginning for the kind of national library he envisioned for the American people. That provision in his offer caused some small debate in the Congress, but nothing much ever came of some questions that were raised by a few congressional members.

The two biggest issues came to be the accurate size of the library and a monetary value the Congress could agree on. Jefferson stipulated in his offer that the purchase price should be assessed by the Congress, not himself. After much debate and delay over those two issues, Jefferson asked George Milligan, a bookseller in the Georgetown section of Washington and a dealer with whom he had previously done business, to count and value the books so that Congress would have some specific numbers to discuss. The book count reported to Congress was 6,487, and the value set by Milligan was $23,950 (Wilson, 1996). With those figures, Congress finally approved the purchase on January 26, 1815. Almost five months elapsed from the time Jefferson first made the offer to sell his books until the day he learned that Congress had approved the purchase. Ten wagons were required to transport the books from Monticello to Washington, D.C.

As the reader would, perhaps, surmise at this point, the absence of a library at Monticello must have had a despondent effect on the avid reader Jefferson. And the reader would be correct. When the wagons left the mountaintop home in April of 1815 with his complete library aboard, the sight left Jefferson in a state of melancholy. In June he wrote to John Adams saying, "I cannot live without books" (Malone, 1981, p. 185). But Jefferson surely took pride in knowing that he had, almost single-handedly, laid a broad foundation for what he expected would one day become a national depository of books embracing the scope of human knowledge. Even John Adams expressed his admiration at such an achievement. He wrote to Jefferson saying, "I envy you that immortal honor" (Wilson, 1996, p. 7). However, the "Sage of Monticello" was not left totally without books. He still owned several hundred volumes at his Poplar Forest retreat. In addition, he continued to buy books at a hurried pace.

In the eleven years between the sale of his Monticello library and his death, Jefferson again built an impressive library in his mountaintop home. As he had written to Adams, he was a man who found living without books to be difficult. By the time of his death on July 4, 1826, he had rebuilt his collection to about 1,600 volumes. His new library included books on many of the same topics that he had accumulated before. The collection also included two editions of *Don Quixote*, a book some have said was the only novel that Jefferson ever reread (Wilson, 1996). Sadly, three years after his death, the indebtedness of his estate resulted in the sale, at public auction, of the second Monticello library.

At Jefferson's death, the Poplar Forest library passed into the hands of his grandson, Francis Eppes. It, too, was sold at auction in 1873. Some of the books Jefferson owned still survive in public and private libraries. They remain treasured holdings by those fortunate enough to have possession. The books that remain in public libraries are sequestered and managed like precious jewels. For those people who privately own copies, the books remain treasured connections to a time and a person that had an enormous impact on making our nation what it is today, educationally, politically, and religiously.

THE IMPACT OF READING

The impact of reading on Thomas Jefferson's life was deep and profound. He had spent his early years in Williamsburg as a student and member of the House of Burgesses writing and promoting his ideas for a free nation, freedom of religion, and education for all. In correspondence with family, friends, and acquaintances throughout the colonies, he continued to represent his ideals, ideals he had formulated from his extensive reading. By the time he went to the Continental Congress in 1775, he had built a substantial reputation as a learned person and an accomplished writer. John Adams remarked to others in the Congress that Jefferson had brought with him "a reputation for literature, science and a happy talent of composition" (Malone, 1948, p. 204).

The wealth of knowledge and writing talent that Jefferson brought to government service frequently placed him in demand by others. He was called on time after time to draft legislative bills, government reports, and documents. Over the course of his long public service career, the number of papers and documents he produced became extensive. While participating in the government of Virginia, he incorporated a wealth of knowledge into proposals, codes, and laws to give Virginians a modern government, one that became a model for other states and the federal government of the United States.

While Jefferson represented his government in France, his knowledge and language diversity won for him easy acceptance among the most influential people. He circulated easily among the leading political figures, artists, writers, scientists, and citizens of French society. The man from Monticello proved to be an able representative of his country because he was learned in the dynamics of governments and people.

During Jefferson's five years in France, he continued to promote education for all. In a 1786 letter to his friend and mentor, George Wythe, he wrote:

> I think by far the most important bill in our whole code, is that for the diffusion of knowledge among the people. No other sure foundation can be devised, for the preservation of freedom and happiness. If anybody thinks that kings, nobles, or priests are good conservators of the public happiness, send him here. It is the best school in the universe to cure him of that folly [Jefferson, 1944, p. 394].

What he had seen of the rule by royalty in Europe had further convinced him that the best form of government was of a kind that Lincoln would later characterize as government of the people, by the people, and for the people. He could see that the freedom to read and learn begun by the American people would made them a stronger people and a stronger nation than those countries in which access to knowledge was limited to a privileged few. In the same letter, he added that even if the rulers of the European nations were to start then to enlighten their people, "a thousand years would not place them on that high ground, on which our common people are now setting out" (p. 394).

The impact of Jefferson's extensive reading led him to understand, perhaps better than anyone else, the importance of reading and its consequence, the spread of knowledge. If the young American nation was to have a free and successful government, he believed that common people must possess an ability to read their daily and weekly newspapers and any books they found of interest. A free government directed by the people would reflect the opinions of the masses. Those opinions would be best diffused through newspapers and books.

In Jefferson's view, reading ability and books to read brings to everyone the power to build freedom and independence of mind, and that should be surrendered to no one. That conviction lead him to introduce to the Virginia Assembly an Act for Establishing Religious Freedom, an act that was adopted in 1786. His thorough knowledge of history had lead him to an understanding of the control that unbridled religious power could exert over the lives of people, as he had observed in certain localities among the American colonies. In his statue he wrote that "No man shall be compelled to frequent or support any religious worship, place or ministry whatsoever … but that all men shall be free to profess, and by argument to maintain, their opinions in matters of religion" (Jefferson, 1944, p. 313). The act established an important principle of human freedom that came to be widely cherished across the United States as our nation grew into a dominant world power.

Thomas Jefferson served his people and the world community well. The humanitarian ideals that he promoted have been widely adopted and practiced. His great sense of human feeling and motive for service to his state and his country was derived in large measure from his reading experience. By the time he had reached adulthood, he had acquired a knowledge base that gave him an understanding of human conduct far superior to most of his contemporaries. The friction between England and the colonies had grown intense. Jefferson's view of England's rule over the mental and economic life of the colonies led him to conclude that a break was necessary. Reading had given him a deep knowledge of human history, and that knowledge had led him to the view that the colonies could never grow and mature as a people so long as they had to remain subservient to the will and control of the king of England. The lack of morality and human compassion displayed by the royal government convinced Jefferson that the conditions and morality of the colonies would follow the same course unless freedom could be wrested from British control.

In his autobiography (Jefferson, 1944), Jefferson identified three periods in world history he had discovered through his reading, in which he believed there had existed an absence of national morality. The first he identified as being under Alexander the Great and his successors. The next was the period encompassed by the successors of the first Caesar. And the third was the time in which Jefferson lived, a time he referred to as "our own age." Among the worst examples of degenerate human morality were the ruthless acts of Bonaparte, "partitioning the earth at his will, and devastating it with fire and sword; now the conspiracy of Kings, the successors of Bonaparte, blasphemously calling themselves the Holy Alliance" (Jefferson, 1944, p.105). That kind of ruthless dominion by absolute rulers over the mind and morality of people shaped Jefferson's view of the future for the colonies if they remained under English rule.

Jefferson saw reading as the most certain vehicle for building a positive national morality. In time, he also grew to enjoy and appreciate fiction as a good revealer of moral perplexity and judgment. Fiction could be entertaining, useful, and pleasant when well written. If people rely solely on real life experiences for acquiring moral lessons, the lessons would be too infrequent to meet the need for positive moral development. Jefferson believed fiction evoked a deeper moral response. Fiction that involves the reader in moral feelings produces an awareness and consideration that leads to the adoption of habits of virtuous conduct. The reader is not concerned with whether the story is real or fiction. The moral encounter is what is important. In a letter written in 1771, Jefferson stated that a lasting sense of "filial duty is more effectually impressed on the mind of a son or daughter by reading King Lear, than by all the dry volumes of ethics and divinity that ever were written" (Jefferson, 1944, p. 358).

In developing habits of moral behavior, everything is useful that establishes principles of virtuous action. In a letter to Peter Carr in 1787, Jefferson advised him to "read good books, because they will encourage, as well as, direct your feelings. The writings of Sterne, particularly, form the best course of morality that ever was written" (Jefferson, 1944, p. 431). Good books, he believed, will develop and promote feelings and guide them to follow moral paths of conduct.

To build the kind of society that Jefferson envisioned, education would be an essential ingredient. He believed that people should govern themselves through representative government. But for such a system to work, citizens must be educated enough to read, analyze, and choose for themselves those they would have lead and manage their government. All children, he proposed, should be taught reading, writing, and common arithmetic. His own reading and study had led him to see that such an advancement in the condition of common people could be achieved under a free government, one created and run by the common people.

Education through schooling and wide personal reading was Jefferson's answer to maintaining free institutions and free people. To him the world of books remained a treasure trove of knowledge waiting to be absorbed by those who wished to be free and independent. He virtually always gave the same advise to anyone seeking his counsel. To a future son-in-law he once wrote advising that he should learn the Spanish language because Americans would have many contacts with the Spanish people in the future (Jefferson, 1944, p. 426). Additionally, the ancient part of American history was written principally in Spanish, further evidence of Jefferson's own wealth of knowledge obtained through reading.

Important in Jefferson's plan for the education of common people were public libraries. At any and every opportunity he promoted the widest diffusion of knowledge through reading. In 1809 he received a letter informing him of the establishment of the Westward Mill Library Society. In a response letter to the society, he wrote, "I always hear with pleasure of institutions for the promotion of knowledge among my countrymen" (Jefferson, 1944, p. 597). His wish was that every county could create a small circulating library to consist of a few of the best books to be loaned to citizens on a responsible schedule. Jefferson believed that such a library system could be established at small expense. In closing his letter, the man of Monticello offered his services to the society if he could be useful.

Jefferson's reading history provided him with many pleasures and opportunities to assist others in his retirement. A thing that he genuinely enjoyed was mentoring those who wanted to acquire an education. When given the opportunity to advise and help young people on their futures, he always advised wide reading and study. To a nephew he wrote that an honest heart was the first thing a person should seek to develop, but the second must be a knowing head. His advice focused on reading the classic works of that day: "I advise you to begin a course of ancient history, reading everything in the original and not in translations. First read Goldsmith's history of Greece. This will give you a digested view of that field. Then take up ancient history in detail" (Jefferson, 1944, p. 374).

In a letter to a friend, Jefferson wrote about his days in retirement and explained how he spent some time helping young men in their pursuit of learning. Many of those he counseled lived near Monticello and made use of his library. In directing their reading, Jefferson kept "their attention fixed on the main objects of all science, the freedom and happiness of man. So that coming to bear a share in the councils and governments of their country, they will keep ever in view the sole objects of all legitimate government" (Jefferson, 1944, p. 603). His guidance proved to be widely sought after. To a student at his new university in Charlottesville, he counseled reading works as they were written by the original authors and in the original language, if known to the student. If not, then read translations of the original works.

A free flow of ideas throughout humanity defined Jefferson's concept of a humane world. He held that nature had uniquely designed the world so that ideas could freely spread for the instruction of all people. He believed that good ideas were like fire or the air we breathe, expanding and flowing through space, incapable of confinement, or sole ownership by any one person or group. In a letter to John Adams in 1821, he noted that printing had led to a vast dissemination of books, which had enlightened the masses and, in turn, extended human freedoms. Such a trend could not be reversed. The "art of printing alone, and the vast dissemination of books, will maintain the mind where it is, and raise the conquering ruffians to the level of the conquered" (Jefferson, 1944, p. 703). The flames of freedom sparked on July 4, 1776, had spread over too much of the globe to be put out by "the feeble engines of despotism" (Jefferson, 1944, p. 703).

Jefferson's preeminence as a man of knowledge did not burst forth through some mystical act of benevolence. He was a reader, and those who read do learn. From early in life, perhaps as early as the age of three or four, he remained an avid reader in a wide range of subjects. Virtually nothing seemed uninteresting to him. Just one year before his death, he wrote to John Adams with the news that, "I have lately been reading the most extraordinary of all books, and at the same time the most demonstrative by numerous and unequivocal facts" (Jefferson, 1944, p. 716). The book to which he referred was a work by Flourend on the functions of the nervous system in vertebrate animals.

In retirement Jefferson's reputation as the "Sage of Monticello" had been achieved through an avid pursuit of learning. Knowledge acquired through reading had led him to the conviction that the human adventure on earth could only be made civil and humane through the widest diffusion of knowledge. When people learn to read and think for themselves, our freedoms will be secured. The example he left to those who study Jefferson's life is clear. Reading and dedication to self-improvement will produce rich rewards in human achievement.

Honors and Memorials

The honors and memorials that have been dedicated to the life of Thomas Jefferson are too numerous to include within the scope of this work. His name has been assigned to innumerable schools, roads, buildings, and monuments erected in his honor. One memorial does, however, merit space. Perhaps the most beautiful and prestigious acknowledgment of his enormous contribution to this nation and its citizens is the Jefferson Memorial located in Washington, D.C. The monument is located on the south side of the Tidal Basin in West Potomac Park, just a short walk from downtown Washington. The colonnaded structure is a simple circular design of white marble erected in a classical style like that introduced into the United States by Jefferson. A nineteen-foot bronze statue of the third president, standing on a six-foot pedestal, dominates the interior. The various wall panels inside the structure are inscribed with excerpts from his writings.

The Jefferson Memorial was dedicated in 1943 on the two-hundredth anniversary of Jefferson's birthday. President Franklin Roosevelt had put down the cornerstone just four years earlier. For sheer beauty, the memorial stands among the best the world has to offer. In the spring of the year, when one stands on the opposite side of the Tidal Basin and looks across the water to the memorial adorned by the Japanese cherry blossoms that surround the basin, the impact is visually inspiring. The memorial is a splendid monument to a man who so enjoyed fine architecture and refined things and whose life was so thoroughly inspired by books.

Abraham Lincoln

A Brief Biography

Abraham Lincoln was the sixteenth president of the United States. Abe, as he is universally known, had no middle name. He was named after his paternal grandfather, an ancestor who was killed by an American Indian in May 1786. Lincoln was born in a log cabin on February 12, 1809, on Sinking Spring Farm near Hodgenville, Hardin County, now named Larue County, Kentucky. His ancestry was English.

Lincoln claimed no religious denomination and never attended any college or university. His personal appearance was best stated in a brief biographical sketch written by him in 1859. In a brief statement he wrote, "If any personal description of me is thought desirable, it may be said, I am, in height, six feet, four inches, nearly; lean in flesh, weighing, on an average, one hundred and eighty pounds; dark complexion, with course black hair and grey eyes — no other marks or brands recollected" (Lincoln, 1859, p. 1).

Lincoln was born into the poverty of a frontier family that moved often and made many restarts while trying to find economic stability. In December 1808 his parents, Thomas and Nancy, bought a broken-down farm on the South Fork of Nolin Creek, which became the site of Abraham's birth. Shortly after his second birthday the family moved to a better farm along Knob Creek that included some fertile bottomland.

During his days as a small boy on the Knob Creek farm, Abe performed chores like most frontier youngsters. He was eight years old when the Lincoln family made another move. In 1816 the family left Kentucky and crossed the Ohio River, made their way sixteen miles father north, and settled near Pigeon Creek, in present Spencer County, Indiana. To reach the site that would become their new home, the family had to chop their way through dense woods. Abraham later described it as a "wild region, with many bears and other wild animals still in the woods" (Herndon and Weik, 1949, p. 21). In this new, unsettled location, Abe helped his father clear some land and build a crude house of logs and boughs that was closed on only three sides and heated only by a fire at the open front. Here the family lived through a cold winter while they built a more permanent home. By the time spring arrived, a few acres of land had been cleared for planting crops.

The Lincolns had been in Indiana for only a short time when they were joined by Thomas and Elizabeth Sparrow, relatives who had reared Nancy Lincoln. With the Sparrows came Dennis Hanks, an illegitimate son of one of Nancy's aunts. Dennis was an energetic youth of nineteen and became a close companion to Abraham. Within a year, the Sparrows became victims of a disease known as "milk sick." They soon died from the illness. Not very long after, Nancy Lincoln became afflicted with the same illness and died on October 5, 1818. Young Abe was only ten years of age. Upon the death of his mother, conditions for Abraham and his sister, Sarah, grew even more desperate and difficult. Without a mother and a woman to manage the home, the Lincolns lived on the edge of dire neglect.

In December 1819, Thomas Lincoln left his son and daughter at their home in Indiana and returned to Kentucky. While there he married Sarah Bush Johnston, a widow with three children. The new Mrs. Lincoln sold her Kentucky home and traveled to the Lincoln home in Indiana with Thomas, her furniture, and three children. Her arrival gave Abe and his sister a new mother. Time proved Sarah to be an excellent stepmother, and Abraham always loved her as he did his own mother until the day he died.

From the day she entered the Lincoln home, Sarah encouraged Abe's learning and took pride in his inquisitive mind. She later recalled his interest in listening to the conversations of guests in the home. After an evening of listening, he would mull over everything he had heard until he understood and had it fixed in his mind to suit him (Armstrong, 1974).

In 1830, when he was twenty-one years old, Abraham migrated with his family to Macon County, Illinois, and found a place to settle near the Sangamon River. After the discouragingly hard winter of 1830 to 1831, the Lincolns started to return to Indiana but stopped in Coles County, Illinois, where they settled and where his parents lived the rest of their lives.

In the spring of 1831 Lincoln left his parents to try to find his own way in life. For the next few years he worked at a number of jobs including that of a deckhand on a flat boat down the Mississippi River to transport produce to New

Orleans. After returning to Illinois from his trip south, Abraham settled in the small village of New Salem. While living in New Salem he engaged in a variety of jobs and adventures. Among them were a partnership in a store that failed after a short run, service with the militia during the Black Hawk War, and a stint as New Salem postmaster, and he learned and practiced the craft of surveying.

In 1834 Lincoln was elected to the Illinois House of Representatives and was reelected in 1836, 1838, and 1840. One of his achievements in the legislature, where he was a consistent supporter of conservative business interests, was to serve as a principal leader in moving the state capital from Vandalia to Springfield.

During his early manhood, Lincoln developed an interest in law. A friend suggested that he study law, a suggestion he accepted. After much reading, studying, and acquiring some experience under the direction of a certified attorney, Abraham obtained a license on September 9, 1836. By that time New Salem was a small village that had begun to decline in commerce and population. Lincoln decided he would have a better, more profitable legal career if he moved to a more populated area. In 1837 he moved to Springfield and joined an established law firm. Except for periods when he served as an elected representative, he would continue to practice law for most of his life until he was elected president in 1860.

In 1840 Lincoln married Mary Todd. Reared in Lexington, Kentucky, Mary was a socially prominent lady with a volatile personality. The marriage proved to be rocky at times, but Abraham exercised enduring patience with his wife's changing moods and desires. Four children were born to the couple, but only Robert Todd Lincoln lived to maturity.

In 1846 Lincoln was elected a member of the House of Representatives in the United States Congress. In 1858 he was nominated to run for the United States Senate against Senator Stephen Douglas. During the senatorial campaign Abraham participated in the famous Lincoln-Douglas debates as each candidate tried to persuade voters to support that person's candidacy. Douglas won the contest and returned to the senate. However, the campaign elevated Lincoln to a new level as a politician.

In the presidential election of 1860, Lincoln was nominated to run as a Republican candidate. In November he was elected the sixteenth president of the United States. Lincoln left Springfield on February 11, 1861, to assume the duties of his new position. Before he reached Washington seven states of the lower South had seceded from the Union, and southern delegates meeting in Montgomery, Alabama, had formed a new, separate government. Determined to hold the Union together at all cost, Lincoln refused to let the South take control of federal property located in the South. When southern soldiers fired on Union soldiers that were defending federal property, the Civil War began. The next four years were difficult indeed for Lincoln, but he persevered and won the war that preserved the Union. As the tide of the war was winding down to a Union victory for the North, Lincoln was reelected to a second four-year term in 1864. But he did not get to serve his second term.

Abraham Lincoln was assassinated in Ford's Theater in Washington, D.C., April 14, 1865, by John Wilkes Booth. He died the next day. Rumors of assassination plots had been raging from the day he was elected to become president. A few days before his death, Lincoln had experienced a horrible dream that the president had been assassinated, a dream he repeated to his wife and a friend. As he recounted the dream, Lincoln became "grave, gloomy, and at times visibly pale" (Oates, 1977, p. 426). Mrs. Lincoln became visibly frightened, prompting the president to say they would discuss the dream no more. Unfortunately, for the nation and the world, the dream did come true. Lincoln had served the nation as president from March 4, 1861, to April 15, 1865.

Reading in Early Life

Abraham Lincoln has been characterized as a product of books rather than schooling. Abraham, himself, recognized that to be true. He once reported his formal schooling amounted to be less than a full year in total time actually spent in school (Herndon, 1949). His first schooling was gained while the family lived on Knob Creek in Kentucky. Abraham and his sister, Sarah, were sent for short periods as students to a local school. They learned their letters A–Z and numbers 1–10. The school was called a "blab school" because the pupils all read their lessons aloud to show they were busy studying (Armstrong, 1974, p. 14). Years later, Abraham continued to read that way. He often annoyed his law partner by reading the newspaper aloud in their office. His reason, he explained, was that he learned better by using two senses (Oates, 1977). First, he saw what he read, then he heard what he read, making the content easier to remember.

Abraham Lincoln's first school was a primitive structure but common for that time and place. The school was built of rough logs daubed with mud. The structure had no windows, but one log was removed the length of the building to allow for light and ventilation. The floor was dirt, leveled and beaten solid. A school session lasted the summer months, as it was too cold to go in the winter.

Lincoln was barely seven years old at the time of his first schooling. His sister, Sarah, went to the same school and took care of young Abe like a mother. She watched him constantly and would carry him in her arms when the roads were muddy from rain. At school he wore homespun clothes, as did all the children, and went barefoot. Sarah didn't want him to play with the boys for fear he might get hurt. But young Abe had a mind of his own and would seek out boys his age for play. In addition to playing with his schoolmates, he also enjoyed bending a sapling bush or tree and riding it like he would a horse.

In school Abraham learned to write letters and enjoyed forming and shaping them. For practice he often scratched letters with charcoal or wrote them in the dust or sand and in the snow when snow fell. He developed into a good speller, sometimes helping his friends during spelling lessons. When a classmate was once stuck on the letter *i* in "defied," Abe got her attention and pointed to his eye. She promptly completed the word correctly (Herndon, 1949).

Many factors worked against schooling for young Lincoln. While growing up he was needed for work on his father's farm. Frontier living conditions were harsh, and every able-bodied person was needed to help earn enough for survival. Schools were widely scattered, and, for most students, attendance required long walks or horseback rides. Teachers were hard to get and often did not remain in place very long. Books and teaching materials were in short supply. In Abraham's case, his father thought that work on the farm should take precedence over reading and study. But, in spite of the unfavorable conditions with which he had to compete, Lincoln did find books and time to read.

Records do not document exactly when young Lincoln first began reading. But evidence indicates he was quite young, perhaps even before he first began school. The family owned a Bible, which may have been the first book he learned to read. He later considered his early education to be poor, stating that, "Still, somehow, I could read, write, and cipher to the rule of three, but that was all" (Oates, 1977, p. 10). The evidence is clear, however, that once he learned, he read every book and paper he could get his hands on and read with a ravenous appetite. However, his early days were quite limited in books and print materials for reading.

When Abraham's father married a second time and brought Sarah Bush home as his wife and stepmother to his children, young Lincoln's interest in reading received a welcomed boost. While his father cared more about the work that Abraham could do on the farm, his stepmother encouraged his reading. Many years later she stated, "I induced my husband to permit Abe to read and study at home as well as at school" (Herndon and Weik, 1949, p. 43 and Tarbel, 1974, p. 72). She added that "Abe was a dutiful son to me always, and we took particular care when he was reading not to disturb him — would let him read on and on till he quit of his own accord" (Herndon and Weik, 1949, p. 33). Sarah provided a stable and loving new home life for both Lincoln children. She quickly grew to love Abraham and greatly encouraged his studious habits. She once said of him, "Abe was a good boy ... never gave me a cross word or look, and never refused, in fact or appearance, to do anything I requested him" (Tarbell, 1974, p. 87).

Soon after entering the Lincoln family, Sarah arranged for the children to attend a few weeks of classes taught by Andrew Crawford at a nearby school. Two years later Abraham attended classes taught by James Swaney. The next year he had a few weeks of instruction from Azel Dorsey. Lincoln learned to enjoy poetry and sometimes tried his hand with simple verse. Often his lines hint of an expectation that books and reading would one day make him an important person, as suggested in the following lines: "Abraham Lincoln, his hand and pen, he will be good, but [God] knows when" (Herndon and Weik, 1949, p. 37). In the Dorsey school Abe was introduced to *The Revised Statutes of Indiana*, a book he borrowed two years later to read and study from cover to cover. It was the first law book the future lawyer ever saw or read.

While in the Dorsey school young Lincoln was introduced to Scott's *Lessons in Elocution*, a book that helped him to develop good speaking skills. In the same school he also read and studied Murray's *English Grammar* and *English Reader*. The time spent in the Dorsey school ended Lincoln's formal schooling. When Dorsey saw him for the last time to say goodbye, he told Abe, "Always remember that lack of a school needn't hamper your learning" (Armstrong, 1974, p. 98). Abe took what his teacher had said to heart as his quest for knowledge never stopped. His friend, Dennis Hanks, said of him, "Abe was a good boy ... he was sometimes uncomfortably inquisitive. When strangers would ride along by the fence, he always ... could be sure to ask the first question" (Herndon and Weik, 1949, p. 24).

When the collection of books that were easily available at school or near his home had been read by young Lincoln, he began to comb the countryside in search of more. Somewhere in his search he secured a copy of Grimshaw's *History of the United States*. The book gave a good account of the discovery of America and its development as a new nation. The fight for independence from England and the heroic leadership and perseverance of George Washington were vividly dramatized as Lincoln read. The book also brought the young reader face to face with the horrors of slavery and its negative impact on the nation and its institutions. Having spent his life on the frontier, Abraham had seen very little of slavery.

During the period 1826–1830, Lincoln read everything he could find and borrow. He borrowed from neighbors and acquaintances in such large numbers that he would tie the books in his big bandana and transport them on a pole swung over his shoulder. One important source of books was Judge John Pitcher, who liked the young reader so much that he made his four-hundred-volume library available to Abe's passion.

While living in Indiana, Lincoln took a job on a ferryboat owned by James Taylor. While living and working with the Taylor family, Abraham read at every opportunity. A son of Taylor later recalled that Lincoln slept upstairs with him and used to read every night "till midnight" (Tarbell, 1974, p. 71). His stock of books at that time was small, but he read those he did have so thoroughly and frequently that he knew them well. The ones we know that he read include Aesop's *Fables*, *Robinson Crusoe*, and *Pilgrim's Progress*. During this period he also began hanging around the log courthouses in nearby towns where he watched young country lawyers cross-examine witnesses and appeal to juries. So thrilled with the legal proceedings was he that he borrowed a copy of *The Revised Statutes of Indiana* and read the volume again.

Every break in his workday Lincoln used for reading, regardless of the nature of the work. When plowing the rough fields he found time to read. At the end of long rows the horse was allowed to rest while he took out his book. Perched on a stump or fence he would read until compelled to return to work. He could become so absorbed in his subject that nothing distracted him. One passerby once reported seeing him on the top rail of a fence reading so intensely that Abe did not see him approach.

Having a limited supply of books available, Abe read and reread some several times. He once remarked that he had read Aesop's *Fables* so many times he could rewrite it from memory "without the loss of a single word" (Armstrong, 1974, p. 89). John Hanks, a relative who lived for a while in the Lincoln home, remembered that when "Abe and I returned to the house from work, he would always read" (Herndon, 1949, p. 39). Abraham told a friend that he had read through every book he had ever heard of for a circuit of fifty miles (Tarbell, 1974).

Any opportunity to acquire reading material did not go unnoticed by Lincoln. A storekeeper in Gentryville subscribed to a Louisville newspaper. Lincoln went there on a regular basis to read the paper and discuss the news with others. He also began to build a reputation as a talker and a person who was tuned in to the issues of the day. He frequently made political speeches to those gathered in and around the store. The ideas he expressed were clear and logical. The jokes and stories he liked to tell were so odd, witty, and original that all the village folk would gather around him and listen to every word. For local people, Abraham became something of a news reporter and entertainer.

The more Lincoln read the more he became aware of the advantages in life that might accrue to him from his vast knowledge. That perception can be discerned in a verse he wrote while still a boy, which stated: "Good boys who to their books apply, Will all be great men by and by" (Herndon and Weik, 1949, p. 37). Abraham took advantage of any opportunity to display his knowledge and skills to others. On one occasion a speaker came into town and made a speech. A friend told Lincoln he could do much better. Abraham stepped forward and gave a speech that so impressed the visitor that he congratulated Lincoln and asked where he had learned so much. Abe explained his study habits, his reading, and what he had read. The visitor encouraged him to "persevere."

Beginning early in his reading life, young Lincoln began developing useful study skills to aid his quest for knowledge. When he came to a passage he wanted to keep and thoroughly learn, he would write it down on paper. If he had no paper, he wrote on a piece of wood until he could get paper, an item that was in short supply in his time and place. Limited resources never discouraged him.

At the age of twenty-one Lincoln's time in Indiana came to an end. In March 1830 he moved with his family to Illinois. They settled near Decatur on the Sangamon River. In the spring of 1831, Abraham made a trip down the Mississippi River on a flatboat to New Orleans. The boat used for this trip was one built by Abraham, his stepbrother, John Johnston, and his mother's cousin, John Hanks. A month was consumed in the boat's construction. When the boat was finished, the crew loaded their cargo and set off down the Sangamon River for the mighty Mississippi, and then down to New Orleans. Shortly into the trip, misfortune struck. The boat got hung on a dam at New Salem, the village where Abraham would later live for a time. As the boat took on water, Lincoln sprang into action. He unloaded a part of the cargo and then drilled a hole in the bow, letting the water run out. He next plugged the hole, helped move the boat over the dam, reloaded the cargo, and proceeded to their destination (Herndon and Weik, 1949). The experience of figuring out a way to get the boat over the dam set the stage for an invention for which Lincoln would receive a patent a few years later.

When Lincoln and his companions reached New Orleans, they spent a month in the city where he saw for the first time the brutal horrors of slavery at its worst. He and his companions walked past a slave auction where a mulatto girl was being sold. The bidders pinched her flesh and made her trot up and down the room like a horse to show how well she could move. He saw slaves in chains "whipped and scourged." The entire scene was so revolting, he moved along to get away from it all. What he had seen left Abraham with a deep sense of gloom and sadness and hate for the whole institution of slavery. To his companions he said, "If I ever get a chance to hit that thing [slavery], I'll hit it hard" (Herndon and Weik, 1949, p. 64). What he saw of slavery on the streets of New Orleans confirmed his worst images of the institution that he had gained through reading.

In September 1831 Lincoln moved to New Salem, Illinois, where, at age twenty-two, he accepted a job as store clerk in Offutt's General Store. New Salem was nothing more than a rustic pioneer town. The store was the gathering place for exchange of local news and assorted tittle-tattle among the local population. Clerking enabled Abraham to meet and get to know a wide range of people in the area. There were discussions and debates on politics and other interesting issues of the day. By this time, he was widely read and was known to be honest and respected by those who knew him, and so he quickly became accepted by the people. They also remembered his inventiveness a few months earlier when he figured a way to get his stuck flatboat loose and over the dam at New Salem.

From some of the new acquaintances made at Offutt's store, Lincoln was able to secure books. He secured and studied *The Revised Code of Laws of Illinois*. With each book on the law he read he became more interested and decided to read law in earnest toward making it a career. He borrowed books from Major John T. Stuart, books he had to hike to and from Springfield to procure. It is said he read sometimes forty pages or more while en route. Often he could be seen meandering at random across the fields repeating aloud the points in his reading (Herndon, 1949). While living in New Salem he also read books in natural philosophy.

In 1832 Offutt's General Store closed, but the experience that Lincoln had gained as a store clerk set the stage for his own venture as a merchant. In just a few months he and William F. Berry formed a partnership in their own general store. Berry turned out to be an alcoholic who neglected the business, while Lincoln spent so much time talking politics with the customers and reading that the business was short-lived. Abraham would spend hour upon hour stretched out on the store counter, or tucked away under a shade tree, reading. Burns, Shakespeare, and law books were among his interest at the time.

From the time he had arrived in New Salem, Lincoln embarked on an intensive program of reading and study. He understood by then the power of knowledge and the opportunities that reading could open to him. He was once heard to remark, "The things I want to know are in books; my best friend is the man who'll git me a book I ain't read" (Sandburg, 1954, p. 37). Books on mathematics, literature, poetry, and language structure and usage absorbed his reading interest. On one occasion Abraham walked six miles to borrow a copy of Kirkham's *Grammar* and spent several weeks studying its content. Sometimes he would stretch out full length on the store's counter with his head propped up on a stack of calico prints and study the book with diligent engagement. He even persuaded the village cooper to allow him to come into the cooper's shop at night and keep a fire of shavings burning bright enough that he could see to read.

At the same time Lincoln was reading with such intensity, the political discussions he engaged in with patrons at the store whetted his appetite for politics. He decided that he wanted to be a public figure of some kind and talked about it with friends. Some advised him to develop good public speaking skills. After searching for help, he found debating clubs in the area for which he would walk seven or eight miles to participate.

In May 1833, Lincoln was appointed postmaster of New Salem, an appointment that was to aid his reading interest. The post office was located in Sam Hill's General Store, a location that gave him an opportunity to read newspapers that came through the post office. In addition, much reading experience was gained when he was asked to read papers and letters to customers who could not read for themselves. From that reading, he acquired a wealth of knowledge and insight into the region, its people, and their concerns and issues.

Many of the postal patrons lived well out in the country. Periodically, Lincoln would stick their mail in the crown of his tall hat and walk from house to house delivering their mail. Thus, an observation of the time held much truth, namely, that Lincoln kept the New Salem post office in his hat.

At times blind luck would intervene to provide Lincoln with important reading material. On one occasion an emigrant came through New Salem in a covered wagon and stopped by the post office. In the wagon the owner carried a barrel full of odds and ends that he wanted to sell because his wagon was overloaded. Good natured as he was, Lincoln bought the barrel and its contents for fifty cents, just to help the man. The barrel was set aside in the store and soon forgotten. Sometime later, when he was cleaning the store, Abraham rediscovered the barrel. Curiosity prompted him to remove the contents. To his great delight, at the bottom of the barrel he found the four volumes of a famous work, Blackstone's *Commentaries on the Laws of England*. He began reading the works and found his mind more thoroughly absorbed than he had ever experienced before.

While serving as postmaster in New Salem from 1833 to 1836, Lincoln read a wide range of books that expanded his knowledge of world history and the world of ideas. Among his readings were Volney's *The Ruins of Empire*, Gibbon's *Decline and Fall of the Roman Empire*, and Paine's *The Age of Reason*. In addition, he performed other jobs to supplement his small income, work that included rail splitting, working at a local mill, being a farm hand, serving as local agent for the Springfield newspaper, and acting as clerk at elections. For a time Abe did some work for John Romine. John discovered that Abe was more into books than manual labor. He later said about Lincoln that, "He worked for me, but was always reading and thinking. I used to get mad at him" (Herndon, 1949, p. 38).

One new trade Lincoln embarked upon in the fall of 1833 was that of surveyor. He was appointed deputy surveyor for Sangamon County. George Washington had begun as a surveyor while a young man, and the identity with a model and hero he regarded so highly appealed to Lincoln. He knew nothing about surveying, so he borrowed some books on the trade and began an intense program of self-study. Many days and nights were spent reading materials on surveying, often staying up until dawn of the new day. Abraham worked so hard in preparation that his friends grew much concerned at his haggard appearance. But in six weeks he had mastered the subject sufficiently so he could begin surveying. Eager to get started in his new job, Lincoln bought surveying instruments and a horse on credit, after which he began surveying roads, school sections, and town sites. Petersburg, Illinois, is a town that was surveyed and laid out by Lincoln in 1836 (Tarbell, 1974). Surveying not only allowed him to apply his reading skills to still another pursuit, it also provided an opportunity for him to meet and serve the people in the region.

Since he also served as the postmaster, Lincoln would take with him on surveying assignments the mail of patrons whose homes he would pass along the way. That personal service won him many friends and a highly regarded reputation as a man. Surveying also nourished his growing political interest. Abraham met and conversed with citizens all over the county. Once people got to meet and talk with him, he won them over. He worked for three years as deputy county surveyor.

READING IN PROFESSIONAL LIFE

At the age of twenty-five, Lincoln ran a second time for a seat in the Illinois state legislature after having lost in an earlier attempt. The second campaign produced a win for the budding politician. At about the same time, he began a concentrated program of reading in law. Books were borrowed from the law firm of Stuart and Drummand in Springfield, Illinois. It was customary in those days for one wishing to become a lawyer to study under the guidance of a trained attorney, but Abraham learned largely on his own. Law books were carried with him virtually wherever he went. People reported seeing him walking alone along a road reading and reciting from his book (Oates, 1977).

On September 9, 1836, Lincoln was awarded a license to practice law. Two days later he tried his first case in Springfield. In April 1837 he moved his home from New Salem to Springfield, where he formed a partnership with John T. Stuart in the practice of law. During his early days as an attorney, a group of young men formed a literary society in which debates were conducted and original poems and other original works were read to members of the group. Such forums gave Abraham a stage for gaining experience in oral and written expression (Herndon and Weik, 1949).

When time came for Lincoln to begin traveling the court circuit to try cases in the small villages and communities across the Illinois countryside, he took books along to read during lulls in court sessions and at night. The bulk of his cases were tried in the circuit courts of about two-dozen Illinois counties, most of them within the large Eighth Judicial Circuit that stretched from Springfield's Sangamon County eastward to Indiana. Twice each year for over twenty years, Abraham spent two to three months riding the circuit in company with the presiding judge and fellow attorneys.

In many of the localities where court sessions were held, living accommodations were limited. Often Lincoln and the attorneys traveling with him had to sleep two in a bed, eight to ten in one room. When others went to sleep, Abe would read by the light of a candle. In such circumstances, he read the several volumes of Euclid. He also bought a book on logic and studied how to untangle fallacies and draw conclusions from established facts. The avid reader often read the family Bible and knew much of it by heart. He could quote whole chapters of Isaiah, the New Testament and the Psalms as well as any clergyman. Quotations from the Bible were often used in talks to juries, in speeches, and in letters written to friends, relatives, and professional colleagues (Sandburg, 1954).

Lincoln's reading influenced his professional life in many ways. He could not separate himself from the books he had read. They were a part of who he was, and their influence was always present in what he did and said. On a trip to Louisville, Kentucky, to visit the Speed family, Lincoln visited the law office of James Speed. While in the office on several visits, James reported that Abraham "read my books, talked with me about his life, his reading, his studies, his aspirations" (Herndon and Weik, 1949, p. 172).

The books Lincoln read on the life of George Washington left him with a deep admiration and respect for our nation's first president. Washington became his hero, a human model that would serve as a guiding light for his life. Abraham found in Washington one who represented man's highest ideals as a person and public servant. We do not have a record of when Lincoln first became aware of George Washington. It may have been during the short time he spent in school. He probably did not have a full appreciation of Washington until he read Grimshaw's *History of the United States*. There may have been other books, of which no record was left, that informed him on the life of Washington. One book, however, does stand tall in Lincoln's appreciation of Washington. That book was *The Life of Washington* by Mason Locke Weems.

Although the record is not clear, Lincoln appears to have first read Weems's book when he was twenty years of age and still living in Indiana. He borrowed the book from a local farmer who had brought it with him when he moved from Kentucky. While it was in Abe's possession, misfortune struck. Late one night, before going to sleep, Abe placed the borrowed book in a place where he usually stored a book while he slept. That place was in a crack between two logs in the wall of the cabin. During the night, rain fell. Water dripped over the mud daubing, allowing muddy water to drip onto the book. The muddy water stained the pages and left the book badly in need of a new binding. Very upset about what had happened, Abe offered to buy the book. The owner, however, struck a deal with the apologetic reader. If he would pull corn fodder for three days, he could keep the book. Abe did the work and kept the book (Herndon and Weik, 1949).

Of all the people Lincoln read about, George Washington was his favorite and the one he considered the greatest of all men. The more he read about our nation's first president, the more it fired his own ambitions. In reading Weems's book, Abraham became enchanted with the story of our nation's beginning. One historian wrote that Lincoln became so engrossed in the Revolutionary War that, "he could almost hear the rattle of musketry and smell the acrid scent of gunpowder in the Indiana wind" (Oates, 1977, p. 11). And who was at the center of the war? George Washington.

Reading the life and adventures of Washington gave Lincoln a deep sense of the American spirit of independence and freedom, the principles upon which our nation was founded, and the great sacrifices made by so many to achieve our freedoms. The book left him inspired by the achievements of Washington and the uniqueness of the young American nation. Who can doubt that what Lincoln learned and felt then was still with him when he had to face the prospect of a divided nation as our sixteenth president many years later? Could he be the one to allow what Washington had created to be torn asunder? We know he could not.

Lincoln left no doubt regarding his admiration and respect for George Washington. In a speech delivered before the New Jersey Senate on February 21, 1861, when southern secession from the Union faced the nation, he recalled how he had read Weems's book at an early age and described how vivid was his memory of Washington and his troops crossing the Delaware River at Trenton and fighting the Hessians under very harsh conditions. To his audience, Lincoln said,

> I recollect thinking then, boy even though I was, that there must have been something more than common that these men struggled for.... I am exceedingly anxious that this Union, the Constitution, and the liberties of the people shall be perpetuated in accordance with the original idea for which that struggle was made [Lincoln, 2003, p. 1].

In addition to Washington, another important discovery Lincoln made, principally through reading, was his intense distaste for slavery. The more he read about the institution the more horrible he believed it to be. A book he read sometime after the Weems book was *Sufferings in Africa: Captain Riley's Narrative—An Authentic Narrative of the Loss of the American Brig* Commerce by James Riley (Riley, 1965). In the book Riley told about his life, career, and lessons learned from his world travels as a sea captain. His ship had been wrecked on the coast of Africa. He and his crew were captured and held as slaves for a long period of time. The experience of being a slave left a deep and lasting impression on Riley. In his narrative he bewailed the brutal fact that in his native country, the United States of America, a million and a half human beings were held in the cruelest bonds of slavery. He pledged himself to henceforth do all he could to redeem the enslaved and destroy the shackles of oppression. From Riley and other readings, Lincoln grew increasingly apprehensive over the agitation surrounding the slavery issue across the nation.

The growing animosities over the slavery issue in the U.S. Congress and across the country began to wear deeply on Lincoln as he traveled the court circuit. Others observed him in times of deep gloom and moodiness when he was not standing before the court. A fellow attorney reported observing Lincoln on one occasion sitting in a corner of the courtroom "wrapped in gloom ... pursuing in his mind some specific, sad subject. He was aroused by the breaking up of the court, when he emerged ... like one awakened from sleep" (Sandburg, 1954, p. 197). Another noted that on a stopover for a court session, the traveling companions went to bed and left Lincoln "sitting in front of the fireplace staring intently at the flames. The next morning he was still there, studying the ashes and charred logs" (Oates, 1977, p. 107).

In 1846 Lincoln was elected a representative to the United States Congress. When he arrived in Washington with his family, they secured lodging in Mrs. Spriggs's boardinghouse across from the Capitol building. Mrs. Lincoln soon grew unhappy with the Washington social scene and, after three months, left the city to live with her family in Kentucky. Her departure left Lincoln alone, when he was not occupied with congressional business, to pursue his reading and study.

In his solitude Lincoln began a focused course of self-education in which he studied mathematics, astronomy, and poetry. He read widely in the books and newspapers available in his expanding environment. When reading he would often lie on the floor with the back of a chair for a pillow. One book read was on the theory of evolution called *Vestiges of Creation*. Poetry proved to be more to his taste than novels. He did, however, enjoy Mrs. Lee Hentz's novels that were popular at the time. Abraham also liked short, spicy stories, one and two columns long, such as "Cousin Sally Dillard," "Becky Williams's Courtship," and "The Down-Easter and the Bull."

One evening Lincoln went to the library of the Supreme Court where he browsed and rummaged for quite a while through books and documents. While rummaging, he collected several for reading. When the hour grew late and the library was about to close, he checked the books out, tied a large bandana around them, ran a stick through the knot, slung the stick over his shoulder, and walked to his room in the boardinghouse where he continued his reading.

Lincoln relished good literature, both reading and using it. When traveling he would sit for hours reading, and sometimes quoting, passages from Shakespeare, Browning, and Byron. Among his favorites were *King Lear, Richard III, Henry VIII, Hamlet,* and *Macbeth*. Later, as president, when he became burdened with the woes and stresses of the Civil War, one of his favorite diversions was in reading Shakespeare. In the evenings, as he waited for sleep to come, he would "read his worn copy of Shakespeare's tragedies, turning again and again to *Hamlet* and *Macbeth*" (Oates, 1977, p. 250).

A poem that Lincoln enjoyed was "Mortality" written by a Scotsman named William Knox. Friends reported that he especially liked the last two stanzas that read:

> Yea, hope and despondency, pleasure and pain,
> Are mingled together in sunshine and rain;
> And the smile and the tear, the song and the dirge,
> Still follow each other, like surge upon surge.
> 'Tis the wink of an eye — 'tis the draught of a breath
> From the blossom of health to the paleness of death,
> From the gilded saloon to the bier and the shroud,
> Oh, why should the spirit of mortal be proud?
> [Oates, 1977, p. 95].

In April 1846 Lincoln wrote to a friend about the poem, which he had read in a newspaper the previous summer, stating, "I would give all I am worth, and go into debt, to be able to write so fine a piece as I think that is" (Oates, 1977, p. 70). Perhaps the poem reflected to Lincoln the periods of dark gloom and preoccupation with death that some acquaintances have reported were a part of his disposition (Oates, 1977).

In 1848 Lincoln was on his way home to Illinois from Washington when the boat on which he was traveling became stranded on a sandbar. The boat's captain ordered the hands on board to collect all the loose planks, empty barrels and boxes and force them under the sides of the boat. The empty casks were used to buoy the boat upward. Gradually, the vessel lifted and swung clear of the sand bar. Abraham watched the operation very closely and probably compared it to what he had done with his flatboat on the Sangamon River in 1831.

Both experiences led Lincoln to think hard on the subject of lifting vessels over sand bars and other obstruction on the nation's rivers. With the help of a Springfield mechanic, he created a scale model of an invention to lift river vessels over obstructions. His law partner later recalled that Abe would occasionally bring the model to the office and whittle on it and talk about its merits and how it was destined to revolutionize river navigation. The partner thought the invention to be impracticable but did not say much out of respect for Abraham's well-known reputation as a boatman (Herndon, 1949). Lincoln took the scale model with him to Washington and hired an attorney to apply for a patent. On May 22, 1849, Abraham Lincoln received patent no. 6469 for a device to lift boats over shoals, an invention which was never manufactured. However, he did become the only person to serve as president that held a government patent.

READING DURING TRANSFORMATION INTO A POLITICAL DIGNITARY

In the years before 1858 Lincoln regularly read two of the leading proslavery journals, the *Charleston Mercury* and the *Richmond Enquirer*, along with the leading histories of the slavery movement. In addition, he and his law partner subscribed to such papers as the *Chicago Tribune, New York Tribune, Anti-Slavery Standard, Emancipator*, and the *National Era*. He read *The Impending Crisis of the South* by Hinton Rowan Helper, a book in which Helper stated that the southern slave society was growing poorer and sinking deeper into debt and poverty while the free labor system in the North was growing richer. His law partner bought a book titled *Sociology* by Fitzhugh in which the author defended and tried to justify slavery in every possible way. Abraham read that book, also. He and his law partner, Herndon, read all the books and papers they could acquire on slavery. Then they would discuss with each other what they understood and believed after the readings. Herndon was even more antislavery than Lincoln, but found Lincoln's views impossible to change. He stated, "I was never conscious of having made much of an impression on Mr. Lincoln, nor do I believe I ever changed his views" (Herndon, 1949, p. 293). From our vantage point today, it seems clear that Lincoln was reading widely to get himself thoroughly informed on the debates raging wildly, both pro and con, on the slavery issue.

In 1858 Lincoln was nominated by the Republican Party to be its candidate for the United States Senate. On June 16, in an acceptance speech delivered to the Illinois Republican State Convention, he outlined a provocative but compelling position on why slavery must be stopped from spreading and ultimately abolished. In the speech Lincoln made the famous declaration that, "A house divided against itself cannot stand." Abraham had read the speech to a group of friends before it was delivered. All but one advised him not to use the "house divided" term. His response was, as reported by Herndon, "The time has come when these sentiments should be uttered; and if it is decreed that I should go down because of this speech, then let me go down linked to the truth" (Herndon, 1949, p. 326).

In a series of debates that followed his nomination for the senate seat, Lincoln debated his Democratic Party opponent, Stephen A. Douglas, in a series of debates that became famous as "The Lincoln-Douglas Debates." Douglas favored the status quo on slavery, but Lincoln was profoundly against it. His position was that slavery was a drain on the national spirit causing regions of the country to be in conflict with each other. In addition, slavery was inconsistent with the principles on which George Washington led our nation to secure its liberty. Slavery was, therefore, morally wrong. Abraham lost his bid for the senate seat, but a far greater prize waited just around the corner.

Soon after the senate contest was over, people began talking about Lincoln as a candidate for president on the Republican ticket in the election of 1860. His widely acclaimed speeches and debates during the senate race had elevated him to celebrity status. He began to receive invitations to speak in nonslave areas of the country. One morning in October 1859, Abe went rushing into his law office in Springfield with a letter inviting him to speak in Brooklyn, New York. After thinking it over, he wrote back saying he accepted the invitation and indicating that he would make it a political speech (Herndon, 1949).

During the time before the speech would be delivered, Lincoln read and scanned a wide array of materials in preparation. At the state library, he read the *Congressional Globe*, the *Annals of Congress*, and in his office worked his way through a six-volume edition of Elliot's *Debates on the Federal Constitution*. This would be a speech not for frontiersman, delivered from the back of a wagon, but one honed for a sophisticated metropolitan audience. When delivered, the speech was well received. Upon leaving New York, he toured the New England states giving political speeches and gaining important exposure and support for his political views.

On May 18, 1860, Lincoln was nominated by the Republican Party to be a candidate for president of the United States. On Tuesday, November 6, he was elected, defeating three other candidates. Lincoln had remained in Springfield during the balloting. When reports confirmed the he had won the presidency, he went with friends to a banquet which Republican ladies had prepared. Upon walking into the banquet hall, he was greeted by beaming ladies with a "How do you do, Mr. President?" (Oates, 1977, p. 190).

Immediately after his election to the office of president, Lincoln began to prepare for the many problems he knew awaited him. One of the most serious issues was what he would do if the southern states attempted to secede from the Union, as some outspoken proslavery voices had declared they would do. That threat was one that weighed heavily on the president-elect's mind. One reporter found him reading a history of the South Carolina nullification crisis of 1832 that President Andrew Jackson had dealt with during his presidency (Oates, 1977). In that crisis President Jackson had signed into law a tariff bill to which South Carolina vigorously objected. The South Carolina legislature declared the tariff void in its state. Jackson threatened to send troops into South Carolina, if necessary, to uphold the rule of law. A compromise was finally worked out, and the state canceled its nullification of the tariff (Schlesinger, 1946). Lincoln was soon to discover that the slavery issue was too intense and ingrained for a compromise that would preserve the Union without war. The southern states did secede and formed a separate government.

Upon taking the oath of office as our nation's sixteenth president, Lincoln faced a multitude of problems and issues. But he never lost sight of the purposes for which he accepted the office. As Commander in Chief of the Union Army, he conducted a war against those who would divide the nation, a war he didn't want, but one he knew must be fought to preserve the Union. For his perseverance and dedication during the darkest hours of that bloody conflict, he was sustained by the memory of George Washington, his hero, who had faced similar toils and burdens during the Revolutionary War. Like Washington, Lincoln knew that the cause for which he fought was right and just, that what he fought for was too important for him to fail. And true to his convictions, he abolished slavery from the country. For his bravery, he was rewarded with election to a second term, a term that would have him be president of a United States of America. But, a complete second term was not to be. Fate intervened.

Lincoln was assassinated on April 14, 1865, and died the next day. He died having practiced the human ideals and beliefs he had acquired throughout his life through reading and interacting with others. The guiding light of George Washington and Abe's abhorrence of slavery that he had acquired through reading and observation gave him the courage and fortitude to persevere during the darkest days of the Civil War. He continued to believe that a house divided against itself could not stand. He would not let the nation be forever divided, allowing a part to practice and spread the institution of slavery. For his ideals and beliefs, Lincoln's mortality was snatched away. In its wake he gained supreme immortality.

Lincoln's untimely death brought to reality a fear that his beloved stepmother had harbored from the time he was nominated for president. In September 1865, Sarah Bush Lincoln talked about her last visit with Abraham in February 1861. She said,

> I did not want Abe to run for President, and I did not want to see him elected. I was afraid that something would happen to him and when he came down to see me, after he was elected, I still felt, and my heart told me, that something would befall Abe, and that I should never see him again [Herndon and Weik, 1949, p. 30].

Sarah passed away at the age of eighty in April 1869, surviving Abraham by about four years.

Lincoln had held a fatalistic view of existence most of his life. He believed that his fate was beyond his control. But in his nation's hour of greatest need, he rose to the top of a brave people and led them in their struggle to preserve their Union. In departing he gave the generations of Americans that have come and will come after him their greatest gift, a free nation, united, and one that is admired around the world. The power of reading had instilled in him the convictions and courage to do what he knew to be right, even in the face of overwhelming obstacles and danger.

THE IMPACT OF READING

It has been said that Abraham Lincoln educated himself for his moment of greatness. That he was special and unique for his time and place is widely accepted. A former school classmate of his once observed, "He was the learned boy among us unlearned folks" (Tarbell, 1974, p. 84). During his developmental years, Lincoln had drawn on the power of reading to gain perspective on the nature of life and human events. Even though he had experienced less than one full year of schooling, he had masterfully overcome any disadvantage such a limitation might have assigned to him.

Having spent most of his early life on the developing American frontier, removed from educated and cultured society, Lincoln made the most of what was available to him. The only books he had to read were those he could pick up within a small radius of his home. He had known and associated only with men and women of the poor frontier towns, and he had never spoken to an audience, except for debating clubs or to a small group by the roadside. Yet, by the age of twenty-three, he had gained enough self-confidence and knowledge to announce his candidacy for the Illinois General Assembly. He knew what his objective was, and he understood what he wanted to be. He knew what he must do to reach his goal in life.

Lincoln's reading instilled in him a well-developed set of principles and ideals that would guide his life. During his long course of self-development, he learned to distinguish the real from the unreal and the true from the untrue. He honed his evaluative skills as he matched his mind and knowledge against the writers of the many books he read. Discussing a book on the life of Edmund Burke, he once observed,

> The author makes a wonderful hero out of his subject. He magnifies his perfections, if he had any, and suppresses his imperfections. He is so faithful in his zeal and so lavish in his praise of his every act that one is almost driven to believe that Burke never made a mistake or failure in his life.... History is not history unless it is the truth [Herndon, 1949, p. 353].

Lincoln's reading became a part of his mind and shaped his vision of history, time, and place. Upon seeing the Niagara Falls, he connected it to all that he had read and learned of the past. He wrote,

> When Columbus first sought this continent, when Christ suffered on the cross, when Moses led Israel through the Red sea, nay, even when Adam first came from the hand of his Maker, then as now, Niagara was roaring here.... The Mammoth and Mastodon — now so long dead, that fragments of their monstrous bones, alone testify, that they ever lived, have gazed on Niagara" [Sandburg, 1954, p. 177].

Lincoln worked hard at learning. He once said that he was slow to learn and slow to forget. He described his mind as being like a piece of steel, "very hard to scratch anything on it, and almost impossible after you get it there to rub it out" (Herndon, 1949, p. 421). A friend once said of Abraham that he read hard books and dug things out (Herndon, 1949). By the age of twenty-four he had developed his mind so fully that he could take hold of a subject and assimilate it to the point it would work for him. The fact that he could, on his own, absorb the knowledge and skills required to become an accomplished surveyor attests to the power of his mind. The mental power and structure required to grasp a complex new subject quickly and completely does not come to one without effort. The future president used reading to build that power.

Reading helped Lincoln develop a deep sense of feeling and interest in people and their needs. He evolved an unselfish nature and a tenderness of heart that allowed him to feel for others. With his broad sense of history, his deep knowledge of the struggles of humankind, he could become deeply troubled over issues that he sensed, more acutely than others, portended serious turmoil and hardship. The slavery issue was such a problem for Lincoln.

Lincoln's own self-development made him acutely aware of the importance of education for the general uplifting of all people. He promoted education for everyone, for he believed that every person should be able to read the histories of his and other countries so as to acquire an appreciation of the free institutions that are so fundamental to free governments. In addition, people should have the advantage of being able to read the Scriptures and other writings of a religious and moral nature for themselves (Oates, 1977).

Lincoln believed that writing and the ability to read what others wrote was the great invention of the world. To be able to connect one's mind with the thoughts and ideas of those men and women, dead or living, across all the distances of time and space since writing began was an astonishing achievement in human history. For Lincoln, books and reading were the great liberators of people. Before printing, the masses did not realize that they were capable of improving their minds. They believed themselves to be the natural slaves of those few who could read books. To free the human mind from the false belief that most people were incapable of personal growth is the greatest step forward yet achieved by humans.

Lincoln saw reading as a tool for gaining access to all that had been discovered by others, to the problems of life already solved. In addition, reading gives an impetus and relish to pursuing the unsolved problems that confront us. When asked by others how to get an education, how to improve oneself, he gave the same advice he had followed; "It is only to get books, read and study them carefully" (Herndon, 1949, p. 261).

The power of reading produced the man we know as Abraham Lincoln. He truly was a product of books rather than schooling. Through focused study and reflection, Lincoln became the man that is recognized the world over as the great liberator of human potential. Not only did he liberate his own potential, he engineered social changes that freed the potential of others. He became a model for all people who aspire to a better station in life. He set the pattern, shaped the mold, showed the way, and proved that people can improve their lives. His law partner said about Lincoln, "Many of our great men and our statesmen, it is true, have been self-made, rising gradually through struggles to the top-most round of the ladder; but Lincoln rose from a lower depth than any of them" (Herndon and Weik, 1949, p. vii).

How fortunate was this nation that such a man was here and ready to serve in its hour of greatest need. Lincoln had worked, studied. and molded his mind and value system. He had defined the ideals that guided his behavior and judgments. He had learned to search for truth and to let truth and honesty, intelligently arrived at, guide his decisions. When the silent, solitary workings of his mind had led him to a conclusion, the power of his knowledge afforded him a certainty of conviction of such depth that nothing could sway him from his beliefs. No influence could lead him to abandon the course his reason told him was correct. That was the power that reading instilled in his life. That power is open to others who are willing to collect it from the thousands of libraries that dot the world's landscape.

Honors and Memorials

Abraham Lincoln is one of the most acclaimed persons who ever lived. He has more national parks named in his honor than any other American. In untold numbers of locations across the nation, statues and memorials, schools and centers have been erected to his memory. A complete listing would be well beyond the scope of this book. However, one memorial should be recognized. That is the Lincoln Memorial located on the Mall in Washington, D.C. The Lincoln Memorial is a huge, impressive structure modeled in the style of a Greek temple. Its design features thirty-six Doric columns on the outside with a massive sculpture of Lincoln on the inside. The majesty of the structure is thought by some to be the most profound symbol of American democracy in the world (Lincoln Memorial, 2003).

Frederick Douglass

A Brief Biography

Frederick Douglass was born in February 1818 on Holmes Hill Farm on Tuckahoe Creek near the town of Easton in Talbot County in the state of Maryland. The exact date of his birth is unknown. His mother was Harriet Bailey, a black slave. Under the laws of slavery in place at the time of his birth, a child born of slaves became a slave. Hence, Frederick was born a slave. His father was a white man that was never identified to Douglass. At birth he was given the name Frederick Augustus Washington Bailey. He later adopted the name Frederick Douglass, the name by which the world came to know him.

Holmes Hill Farm was part of an estate owned by Aaron Anthony. Anthony also managed the plantations of Edward Lloyd, one of the wealthiest men in Maryland. At Holmes Hill Farm, Frederick's mother labored as a field hand, working long hours in the cornfields. For that reason, young Frederick was sent to live with his grandmother, Betsy Bailey, who lived in a cabin a short distance from the farm. His mother made brief, infrequent visits to see Frederick, visits that were made at night in the darkness of the cabin in which he lived. He once wrote that he only saw her four or five times, leaving him with only a dim memory of her throughout his life (Douglass, 1982).

In 1824 at the age of six, Douglass was sent to live on the Lloyd plantation. The plantation was located on Wye River and was the site of the home of Aaron Anthony. The distance between Holmes Hill Farm and the Lloyd plantation made visits by his mother very difficult. Frederick saw her one last time within a few months after he was moved. His mother died within the year after that visit.

While living on the plantation young Frederick developed a natural charm and personality that made him easily likable to both whites and blacks. His chief friend and guardian became Lucretia Auld, the daughter of his owner. She had recently married a ship's captain named Thomas Auld. One day Lucretia told Frederick that he was going to be sent to live with the family of her brother-in-law in Baltimore. Within three days, he had been scrubbed clean, dressed in a pair of pants, and sent on his way to the city.

The move to Baltimore in March 1826 introduced a dramatic change in Frederick's young life. He lived with the Hugh Auld family in the Fells Point section of Baltimore. His job there would be to run errands and look after the Auld's small son, Thomas. Initially, Frederick found Mrs. Auld, Sophia, to be a gentle and kind mistress. She took pride in his growth and development and he worked hard to please her. Not long after he became comfortable and settled into his new life, an unexpected event threatened his sense of security. Mr. Auld scolded Sophia for her gentle and caring treatment of young Frederick, resulting in a complete change in her disposition toward him. But he continued to live with the Auld family for seven years.

A dispute between the two Auld brothers in 1833 resulted in Frederick being transferred to a farm to live and work. Life on the farm was very difficult for the youngster who was approaching manhood. He was put to work as a field hand where he went hungry most of the time. He and other slaves often had to steal food to keep from starving. When caught, as they sometimes were, they were beaten with a whip. Frederick and his owner had frequent disagreements and conflicts. Eventually, his owner concluded that Frederick was so difficult to manage that he needed obedience training.

In January 1834 Douglass was sent to work for Edward Covey. Covey was a poor farmer who had built a reputation around the area for being an effective "nigger breaker" of young undisciplined slaves (McFeely, 1991, p. 44). By the end of his first week with Covey, Frederick had received a severe beating for letting an oxen team run wild and destroy a wagon. True to the reputation he had acquired, Covey beat his slaves, spied on them as they worked to see if they slacked on the job, and worked them from dawn until nightfall in all kinds of weather. Because Covey assumed a religious faith, his one humane concession was to let his slaves have Sundays free from work. Covey also fed his slaves better than Frederick's owner in order to keep up their stamina for the hard manual work he expected them to endure. Even though life under Covey was harsh and trying for Douglass, he did realize a positive byproduct. He was quickly becoming a man. That became clear to both Frederick and Covey one day in August.

After an extremely serious beating one day by Covey, Frederick ran away and went to find his owner. After listening to Frederick's description of his severe beatings, the owner took no sympathy and sent him back to the Covey farm.

Upon his return, Covey grabbed Frederick and began trying to tie him to a post so that he could beat him again. Knowing what was about to come his way, from somewhere deep inside himself, Frederick mustered the courage and strength to fight back. For almost two hours Covey and Frederick tussled and wrestled around the farmyard until both were exhausted. Covey finally gave up and never attempted to whip Douglass again.

At the age of eighteen Douglass was arrested and confined to jail for developing a plan to escape from slavery to the North when authorities learned about the plan from one of the participants. After Douglass spent a week behind bars, his owner paid his fine and sent him back to Baltimore to live again with the Auld family. While in the city he learned the ship-caulking trade and began participating in several social activities. He learned to play the violin and met a young woman named Anna Murray. Anna was a free black person who worked as a servant for a prominent Baltimore family. She was five years older than Frederick, was plain and uneducated, but Frederick admired her qualities of honesty, efficient work ethic, and noble character. Love soon conquered, and they became engaged to marry in 1838 (Thomas, n.d., p. 4).

Douglass never lost hope that he would one day be a free person. With Anna's help and support, on September 3, 1838, he jumped aboard a train dressed as a seaman and rode out of Baltimore. With seventeen dollars in his pocket, some of it given to him by Anna, he worked his way to New York City (Quarles, 1968). Being careful about where he went and with whom he spoke, he walked the streets and finally spent his first night in New York sleeping behind some barrels stacked near a wharf. Realizing the next day that continuing to roam about the city would endanger his freedom, he placed his trust in a sailor he saw on the street. After he shared his confidence with the seaman, the new acquaintance took Douglass to the house where his prearranged plans directed him, a place where he could receive help. When he was at last safe and secure in the home of friends to runaway slaves, Frederick rejoiced in a "moment of the highest excitement I ever experienced.... I felt like one who had escaped a den of hungry lions" (Douglass, 1982, p. 143).

The home to which Douglass had been directed was that of David Ruggles, an officer in the New York Vigilance Committee. That committee worked with the "underground railroad" in assisting escaping slaves to freedom. Soon after discussing his circumstance with Ruggles, Frederick sent for Anna to come to New York. The two were married September 15, 1838. The next question for the newlyweds to address was where they could live and find work. Ruggles pointed out to them that slave catchers watched the streets and wharves of New York for runaway slaves that they could catch and return South for money. He recommended that they settle in New Bedford, Massachusetts, a small port town on the Atlantic coast that would be safer from slave catchers and where he could probably find work as a ship's caulker. The couple accepted the recommendation and settled in New Bedford.

In his new life as a free man, and a married man that would soon become a father, Douglass took whatever work he could get to support his family. He also became involved in the slavery abolitionist movement that was gaining acceptance in the North. In August 1841, he made a compelling speech to the audience at the annual meeting of the Massachusetts Anti-Slavery Society. The speech was so powerful that he promptly was recognized as an electrifying speaker and was immediately hired to be an agent and lecturer for the society. The new job would pay him a living wage and would also set the pattern for the remainder of his life. From that day forward he lectured and wrote on behalf of freedom for slaves and became famous as an abolitionist and fighter for equal rights for all citizens.

READING DURING EARLY LIFE AS A SLAVE

When young Douglass was sent, at the age of eight, from the plantation to live with the Auld family in Baltimore, his exposure to books and printed language had been near zero. Soon after moving into the Auld home, he discovered that his mistress, Sophia Auld, enjoyed reading the Bible out loud when her husband was away at work. She would often hold her two-year-old son on her lap and read stories to him. She soon began to pull Frederick into her reading sessions. The mistress liked the young slave and was pleased with the interest he displayed in what she read. Her read-aloud sessions soon awakened in Frederick a curiosity about printed words. He listened to the words and tried to match them to their printed form in the book. What he learned from those sessions created a burning desire to learn how to read for himself. Feeling at ease with his kind mistress, Frederick asked her to teach him. Stimulated by the challenge, she promptly began instructing him in the letters of the alphabet.

Within a short time Frederick had learned the alphabet and could spell words of three to four letters. The young slave student learned quickly, and Sophia found joy in his progress. She gained a real sense of accomplishment as a teacher. So pleased was Sophia, she excitedly told her husband what she had been doing. Her joy was quickly dashed.

Mr. Auld scolded his wife and told her that what she was doing was both wrong and unlawful. She seemed unaware of the social and legal constraints inherent in the master-slave culture. He forbade Sophia to continue her instruction to Frederick, saying that it would only lead to difficulties. A slave should be taught only how to obey the will of his master. If she taught him how to read there would be no keeping him. Learning would make him unfit to be a dutiful slave. He would become discontented and unhappy, and in the end, would run away, never to be a slave again.

Douglass overheard the rationale explained for not teaching a slave to read. He at once recognized the connection between ignorance and slavery. Slavery could only exist where those in bondage were kept ignorant and unable to learn on their own. Suddenly, he understood it all. The reasons that Mr. Auld had given as to why he should not be taught to read were for Frederick the very reasons why he must learn to read. He, then and there, determined that he would learn to read no matter what he would have to do to acquire the skill. He understood that Mrs. Auld would no longer be able to teach him, but he would find a way (Douglass, 1982).

Frederick lived with the Auld family for the next seven years. Mrs. Auld turned cold and sometimes cruel in her treatment of him. The gentle nature of her soul turned blind to human warmth toward slaves. She had learned that slavery and education were incompatible. She watched Frederick carefully and tried to prevent any move he made to learn to read. She removed his freedom and access to books and newspapers in the home. If she saw that he had surreptitiously acquired reading material, he was scolded and told to remember his place. With the passage of time, she grew to be more violently opposed to his learning than even her husband. But it was too late. Nothing could douse the fire of ambition in young Frederick she had started with an introduction into the mysteries of printed and written language.

During the course of time that Douglass resided in the Auld home, he did learn to read and write, even without a teacher to guide his growth. In the place of instruction, he created devices of his own that rendered help when needed. He began by making friends of the white boys he met on the streets of Fells Point. He converted them into his teachers. When he went on the streets to run errands, he always carried a copy of Webster's spelling book in his pocket. To support his quest for reading help, Frederick would put bread from the Auld kitchen in his pockets, for they always had an abundant supply of good bread, and use it as "tuition" for reading assistance from his poor, and often hungry, white street friends. When he was on an errand for Mrs. Auld, he ran it quickly to leave as much time for reading as he could squeeze from his allotted time away from the house.

By the time he reached the age of twelve, Douglass had developed into a good reader. He had learned much about slavery and the condition in which he found himself. Increasingly, he thought about freedom and how it might be achieved. The thought of being a slave for life weighed heavily upon his soul (Douglass, 1982). About that time he heard his friends talking about a book from which they were going to learn some pieces. With fifty cents he had saved, he went to a bookstore on Fells Point and bought a copy of the *Columbian Orator*. At every opportunity where he would not risk being caught, he read the book. Inside he discovered a fictional dialogue between a master and a slave.

As portrayed in the book, the slave had been recaptured after having escaped. The master scolds the slave for being so ungrateful for all that the master had done for him. The slave responds that he understands his condition and will accept his fate. That response leaves the master troubled. He had expected more of a protest. He then invites the slave to state his true feelings. The slave then describes his feelings of hopelessness and limitations as a man because he is not free, as is the master, to develop his own potential and pursue his own life. The master attempts to defend slavery, but the slave is so convincing in his arguments for freedom that the master decides to set the slave free. The dialogue represented, for Douglass, "the power of truth over the conscience of even a slaveholder" (Douglas, 1982, p. 84).

The content that he read in the dialogue deeply affected Frederick. He read it at a time when the forlorn state of his existence made him wish he were a dumb beast that could not know the depravity of his condition. The power of language and the ideas with which the fictional slave acquired his freedom gave Frederick hope that one day he might be able to achieve a similar result for himself. He also knew about real-life slaves who had escaped to freedom. Having now learned through reading something of the nature of human bondage, having learned that real human voices spoke out against the institution, he craved to learn more.

In the *Columbian Orator* Douglass read many speeches delivered by famous people on the subject of emancipation and freedom in a variety of contexts. On the streets and wharves of Fells Point he eavesdropped on any conversation when he heard slavery being discussed. A word he kept hearing was "abolition" (Douglass, 1982). The context in which he heard the word used left him unsure of its meaning. He finally found a dictionary and looked the word up. The definition still left him unsure of what abolition had to do with the issue of slavery. Wanting very much to learn the connection, he continued to listen and to read anything he could find that would add to his understanding of the word.

One day Douglass got his hands on a copy of the city newspaper, the *Baltimore American*, and found a column that explained what abolition really meant. After reading the column, the idea of abolition and abolitionist movement became clear. He then understood so much that had puzzled him: the secretiveness around slaves, the bitterness and fear, and the uncertainty of something not defined when white slave owners were confronted with the idea of abolition.

Frederick's emotional stance with the word "abolition" was very different from that of slave owners. For him, abolition became a kind of soothing agent. The more he read, the more he realized abolition was a giant issue between North and South. On the streets he grabbed every newspaper and read every word he could find on the subject. There were columns copied from abolitionist papers in the North and then rebutted by slave-supporting journalists that favored the position of the South (Douglass, 1855). Those discussions he read with keen interest over and over again. The issues spoken against slavery and those for the institution he grew to know thoroughly. For Frederick, abolition spelled hope and gave him a comfortable sense that he was not alone in his hatred of slavery. He found comfort in learning that the horrors of bondage had not been concealed from the world.

The more Douglass read, the more he hated slavery. Slaveholders, he believed, were nothing more than robbers, stealing the humanity of others for their own gratification. Mr. Auld had been right when he said that to teach a slave to read would make him unfit for slavery. The more Frederick learned, the more discontented he grew in bondage. Freedom! Liberty! Every sound and every object seemed to pronounce his confiscated birthright. A beautiful day, a lovely tree, a sparkling bay were all made more wretched by his deplorable condition. Ever more determined, he would find a way out of slavery.

Now that he had become a good reader, Douglass set for his next goal that of learning how to write. He began by copying letters at the shipyard that he watched carpenters write on boards made for ships under construction. The letters written on the boards represented where each board would be fitted on the ship. For example, L A meant larboard aft. When he was left at home alone, he would copy the writing that his little charge, the Auld's son, Thomas, had written and brought home from school. He would then go on the street and challenge his white friends, who were trained in school, that he could beat them in writing. When they wrote something to show that they were better, Frederick watched carefully and learned how they formed their letters and words. Through such clever tactics, he learned to write.

Once he had acquired basic ability in writing, Douglass set about to improve his skills. One technique employed was copying the italicized letters and words in Webster's spelling book until he could write them correctly from memory. In his sleeping room, a loft over the kitchen that the Auld family rarely visited, he set up a flour barrel and a chair to use as his desk. There he spent many hours copying and practicing letters and words from the Bible, the Methodist hymnbook, and other books he had accumulated in his room. Frederick often practiced late into the night while the Auld family slept. Sometime during this period he read a speech by John Quincy Adams in which Adams presented petitions to the House of Representatives calling for the abolition of slavery in the District of Columbia. He then shared that speech with other slave boys.

In March 1833, when he was fifteen years of age, Douglass was returned to the Auld plantation. For the next three years he would be assigned to work as a field hand on plantations near St. Michaels. While on the plantations he continued to read and discuss what he had learned about slavery with his fellow slaves. Periodically, he created what he called "Sabbath schools" that met on Sundays. These schools were sometimes broken up by slave owners and not allowed to continue. During the sessions when he was able to conduct classes, he taught other slaves to read and discussed what he knew about slavery, the abolition movement, and the truth regarding the Bible. Truth about the Bible he believed to be important because he had found that many slaves had been taught to believe that the Bible required them to accept slavery as their duty in life, a condition that had been planned and ordained by God (Douglass, 1855).

As he began approaching manhood, Douglass did not accept the interpretation that some gave to Biblical scripture wherein slaves should be obedient and stay with their masters. His inherent dislike of bondage and his knowledge gained through reading had given him a big appetite for freedom. His waking hours were devoted to reading, learning, planning, and waiting for an opportunity to gain freedom. That day came on September 3, 1838.

Reading as a Free Man

Frederick Douglass did not enjoy easy access to books and newspapers until he escaped from slavery. Although he had become an accomplished reader, the circumstances of his bondage had provided only limited access to reading material. Once he became free, reading became a principal avenue through which he could advance his station in life. Documents related to his life in freedom provide only a limited amount of information about his reading and the books he read. However, his career as a speaker and writer required him to read widely. Evidence of his reading will be reviewed with special attention to the content of his speeches and written works for insight into his reading interests.

After Douglass escaped to freedom and settled in New Bedford, he and Anna found life much better than what they had experienced in Baltimore. They settled into the black community and began their life together as man and wife.

But, to his dismay, he still found that his skin color worked against him. He was unable to get work as a caulker because white workers would not allow black skilled tradesmen to work beside them. Frederick had to turn to taking any menial jobs he could pick up to earn money. He loaded and unloaded ships, dug cellars, sawed wood, shoveled coal, cleaned cabins, and moved rubbish from back yards. After some time in New Bedford, he obtained work with fixed wages in a whale-oil refinery.

At the end of each workday, Douglass continued to read and study for his educational development. As a free man, he had ready access to the newspapers, magazines, and books in which the knowledge he craved could be obtained. He regularly read the *Liberator*, a publication devoted to the abolition of slavery and human rights for all. He liked the attacks the paper made on southern slaveholders and the program it promoted for abolishing slavery. In New Bedford he became a regular attendee at lectures of the American Anti-Slavery Society. At a meeting of Negro citizens of New Bedford, Douglass praised the *Liberator* for its devotion to freeing slaves.

Over the course of the next two years, Douglass became more and more involved in the slavery abolitionist movement. In August 1841 he made a compelling speech to an antislavery audience and was immediately hired as a lecturer to travel the region and promote antislavery issues. For the next three years he and other members of the Anti-Slavery Society traveled and spoke against slavery and the laws that supported the institution. With each speech, Douglass gained stature and fame as an orator and a spokesman against slavery.

Douglass's skills as a speaker began drawing large audiences. He used wit, sarcasm, a sense of humor, and an arresting command of words and oratory skills. Some who listened to his presentations thought he had few equals as a speaker. The subject of his presentations included his own days in slavery and how he had survived, along with descriptions of the horrible conditions under which so many slaves had to live. His personal story was so compelling that it captivated virtually everyone who listened to his adventure. The story generated so much interest that he was urged by friends to put his experience as a slave into a manuscript and get it published.

During the winter of 1844 to 1845, only six years after escaping from slavery, Douglass curtailed his work on the lecture circuit to write the story of his life. He titled the work *Narrative of the Life of Frederick Douglass, An American Slave* (Douglass, 1982). The autobiography was published in 1845 and was the first of three autobiographies he was to write. The book proved to be an immediate success in the United States and soon appeared in three European editions. Highly admired and praised, critics said the book could not possibly be the work of an ex-slave. But those who had heard Douglass on the lecture circuit knew very well that the words in the book were his words. His power with language had come a long way since the days when he stood by the chair of Mrs. Auld and looked at the words while she read aloud.

The book, along with Douglass's lectures, established him as a person who had a great facility with words and foreshadowed his contribution to printed works later in his career as a writer and publisher. With the success of his book, his fame spread far and wide. But his success presented him with a ticklish condition. Federal laws still gave his owner in Maryland the right to him as property. Legally, he could be seized and returned to his owner and slavery. In the United States, he would have to be constantly on guard against slave catchers. To remove that concern from his life for a while, he decided to pursue a dream he had held for quite sometime. He decided to visit the British Isles.

In August of 1845 Douglass set sail for Great Britain aboard the ocean steamer *Cambria*. He reached Liverpool on August 28. Three days later he traveled to Ireland for a three-month speaking tour. He was well received in Ireland and spoke to large, enthusiastic audiences. While traveling around the island nation he was humbled by the depth of poverty and malnutrition he observed across the countryside. The thin-armed children and mothers showing defeat in their faces that he witnessed touched him deeply. He connected the condition of the Irish poor to the poor slaves in the United States and to the poor around the world. In his view poor people everywhere were mistreated and reduced to human bondage by those with power and economic advantage (McFeely, 1991).

While abroad, Douglass spent almost six months in Scotland. There he found a big audience for his views on slavery. Scotland proved to be a home for the more radical antislavery positions, thus he felt very much at ease among Scots. The Glasgow and Edinburgh Emancipation Societies had already called for the abolition of slavery worldwide, but especially in the United States.

The later half of 1846 Douglass was in England spreading his antislavery views. His message and his speaking style earned him scores of friends and admirers. He became so comfortable with the English people that he seriously considered making England his permanent home. After talking to friends and family, he came to realize that such a move would be difficult and probably impractical. However, when and if he did return to the United States, he still had to face the horrid prospect of slave catchers trying to return him to his legal owner in Baltimore.

While Douglass toured the British Isles, his owner sold his rights to Douglas to another owner in Maryland. The new owner vowed that he would sell Frederick in the Deep South where slaves most dreaded the long hot summers in the cotton fields. With such a threat looming if he returned to America, a group of

English friends raised money to purchase his freedom before he returned. On October 6, 1846, his new owner agreed to sell his claim to Douglass for the sum of $710.96 that had been raised in Britain. He became a free man on December 12, 1846, when papers for manumission were filed in Baltimore County court. He was twenty-eight years of age (Thomas, n.d.).

Before leaving England, Douglass made a speech on slavery in which he quoted a poem, further documenting his wide reading and study of the literature related to slavery.

> What mothers from their children riven
> What! God's own image bought and sold.
> Americans to market driven,
> And bartered like the brute for gold.
> [Quarles, 1968, p. 40].

In spring 1847, Douglass returned to the United States and announced plans to publish a newspaper that would have as its principal focus the abolition of slavery. To avoid competing with the *Liberator* on its home turf, he decided to move to Rochester, New York, and make it his home and publishing base. Rochester was a good site for Douglass since it served as a safe stop for runaway slaves on their escape route into Canada. For them the city served as a bright northern star that could lead them to freedom. The location fit nicely with the antislavery stance Douglass' paper would promote. He thus named his newspaper *North Star*.

The first issue of *North Star*, a four-page weekly, was published on December 3, 1847. Early issues received a number of complimentary reviews. Copies were sent to distant lands like Canada, Mexico, Australia, and, of course, to his friends in Britain. However, the early enthusiasm for the newspaper began to wane when the economic realities incident to producing the paper began to create financial stress for its publisher.

The cost of producing a weekly paper was high, and subscriptions came in at a disappointingly slow rate. An English printer who came to the United States to help Douglass produce the weekly found the expensive press that the inexperienced Douglass had bought to be inadequate for the job. He finally hired the printing out at a substantial cost. Douglass was forced to spend his own savings and donations from supporters to keep the paper afloat. When funds grew so short that the publication was in danger of folding, he returned to the lecture circuit to earn money and sell subscriptions. By the spring of 1848, he had to mortgage his home. However, help soon arrived in the person of Julia Griffiths, a friend he had made in England who had helped to raise money to start the paper.

Griffiths soon assumed an important role in the production of *North Star*. She became Frederick's chief assistant and began fighting for the paper's survival. Her contribution involved fund-raising and improved financial management. Julia soon had the paper's financial affairs in order, an accomplishment that allowed Douglass to regain full possession of his house. By 1851 he wrote to a friend that the paper was doing well and making a bit of a profit. He then changed the name of the publication to *Frederick Douglass' Paper*.

During her time with Douglass, Julia Griffiths and he became more than colleagues producing a newspaper. They developed a very close friendship and became traveling companions. At a time when black and white relationships among men and women were sensitive virtually anywhere in the United States, the couple became the object of much gossip and criticism. Those in the antislavery movement were especially critical, saying that the gossip surrounding the two was hurting the antislavery cause. But Frederick refused to curtail his cozy relationship with Julia. They continued to work closely on the newspaper and travel together to his lecture engagements.

As a newspaper publisher, Douglass read widely on current issues and the history of America. The knowledge he gained was frequently revealed in both his writing and speaking. On the fourth of July in 1852 he gave a speech in Rochester on the topic "The Hypocrisy of American Slavery." In the speech he displayed a thorough knowledge of the laws that had been written and adopted by many states to hold Negroes in bondage. In part he said, "There are seventy-two crimes in the State of Virginia, which, if committed by a black man (no matter how ignorant he be), subject him to the punishment of death; while only two of these same crimes will subject a white man to like punishment" (Douglass, 1852, p. 2).

In a similar speech given in England in 1846, Douglass had displayed a thorough knowledge of the inconsistent application of laws in America as they related to slaves. He stated, "I think no better exposure of slavery can be made than is made by the laws of the states in which slavery exists. I prefer reading the laws to making any statement in confirmation of what I have said myself." After citing several laws that demonstrated discrimination against slaves, he added, "The laws referred to, may be found by consulting Brevard's *Digest*; Haywood's *Manual*; *Virginia Revised Code*; Prince's *Digest*; *Missouri Laws*; *Mississippi Revised Code*" (Douglass, 1846, p. 5& 6). The evidence provided by Douglass himself reveals how avidly he read into national and state laws that were created to keep slaves in bondage.

In 1855 Douglass published his second autobiography, *My Bondage and My Freedom*. Said by many to be a more complete and balanced account of his life than the first, it depicted a more penetrating look into the heart and soul of slavery. Julia had become so important in his life and work that it is believed she played an important role in the completion of the book. The couple was also deeply involved in the Underground Railroad, the network of people who helped runaway slaves escape into Canada. As they worked through the year of 1855, the criticism surrounding the relationship between the ex-slave and the woman from England grew so intense that it could no longer be ignored. Before the year came to an end, Julia had packed her bags and returned to England. She continued to write articles for the publication, and she and Douglass remained lifelong friends, even though they saw very little of each other from that time forward.

Meanwhile, in Hamburg, Germany, Ottilia Assing had been reading Douglass's second autobiography. Upon learning about the plight of slaves in America from *My Bondage and My Freedom*, she decided that she must travel to America and meet the author and abolitionist. Upon reaching Rochester she walked out to his home, located just out of town on South Avenue, and met Douglass. The two immediately liked each other and enjoyed talking and found they held much in common. A firm friendship was formed between the two that day. Ottilia decided to remain in the United States and settled in Hoboken, New Jersey, where a large number of German immigrants already lived. There she taught German and wrote articles for German and American journals. Her principal interest, however, was in helping Douglass produce his paper.

The distance from Hoboken to Rochester did not hamper the new friendship between Ottilia and Douglass. She began making long summer visits to the Douglass home, where the friendship continued to grow. With Frederick always eager to learn something new, her cultural sophistication appealed to his strong interest in self-development. To his delight, she taught him the nuances and intrigues of European culture. With his consent, she translated his new autobiography into the German language. The book was published in Hamburg in 1860. From the collaboration on the book, their friendship moved to a partnership in Frederick's work. Together they worked to bring an end to slavery and achieve equal rights for all political minorities in the United States.

Before the election of 1860 brought Abraham Lincoln to the office of president of the United States, another event would intervene in Douglass's life to interrupt his fight to abolish slavery. Frederick had met John Brown in 1848. Since both were fiercely interested in eradicating slavery from American soil, they shared a common bond. However, the abolition of slavery was about the only connection they held. Brown held some fanatical ideas that Douglass believed were unrealistic, but if Brown could initiate a successful move to abolish slavery, Frederick was willing to listen to his ideas. One idea was to initiate a slave revolt. Such a prospect had always been horrifying to the white slave owners in the South.

In February 1858, John Brown spent some time at the Douglass home in Rochester while working out a slave revolt plan. In August 1859, Douglass received a note from Brown asking that the two of them meet secretly at a stone quarry near Chambersburg, Pennsylvania. At the meeting Douglass learned of Brown's plan to raid the federal arsenal at Harper's Ferry for the purpose of securing guns and ammunition to support the slave revolt. Brown asked Douglass to join him. Frederick refused. He knew that such an act would enrage most Americans and do far more to inhibit his work than to provide it with aid (Thomas, n.d.). That was the last time that Brown and Douglass met. On October 16, 1859, Brown and his small band of followers seized Harper's Ferry.

Douglass did not support or participate in the raid on Harper's Ferry. The event did, however, immediately impact his life. Back on December 7, 1857, he had written a note to Brown inviting him to visit the Douglass home. The note was discovered and seized by authorities. It was then published in the newspapers, creating a suspicion among the public that Douglass was somehow involved with Brown in a conspiracy to incite a slave revolt. Within a week, realizing that his freedom and safety were in jeopardy, Frederick fled to Canada to evade arrest on a charge of being a Brown accomplice. The departure turned out to be timely. The next day, United States marshals were reported to have arrived in Rochester.

Well before the date of Brown's raid, Douglass had been planning a second trip to England. With his safety in doubt at home, he decided to sail from Canada to England. For the next six months he toured England and Scotland speaking out against slavery and praising John Brown for his work in bringing the slavery issue before the world. During the tour he received word that his ten-year-old daughter had died. He promptly returned to the United States.

Back on his home turf, Douglass continued to speak out against slavery and draw attention to its incompatibility with the American spirit of freedom. He had read and studied the issue so thoroughly, he could cite one American after another as to what they had said and wrote on the issue of human freedoms. In a speech delivered in Boston in 1860, on the right of free speech for all Americans, he cited Daniel Webster as one example.

> No right was deemed by the fathers of the Government more sacred than the right of speech. It was in their eyes, as in the eyes of all thoughtful men, the great moral renovator of society and government. Daniel Webster called it a homebred right, a fireside privilege. Liberty is meaningless where the right to utter one's thoughts and opinions has ceased to exist [Douglass, 1860, p. 2].

Throughout his hundreds of speeches he demonstrated evidence of voluminous reading.

Frederick Douglass had often forecast that a time would come when good would overpower bad and overcome the evil institution of slavery (Douglass, 1855). The election of Abraham Lincoln as president began to fulfill that promise. On January 1, 1863, Douglass joined in celebrations when Lincoln issued the Emancipation Proclamation, declaring an end to slavery in those southern states that were in rebellion. Assured now that the long-awaited tide for freedom for all slaves was moving toward a successful climax, in February Frederick became an agent for the Union to recruit Negro soldiers into the northern Union army. In the summer of 1863 he met with President Lincoln at the White House to discuss the treatment of Negro soldiers, such as less pay and poorer facilities for them than for white troops. Douglass had believed that Lincoln was often too slow in addressing problems and making decisions. Lincoln reassured Douglass that he should not mistake slow, steady progress for a lack of commitment to the war or the welfare of ex-slaves and Negro soldiers. Douglass left the White House charmed and reassured by what the president had said to him.

In the summer of 1864 Douglass again met with President Lincoln to discuss the upcoming presidential election in which Lincoln would seek a second term. Douglass held some reservations about Lincoln's commitment to total abolition of every vestige of slavery throughout the United States and equal opportunity for freed slaves after the war. In the end, however, he decided that Lincoln was the best choice available and endorsed the president for a second term. On March 4, 1865, he attended Lincoln's second inauguration and was personally greeted by the president at the Inauguration Ball.

The president was assassinated on April 14 and died the next day. Following that tragic event, Douglass met with other mourners at City Hall in Rochester for a memorial service. Called upon to speak, he gave praise to the fallen president for his role in bringing an end to human bondage in the United States. In August, Mary Todd Lincoln, the slain president's wife, gave Douglass a walking cane that had been owned by her husband, specifically in recognition of his work in recruiting Negro soldiers for the war.

The Union victory in the Civil War marked an end to the long-frustrating campaign Douglass had waged to achieve freedom for all slaves. With one goal achieved, it was time to begin another. For the remainder of his life he would fight for equal rights and opportunities for all political and economic minorities.

One of the rights that Douglass worked hard to achieve for Negroes was the right to vote in political elections. He spoke and wrote often and passionately on the subject. What he expressed demonstrated a wealth of knowledge about other peoples and cultures when he compared their rights and laws to those for Negroes in the United States. In 1867 he published an article in the *Atlantic Monthly* titled "An Appeal to Congress for Impartial Suffrage" in which he called attention to inequities in the American system. In urging the nation to incorporate the Negro into its enfranchised structure, Douglass cited examples in other countries where much good had been achieved through similar acts for their citizens, while some still remained to be reconciled.

> Look across the sea. Is Ireland, in her present condition, fretful, discontented, compelled to support an establishment in which she does not believe, and which the vast majority of her people abhor, a source of power or of weakness to Great Britain? Is not Austria wise in removing all ground of complaint against her on the part of Hungary? And does not the Emperor of Russia act wisely, as well as generously, when he not only breaks up the bondage of the serf, but extends to him all the advantages of Russian citizenship? Is the present movement in England in favor of manhood suffrage — for the purpose of bringing four millions of British subjects into full sympathy and cooperation with the British government — a wise and humane movement, or otherwise? [Douglass, 1867, p. 3].

In January 1870 Douglass, with a group of colleagues, began publishing a newspaper in Washington. He split his time between his work in the nation's capital and his home in Rochester. In June 1872 fire destroyed his Rochester home, along with many of his important papers. In July he moved his family to Washington. After suffering serious financial losses from a failed bank he served as president, in 1874 Douglass shut down the newspaper he had been serving as editor in Washington. For the next twenty-one years he would write and speak for the improvement of rights for ex-slaves. During that time he also held several government appointive offices.

In 1877 Douglass accepted an appointment by President Rutherford B. Hayes as United States marshal for the District of Columbia. In 1878 he purchased Cedar Hill, a fifteen-acre estate in the Anacostia section of Washington. In January 1881 he accepted an appointment by President Garfield as recorder of deeds for the District of Columbia. On August 4, 1882, his wife of forty-four years, Anna, died. While serving as recorder of deeds, Douglass hired a white secretary named Helen Pitts. In 1884 he secretly married her. When the news became public, he had to face a considerable amount of criticism and consternation from family and friends, both white and black. In 1886 he resigned as recorder of deeds, and later that year he and Helen went on an extended trip to Europe.

In 1881 Douglass completed and published his third, and last, autobiography. Written after the death of President Lincoln, a president Douglass had supported and worked for, the author discussed the life of Lincoln in the book and demonstrated that he had read and studied Lincoln's life in considerable depth. In part, he said of Lincoln,

> The hard conditions of his early life, would have depressed and broken down weaker men, only gave greater life, vigor, and buoyancy to the heroic spirit of Abraham Lincoln.... All day long he could split heavy rails in the woods, and half the night long he could study his English Grammar by the uncertain flare and glare of the light made by a pine-knot [Douglass, 1881, p. 499].

In an essay written in 1881 Douglass wrote about the Norman invasion of England, demonstrating a thorough knowledge of English history. He wrote, "Though the Saxon has for centuries been giving his learning, his literature, his language, and his laws to the world more successfully than any other people on the globe, men in that country still boast their Norman origin and Norman perfections" (Quarles, 1968, p. 81). In an 1894 speech he returned to his reading of English history when he spoke again about the Saxons and Normans.

> The history of the great Anglo-Saxon race should encourage the Negro to hope on and hope ever, and work on and work ever. They were once the slaves of the Normans; they were despised and insulted. They were looked upon as coarser clay than the haughty Norman... Their language was despised and repudiated, but where today is the haughty Norman? What people and what language now rock the world by their power? [Quarles, 1968, p. 97].

In the same address, Douglass displayed knowledge of Russian history when he stated, "When Russia emancipated her slaves to the number of twenty million, she gave the head of each family three acres of ground, and implements with which to till the soil, that emancipation was merciful to the serf and honorable to a despotic government" (Quarles, 1968, p. 95).

On July 1, 1889, Douglass accepted an appointment as minister to Haiti by President Benjamin Harrison. During his tenure in Haiti he grew discouraged by political designs in Haiti on the part of some American officials. Feeling that he had contributed all that he could, he resigned the position in July 1891. In 1892 to 1893 he served as commissioner of the Haitian exhibit at the Chicago World's Fair. During this period he continued to speak out for equal rights for minorities and to spread his fury against the lynch laws that had sprung up across the South, laws that permitted the lynching of many ex-slaves, often on fabricated charges.

On February 20, 1895, Douglass attended a women's rights rally during a morning session of the National Council of Women in Washington. He returned to his home at Cedar Hill in the late afternoon for dinner with Helen. While waiting with her for a coach to take them to an evening service at their church, he collapsed and died instantly. After services were held in both Washington and Rochester, Frederick Douglass was laid to rest in Mount Hope Cemetery in Rochester on February 26, 1895.

The death of Frederick Douglass brought to an end a life that had been nourished by his ability and interest in reading. Books and newspapers filled his need to know and understand so much that had been denied him during his days in bondage. Words and ideas excited his abundant intellect and keen interest in the world. As his knowledge grew, his interest grew. Books became a cornerstone of his daily life. In his first Rochester home, he created a small study in which he kept a small library and lists of words he found hard to spell when writing. When his German friend Ottilia came for summer visits, she would sit with him outside and read to him books that he enjoyed. In the summer of 1868 she read works by Goethe and Feuerbach. In addition, *Hard Times* by Dickens and *Rise of the Dutch Republic* by Motley were read. Frederick enjoyed discussing with others the books he had read, and Ottilia fulfilled that need.

One area of reading interest that occupied Douglass over most of his postslavery life was that of racial definition. Early in his Rochester years he had read a book titled *Natural History of Man* by James Prichard. In the book he saw a picture of an Egyptian pharaoh that reminded him of his mother. Contrary to the prevailing point of view at the time, he came to believe there existed a direct racial link between the Egyptians and African Negroes. Racial characteristics became a subject of serious study for Douglass. As he moved into the final days of his life, his, by then, large library at Cedar Hill included many books on the subject (McFeely, 1991).

Books and reading were to Frederick Douglass what bread is to a starving man. They were his nourishment, his intellectual bread of life. Born with a powerful capacity and desire to learn, he developed that aptitude through books. Upon learning to read, he also learned that he could never accept slavery as his condition for life. The impact reading exerted on his life grew to be profound and would remain enduring.

THE IMPACT OF READING

Upon learning to read, Frederick Douglass became fully conscious of his human condition as a slave. That awareness impacted his mind and emotions with a deep-seated discontent. Books and newspapers opened his soul to the horrible state of his condition. Such a condition for life he could not and would not accept. A burning need to change his condition drove him ever forward in quest of the knowledge that could lead him to freedom and a better life.

Frederick had read the writings of Thomas Jefferson (Quarles, 1968). He knew that Jefferson had declared that all men are created equal in the Declaration of Independence. He had found no exclusion that exempted slaves from that declaration. He had read the words of Jefferson in which he stated that "governments derive their just powers from the consent of the governed" (Jefferson, 1944, p. 22), and that statement didn't exclude slaves. His reading had made Douglass fully aware that great men and women had spoken out against the institution slavery. He was no longer left to accept as truth only that which white slave owners interpreted for him. Through his own diligence, he had acquired a very different perspective.

Frederick's reading lifted his vision to a broad view of life and the acts of people. When governments acted in ways that worked against human advancement, he could always find a ray of light and hope for the future in what he witnessed. When national and state governments created laws to extend slavery to new states and to return runaway slaves, such acts were depressing. But Douglass believed that the Constitution of the United States and its Bill of Rights offered hope and the best guarantee for people in slavery to ultimately achieve freedom. He trusted that the words of Jefferson would one day come to be true for all people. Reading and study had given him that ideal.

Reading instilled in Douglass a power that elevated him intellectually above most of his contemporaries. He used the power of language to frame issues in such ways that others paid attention to what he had to say. In 1881 he wrote an essay on prejudice in which he defined it as "a moral disorder, which creates the conditions necessary to its own existence, and fortifies it self by refusing all contradiction" (Quarles, 1968, p. 80). He had read about prejudice in other cultures and had drawn parallels with what the Negro slaves and ex-slaves encountered in America. He knew how the Norman invaders of England had conquered the Saxons and ruled them for a long period of time. When the Normans were overthrown, they still looked down on the Saxons, seeing them as crude and less strong than were the Normans.

In speeches and discussions on slavery, race, and prejudice, Douglass could size up an opponent, see at a glance the weak points in his position, and slay him with facts and principles. Through the power of reading he had acquired a commanding grasp of the fine points of truths and untruths in what people said and did. Using the power of his expanded vision, he fought hard as an abolitionist and reformer. As an abolitionist, he worked diligently to bring an end to slavery. As a social reformer, he campaigned vigorously for a nonviolent end to school segregation, for equal housing, for equal employment opportunities, and for equal voting rights. He held such an exhaustive grasp of the principle issues of his day that he was referred to by some as "the Sage of Anacostia; ... wise, thoughtful, sound of judgment, discriminating, far-seeing" (Quarles, 1968, p. 123).

Frederick Douglass considered himself to be a self-made man. He had risen from slavery to become an international celebrity. The celebrity and influence he had generated opened important doors of acceptance and opportunity, ones that granted him occasions to walk and talk with important people, including American presidents. From his reading, Douglass had noted many passages that he believed helped to define him as a self-made person. Among his favorites were lines from Shakespeare: "The fault, dear Brutus, lies not in our stars, but in ourselves, that we are underlings," and from the biblical New Testament: "He that overcometh" held important meaning for him (Quarles, 1968, p. 175). Others saw Douglass in a similar way. One author describes him as "an example of self-elevation under the most adverse circumstances" (Quarles, 1968, p. 113).

Douglass saw himself as one who had attained knowledge, usefulness, power, position, and fame in the world without the aid of importance by birthright, favorable environment, or formal education. He had overcome all of the limitations of his station in birth to achieve an acclaimed place in the annuals of human history. For that he was proud. Today, he stands tall in our history as one of a small number of Americans who rose from the lowest, most adverse social state to achieve eternal honors and memorials for helping to make America a nation of free citizens with guaranteed constitutional rights for all.

HONORS AND MEMORIALS

The life of Frederick Douglass had been honored in many forums. Scores of schools, bridges, and landmarks have been named in his honor. Perhaps the most impressive memorial is the last home he lived in, a home he named Cedar Hill. On February 12, 1988, the National Parks Service designated Cedar Hill, located in the Anacostia section of Washington, D.C., as the Frederick Douglass National Historic Site. He had lived there from 1877 until his death in 1895. The site includes his home and a visitor center that offers exhibits and a film on the important events and achievements in the life of Douglass. The exhibits include the walking stick that once belonged to President Abraham Lincoln that was given to Douglass by the president's widow, Douglass's death mask, photographs of his family, and many of his cherished possessions.

Susan B. Anthony

A Brief Biography

Susan B. Anthony was born on February 15, 1820, in Adams, Massachusetts. Adams is a Quaker town located in the Berkshire Hills in the northwestern part of the state and was named after the Boston revolutionary leader Samuel Adams. The Berkshire Hills region is credited by some as having produced a breed of Americans noted for independent thought, innovative ideas, and bold achievements (Harper, 1998). Susan was born into a family that represented that heritage. Her mother, Lucy, was reared in the Baptist church while her father, Daniel, was a practicing Quaker.

From the beginning of their marriage, Susan's parents cast themselves as independent people. Daniel was a schoolteacher, and Lucy was a student in his class. While they were engaged in the process of schooling, teacher and pupil fell in love and were married. Lucy became a practitioner of the Quaker faith instead of the Baptist denomination of her parents, while Daniel became the first member of his family to marry outside the Quaker faith. Thus, Susan was born in a region and into a family in which independent thought and action were practiced.

Growing up on the American frontier of her time, from early childhood Susan was fascinated with the natural world that dominated her environment. Within her emerged a spiritual force rooted in the majesty and wonder of the great outdoors. As a small girl, she and her sisters roamed the hills and pastures around their home admiring the flora and fauna that encircled their small world. The sisters played in the cold winter snows and picked wildflowers in the mild summer's warmth. Susan enjoyed sitting in the grass while watching insects at work and admiring the quiet beauty of approaching dusk as the sun set behind a nearby mountain. A love of nature became one of the enduring joys that sustained Susan throughout her life.

In 1826 the Anthony family moved to Battenville, New York. At Battenville the father built a new cotton mill and opened a merchandise store. Unsatisfied with the educational opportunities available for his children in the region, he opened a school in his home and hired a teacher to teach both his children and, for a small tuition, those of his neighbors. Susan attended her father's school until she reached her mid-teen years. At the age of fifteen, she became a teacher in the same school during the summer, when only the very young were in attendance. Drawing on that experience, she went forth to teach in other schools in the region. As a student and teacher, Susan displayed many of the characteristics associated with her father: his drive to achieve, his intellect and flow of ideas, and his penchant for taking on challenges not yet conquered by others.

A downturn in economic conditions forced Susan's father to declare bankruptcy in 1838. Under laws in place at the time, all family assets were the property of Mr. Anthony. That included even the children's clothing, pins and needles used for sewing, and the things given to Susan's mother by her parents. All assets were seized by debtors and sold at auction to pay the father's debts. The family was left homeless, owning nothing except the clothes they wore.

To get started again, the father rented an abandoned tavern about three miles from the home they had lost. With help from relatives, the family slowly began to rebuild a home and their lives. The event of losing everything merely because a woman could not hold any property in her name made a deep and influential impression on young Susan, one that would substantially mold her life for evermore.

During the next several years Anthony's exposure to the larger world would finally define her course in life. At the age of nineteen, she left the home of her parents to teach in New Rochelle, New York. On the boat trip to New Rochelle she frequently overheard southern slave owners defending slavery to those who were opposed. The arrogance with which white slaveholders tried to justify the institution horrified Susan. On a stopover in Brooklyn, she attended a Quaker lecture on the subject of prostitution and learned about the degradation it brought to the people and communities involved in the practice. As she settled into life in New Rochelle, she learned about alcoholic intemperance. From her exposure to a larger world, she became aware of how government monetary policies had driven so many people to the poor house, people like her own family.

While in New Rochelle, a series of events began to help Anthony sort out who she wanted to be as a person. She observed open prejudice against blacks by whites when she formed friendships with three black girls. When she wrote to a male friend back home, informing him that she was taking algebra lessons on her own, he wrote back that algebra was not a proper subject for a woman, that it had no place in a woman's world. That kind of attitude by men toward women angered Susan and drove her forward in pursuit of what she had chosen to learn. Slowly, but surely, she was beginning to define herself as a unique person that was living in a world of tradition and defined roles for women.

In 1845 the Anthony family moved to a farm at Rochester, New York, near the Erie Canal. The home soon became a gathering place for anti-slavery activists. Among the many abolitionists to visit the home was the famous ex-slave, Frederick Douglass. The center point of conversation during frequent visits by abolitionist activists was how to bring an end to slavery in the United States. Susan found herself participating in many important discussions with leading opponents of slavery. Increasingly, she grew more conscious and concerned with the absence of voting rights for so many American citizens, both women and blacks, two groups that constituted well over half of the adult population.

In 1846 Anthony accepted a teaching position with Canajoharie Academy at Canajoharie, New York. In that new setting she underwent a notable change in her personal life. Susan dropped her Quaker dress, speech, and mannerisms. She dated and danced and enjoyed a rich social life. Several young men showed an interest in her, but no one ever made a sufficient impact to form a relationship. Perhaps, unknowingly, the young men were competing against a more powerful force in her life. Amid the natural beauty of Canajoharie, Susan spent quiet time reflecting on her life and her future. She often walked with her students, and sometimes alone, on the banks of the Mohawk River and watched water tumble over a high falls and then drop into a gorge far below. Perhaps some decisions were made there in the serenity of nature where she gained the spiritual nourishment that gave her confidence about her future. The days just ahead would find Susan getting deeply involved in the tide of social movements that began to swirl around her.

By 1850 Anthony had largely given up teaching, except for an occasional substitute role. She was once again living with her parents and working many hours on the family farm. Her interest had been moving for sometime toward the antislavery and voting rights for women issues. While looking for ways to get involved in the social movements, she continued to participate in social discussions around her parent's dinner table. She soon joined the Daughters of Temperance group, the only organized woman's group in Rochester. By the time she reached the age of thirty, she had determined that social work in the interest of slaves and women should become her life's work.

In 1852 Anthony attended the state convention of the Sons of Temperance. During the proceedings of the convention she rose to speak. When told by the male moderator that women were invited only to listen but not to speak, Susan and several other women walked out of the meeting. Susan gathered all those who had walked out with her and formed a women's meeting to be held that evening in a local church. After advertising the meeting in the evening paper, a sufficiently large group gathered and formed themselves into the Woman's State Temperance Society. The society held its first state convention in Rochester in April. At the convention Susan engineered the election of Elizabeth Cady Stanton as president of the society, and Susan became its secretary. The two women would become close friends and major players in the movement to gain voting rights for women. However, Susan would always be considered the driving force behind the movement.

In the second half of the nineteenth century, Susan B. Anthony reigned as the leading advocate for voting rights for women in the United States. More than any other individual, she devoted virtually the entirety of her adult life to that purpose. Never married and never a mother, her mission was her life. She traveled the country speaking anywhere and everywhere she could garner an audience to promote her cause. Many days and lonely nights were spent traversing through wilderness country using primitive modes of transportation. The audiences to which she spoke often included male hecklers who looked at her as a feminist radical before that term became common in American usage.

Anthony found her goal opposed by groups who believed the time for voting rights for women had not yet arrived. Few women were willing to step up and voice support for a cause their fathers and husbands strongly opposed. Male-dominated federal and state legislative bodies were her natural opponents. Without the power of the electoral ballot, women had no leverage with politicians who refused to risk alienating their male constituencies. Such were the times and conditions in which she had to pursue her mission.

Anthony was only one of many Americans that worked for female voting rights. Other women and some few men participated in the long and hard-fought effort to win that right. But in the history of the women's movement, it is Susan B. Anthony who reigns as the intellectual and spiritual force that propelled the adoption of the Nineteenth Amendment to the United States Constitution that granted that right. Unfortunately, she did not live to see the successful conclusion of her long and determined struggle.

Reading in Early Life

In the early history of the United States, families living on the American frontier had to make their own provisions for the education of their youth. Such was the case with Susan B. Anthony's grandparents. Her paternal grandfather built a school next to his home and hired a teacher to train his children and those of his neighbors. Susan's father acquired an education in the family school and later served it as a teacher for a short while. Susan B. Anthony was born into that environment. Her family was one that placed value in education, and Susan was a product of that heritage.

When Susan was just three years old, she and her older sister, Guelma, were sent to live with their grandmother Anthony for six weeks during the birth of a fourth child into her family. During their stay a teacher in her grandfather's school taught the two sisters how to read. They both proved to be quick learners and thoroughly enjoyed the experience of learning to read. Susan was quoted as saying, "We just loved those books and we pored over them too much" (Anthony, 1954, p. 26). Further evidence of early language development in the two sisters is a game they played with a man who lived directly across the road from the Anthony home in Adams, Massachusetts. Sam Bowen would sit on his steps and call out words across the road to the young sisters sitting on their steps. They would respond by spelling the words back to Sam. He seldom was able to stump them and came to regard both as unusually bright.

Having learned to read at an early age, Susan grew into a widely read person. Her home and the family school contained books, books she read. She later recalled attending her father's school, located in their home, where she was introduced to poems and "school books with pictures" (Anthony, 1954, p. 37). She attended that school until she reached her mid-teen years. Her family, along with friends of the family, subscribed to the antislavery newspaper the *Liberator*, which she also read regularly. Reading and family discussions of the issues surrounding slavery and female disenfranchisement gave Susan an early introduction to issues that would become the focus of her life and work. For the duration of her life she would remain an avid reader who used books and newspapers to improve her knowledge and skills in those areas where she felt a need to be more fully trained and informed.

In 1837 Anthony entered Miss Moulson's Seminary for Females located near Philadelphia, Pennsylvania. While a student, she studied science, some literature, the Bible, and language composition. A male teacher introduced her to the subject of algebra, a subject that Susan learned to love and continued to study on her own after she left the school. Susan attended the seminary for six months before her father went bankrupt in his businesses and had to close his home school and withdraw Susan and her sister from Moulson's Seminary. The bankruptcy presented the family with a harsh reality they had not experienced before. Susan recorded in her diary at the time that she would probably never attend school again (Barry, 1988). The economic plight of the family would require each of the family members to grow and acquire useful knowledge through his or her individual drive and determination.

At the age of nineteen, Anthony left her parents' home to teach in New Rochelle. While teaching, she learned something of the unstable political conditions of the times through reading the New York newspapers. Between classes at school she also read scores of books that gave her a non–Quaker view of life outside her home environment. The books she read during this period included some works by Harriet Martineau, novels by George Sand, a history of women by Lydia Maria Child, and some essays by Margaret Fuller. Her readings lead her to a more liberal point of view toward life and the world she was growing to learn more about. A rapid growth in knowledge enriched her understanding of human issues and built a strong courage of convictions toward what she came to understand as truth. Susan came to accept positions on social issues that she had previously rejected. Her friendship with three black girls in a climate of racial separation marked the emergence of a reform-minded disposition that she had been gradually constructing as she read and saw more of a larger world that was new to her.

At the end of summer in 1839, Anthony's employment in New Rochelle ended, and she returned to her parent's home to attend the wedding of her older sister, Guelma. She next accepted a teaching position with a school district near her home. From that position she soon moved to Albany to teach in a private home school of a merchant. While there she became more acquainted with the antislavery movement and attended some lectures given by its leading personalities. While attending a Whig Party political convention she again heard speeches that criticized monetary policies that made life difficult for common people.

After Albany, Anthony returned home to a teaching position in a local school where she learned that men teachers were paid four times that of women. That discovery distressed her and added to her growing awareness that she lived in a world that was dominated by men who would deny women equal treatment and access to influence.

In 1843 Anthony accepted a position as governess in the home of a Taylor family in Fort Edward, New York. While living there, she read the *New York Herald*, thereby increasing her knowledge of politics and the growing storm surrounding the slavery issue. She also devoted some time to further her study of mathematics and read more literature. Her Uncle Joshua had once advised her to "make people think you know it all," (Dorr, 1928, p. 34) advice that was not lost on Susan. During this period of her life, she also lived for a time in the home of her dear friend, Elizabeth Cady Stanton. Together she and Mrs. Stanton spent hours reading newspapers, magazines, public documents, proceedings of Congress and the state legislatures, accounts of conventions, church and reform assemblies, and any documents having to do with the rights of women anywhere in the country.

When her family decided to move to a farm at Rochester in 1845, Anthony moved with them. The following year she accepted a teaching position with Canajoharie Academy at Canajoharie, New York. While teaching at the Canajoharie Academy she embarked on a self-study program to improve her skills as a teacher. She read books like Comstock's *Chemistry* and Abercrombie's *Intellectual Faculties*. In Canajoharie she lived with her married cousins, dropped much of her Quaker speech and mannerisms, and began to dress like her cousins, who dressed like the ladies at the Academy. While in the home of the cousins she read Godey's *Lady's Book*, a book that influenced her thinking about dress and personal appearance. By the time she finally decided to give up teaching for good and devote her life to the slavery abolition and women's voting rights movements, she was widely read and well informed about the young American nation and its social inequalities. Her avid reading would continue when she became deeply involved in promoting both causes, although her busy schedule would make reading time more difficult to find.

READING IN EARLY YEARS AS A SOCIAL RIGHTS ACTIVIST

By 1850 Anthony had largely given up teaching, except for an occasional substitute role in the Rochester schools. Much of her time was spent working on the family farm. Her engagement in several social issues continued to grow and absorbed more of her time. As she approached the age of thirty, she became increasingly focused on the two issues that most commanded her time and emotion: the abolition of slavery and the right of women to vote. Those two issues would become her life's focus, with woman's suffrage eventually becoming her chief commitment after the close of the Civil War.

Slowly but surely, Anthony became absorbed with woman's disenfranchisement. To her it was a wrong that needed to be made right. The issue seemed to her to be compelling enough that she should never marry. In her view, marriage between a man and a woman could not be a marriage of equals as long as women were denied an equal right to vote. There could be no fairness in a relationship where one person could theoretically rise to the presidency of the United States and the other didn't even have a right to vote in the electoral process (Barry,

1988). Additionally, Susan had watched her married sisters go through changes in their lives that she could not accept for herself.

When Anthony became deeply involved in the women's voting rights movement, she often used reading to help rejuvenate her spirits when progress appeared slow or nonexistent, as it often did. In 1854 she bought and read *Bertha and Lily: Or the Parsonage of Beech Glen* by Elizabeth Oakes Smith. In the story, Bertha, a spinster, had achieved complete happiness. She reveled in her freedom to do as she pleased without having to answer to anyone. For Susan, Bertha represented a model for her own life. She discovered in the story of Bertha some genuine truths about equal rights and an equal life for women, equal to the rights and freedoms that men enjoyed. They were the kind of truths that Susan had been fighting to achieve for all women (Barry, 1988). Susan became so enchanted with the book that she wrote the author, praising her message and suggesting that a cheaper edition should be published so that even the poorest women could buy a copy.

During her busy schedule on behalf of the movement, Susan would sometimes exhaust herself and become ill or be forced to take a break. Those respites from work were usually times that she could devote to reading. In 1855 she developed a nagging back pain and went to Worcester Hydropathic Institute in Worcester, Massachusetts. While there she had free access to her physician's personal library, an access that she used to good advantage. Hours were spent in the sunshine reading such works as *Sartor Resartus*, works by Gerald Massey, George Sand's *Consuelo*, Mme. De Stael's *Corinne*, Frances Wright's *A Few Days in Athens*, and other books she never expected to have time to read. In the summer of 1859 she again experienced a period of back pain and depression. Her doctor advised rest. During that period of recovery she spent time reading to improve her "literary culture." Among the selections read was the *Life of Charlotte Brontë* by Gaskell.

In 1856 Anthony signed on as a speaking agent for the American Anti-Slavery Society at $10 per week. Having previously been supported financially by her father because she had earned very little money thus far in her work, the weekly salary gave her a degree of financial independence, something that was personally new for her. Her new sense of financial freedom made her ever more aware that financial resources were necessary for women to have any real sense of freedom in thought and action. That recognition further crystallized her resolve to fight for women's voting rights, a right she believed would lead to greater economic independence for women. An unexpected act of support for her work would soon make her realize even more personally the importance of economic independence to real freedom.

In 1858 a secret donor donated $5,000 to the Women's Rights group to be used in its work. Susan and two others were assigned as a committee to decide how the money would be used. With the support of the committee, Susan made arrangements to send out a group of speakers at $12 per night to crisscross New York promoting women's rights issues. The speakers would speak on the need for a law that would give women equal rights with men in the custody and guardianship of children and then collect petitions to support legislation to win that right. Her diligent effort paid off.

In 1860 the New York legislature passed a law that gave women in the state the right to control inherited property and to own and control their personal earnings. A married woman could make contracts and go into business on her own; a married woman could sue or be sued; any money recovered would be her property, and every married woman would be joint guardian of her children with her husband, with equal powers regarding their welfare and rearing. Susan's dedication to rights for women had achieved a giant step forward. There would be others to follow.

When she could find time for reading in her busy life, Anthony's two favorite authors were Charlotte Brontë and Elizabeth Barrett Browning. She found in their works excellent models for the ideal woman, what Susan called the "new true woman." They were women who could overcome the "aristocracy of sex" and compete on an equal footing with men (Barry, 1988, p. 106). In addition to Brontë and Browning, Susan read a wide selection of books that portrayed the strong-minded women of that day, including the works of controversial French writers like Madame de Stael and George Sand.

The character in *Jane Eyre* by Charlotte Brontë was a "new true woman" like that envisioned by Anthony. Jane was a fictional nineteenth-century woman who commanded her independence and refused to have her own identity as a person subjugated in marriage as so many women had done. In 1857 Susan read Browning's *Aurora Leigh*, a book she liked so much she kept it with her for the remainder of her active suffrage life. From time to time she would reread her favorite underlined sections (Barry, 1988). Brontë and Browning's characters embodied the kind of vision that Susan continued to work to achieve for all women. Additionally, Susan and her friend Mrs. Stanton read Mary Wollstonecraft's *A Vindication of the Rights of Women* in which the author promoted the idea of a fuller education for women. The two rights advocates then began promoting a program for a more complete and widespread education for women.

When the Civil War forced a major reduction of attention to slavery and women's rights issues, Anthony found some time to indulge in some reading for self-education. Her diary for 1860 listed the following books she had read or was reading: Buckle's *History of Civilization*, Darwin's *Descent of Man*, and poems by Ralph Waldo Emerson (Harper, 1998, p. 198).

In the early months of the 1860s, Anthony and her coworkers conducted an antislavery campaign across New York in which they promoted the position of absolute abolition of slavery. "No union with slaveholders! No compromise!" became their slogan (Anthony, 1954, p. 149). In virtually every city their reputation as women's rights and antislavery advocates preceded them. They encountered protesters at every turn, and Susan, as the leader of the group, became a prime target of the mobs. One evening in Syracuse, mannequins of her and a local supporter were dragged through the streets and burned in the public square.

By this point in her life, virtually everyone recognized that Anthony had become a national figure engaged in work that was controversial and often confrontational. Although she was single and spent many lonely days and nights traveling, canvassing, and campaigning for her causes, she was never emotionally and spiritually alone. She had books to fill her lonely hours, and her family at all times remained like a bedrock of support for her work. It made no difference if she dressed differently, as she sometimes did; inflamed crowds to anger, as often happened; or set herself apart from the main social thinkers and politicians of the day; her family remained loyal and steadfast behind her. Individually, Susan was a strong person who could, when needed, dig deeply inward and draw on inner reserves of strength. That which came from her family gave her that strong sense of confidence and personal security she so openly displayed in her work.

As the Civil War moved into a major military conflict between North and South, the nation's interest became absorbed with promoting the war effort on both sides. The campaigns that had so absorbed Anthony in the preceding years had to retreat to very few and very minor events. Susan returned to her father's farm and took over the farm operation. Her father was away most of the time working an insurance business with which he had become involved. Among all her farm chores she found more time to read than she had previously enjoyed. The many books read during this period included Browning's *Portuguese Sonnets*, a book named *Adam Bede* by George Eliot, and a poem she praised, "Casa Guidi Windows," calling it "a grand poem so fitted to our terrible struggle" (Dorr, 1928, p. 152). Others included Darwin's *Origin of Species*. Her reading included much serious content but also many novels, some by George Elliot. During the period while the war raged, she and Mrs. Stanton read many of the same novels and exchanged commentary on their readings (Dorr, 1928).

At home Anthony continued to read the antislavery newspaper the *Liberator*. Even after President Lincoln issued the Emancipation Proclamation in September 1862, she and other abolitionist felt that the proclamation did not go nearly far enough. Total freedom and equal rights for slaves and no compromising with the South remained their battle cry, a battle cry the *Liberator* continued to promote. Susan had been an avid reader of newspapers since her childhood and would continue that practice for the remainder of her life. One Sunday morning, when her father was at home, the two were reading the *Anti-Slavery Standard* and the *Liberator* when he was suddenly stricken with severe stomach pains. His condition grew worse, and he died two weeks later.

Anthony's drive to get a constitutional amendment granting women the right to vote had led her to read and study at length the major documents that defined and structured our federal and state governments. She acquired through that reading a working knowledge of the laws that had been adopted to regulate and direct the workings of our institutions. In her speeches Susan quoted from the Declaration of Independence, the United States Constitution, the New York State Constitution, the writings of founding father James Madison, works written by Thomas Paine, decisions of the U.S. Supreme Court, and most of the leading radical Republican senators of her day to support her position that women had a legal right to vote as United States citizens (Linder, 2001, p. 5). Her speeches demonstrated an extensive knowledge of the laws and the positions of many people on women's suffrage, knowledge she had gained through devoted reading and study.

Knowledge gained through reading frequently served Anthony as a handy reference when she wanted to make a point about an issue. On one occasion a male acquaintance of the Anthony family was accused of adultery with a woman who was also well known to the Anthonys. Both of the accused were highly visible to the membership of the suffrage movement. Upon learning of the affair, Susan became so distressed that she pulled out a book, Hawthorne's *Scarlet Letter*, and read it to her family to show how others had faced and dealt with temptation.

After the war ended, Anthony traveled to Kansas to work for her brother in his newspaper enterprise. While relaxing in her office one day she read a news article about a proposed amendment to the Constitution that would give voting rights to freed slaves but would withhold that right from the ex-rebels of the South. In the proposed document, the word "male" defined who would be granted voting rights and who would not. Clearly, women would not be included. Alarmed at such a prospect, she soon left Kansas and returned east.

To try and thwart the obvious omission of women in the proposed constitutional amendment, Anthony worked to create a movement that would unite the women and antislavery groups into a combined association that would become the National Equal Rights Association. The antislavery group decided they had a better chance of gaining voting rights for Negro men if they remained a separate association. Too much opposition existed against woman's suffrage, and the chance for Negro men would be defeated along with that of the women. The attempted merger failed. The women's group, thereupon, adopted the name American Equal Rights Association and continued their fight for passage of a voting rights act that would include women and Negroes.

In 1868 the Fourteenth Amendment became law and declared that all persons born or naturalized in the United States are citizens of the United States and the states wherein they reside. The amendment ensured that ex-slaves were legal citizens but did not guarantee Negroes or women voting rights across the nation. In 1869 the U.S. Congress adopted the Fifteenth Amendment to the Constitution, and by 1870 enough states had ratified the act for it to become national law. The amendment gave Negro males the right to vote. Women, of any race, even though they were legal citizens as guaranteed in the Fourteenth Amendment, still had no legal right to vote. That omission would lead Susan to embark on one of the boldest ventures during the course of her long struggle for women's right to vote.

On November 1, 1872, in the city of Rochester, Anthony and fifteen other women presented themselves in the registration office of the Eighth Ward for the express purpose of registering to vote, something that no woman had ever done before. The male registrars denied them the right to register, so Susan proceeded to read to them the voting law contained in the Fourteenth Amendment and the election laws of the state of New York, neither of which specifically denied women the right to vote. Her view held that the laws stated that males could vote, but they did not state that women could not vote. The male registrars finally gave in and permitted the women the right to register.

On November 5, the day of the election, the sixteen women appeared at the polls, and after some small attempts to stop them from voting, each cast her vote for candidates of her choice. With their ballots now mingled in the ballot boxes with all the male votes cast, the votes would have to be counted. The women had voted in a presidential election and nothing could change that. On November 28, Susan and the other fifteen women were arrested for voting illegally. Each one was required to pay a bail before she could be released. Susan refused to pay. Her case was then moved to Albany where she was indicted by a grand jury of men. Her new bail was set at $1,000. Again, she refused to pay.

Within a short period of time, unknown to her, Susan's attorney paid her bail, and she was released. When asked why he had paid her bail, her attorney answered that he could not suffer to see an important lady go to jail. While she awaited the beginning of her trial, Anthony spent the time touring and lecturing on her belief that women could legally vote under the Fourteenth Amendment.

The trial of the leading women's rights advocate in the country began on June 17, 1873. The case proclaimed such widespread notoriety that it was attended by scores of notable people, including ex-president Millard Fillmore. After two days of testimony by both prosecution and defense, the presiding judge ordered the all-male jury to find her guilty, which they proceeded to do. Before pronouncing sentence, the judge asked Anthony if she had anything to say. That proved to be a big mistake.

Anthony promptly launched into a long and wordy lecture on discrimination against women in the male-dominated society. Many times the judge tried to take back the floor, but she refused to stop. After a time she did finally wind down. Her final words to the judge were, "I shall earnestly and persistently continue to urge all women to the practical recognition of the old revolutionary maxim, that 'Resistance to tyranny is obedience to God'" (Linder, 2001, p. 11). The judge fined Susan $100 and the cost of the prosecution. She again refused to pay but was not imprisoned. There appeared to be a surreptitious motive by the court for not incarcerating Anthony.

By the rules of the court practiced at the time, if Anthony was not imprisoned, there could be no right of appeal from the guilty verdict. She asked the judge to imprison her, but he refused. It seemed clear then, as it does today, that the court and the government did not want her to have a basis for appealing the guilty verdict, an appeal that would almost certainly gain a national audience. The trial had been a sham procedure, and everyone knew it. No serious effort was ever made by the government to collect the fine and Susan never went to prison. With the trial completed, the case dropped from public interest, and Anthony went on with her campaign to win voting rights for women.

READING DURING THE WOMAN'S VOTING RIGHTS STRUGGLE

In October 1880 Susan and Mrs. Stanton began work on a project that was to consume a huge block of their time and energy. They began writing a history of woman's suffrage. Work on the first volume began in October 1880 and was published and ready for sale by May 1881. While they both shared in the demands required of the project, Susan did more of the research and ordering of documents while Mrs. Stanton did more of the writing. After a break for summer, work on volume 2 began in November and was ready for publication by May 1882. Mingled with their ongoing work in promoting the movement and some time taken for travel, volume 3 took longer to complete. Published in 1886, it carried the movement to the date of completion of the volume. While engaged in the research required for the lengthy volumes, Susan spent an enormous number of hours reading and ordering the documents that represented the work that had consumed so much of her adult life.

Needing a break from her arduous work schedule, Susan and a friend, Rachel Foster, boarded the British *Prince* and sailed for a European vacation in 1883. The two travelers toured the continent, visiting many of the famous places and historical sites. Susan marveled at the ancient culture she witnessed, at once declaring her astonishment over the "wealth of marble — not only statuary, but stairs, pillars, and massive buildings" seen in so many cities (Anthony, 1954, p. 357). While touring England, Anthony's reading interest led her to visit the home of the famous novelist sisters, Charlotte, Emily, and Anne Brontë. She had read many novels written by the sisters and found that their works reminded her of her life with her sisters.

Susan had also read Mrs. Gaskell's *Life of Charlotte Brontë*, a book that further extended Anthony's appreciation of one of her favorite authors. Having lived as a single woman who gave no indication of ever having a serious romantic attachment to a suitor, Susan's image of love and marriage had been gained from novels like those written by the Brontë sisters. When one of her nieces was married, she recommended to the bride that she read the novel *Shirley* by Charlotte Brontë. Susan even went out and bought a copy to give to the bride (Anthony, 1954). Other books that were in Susan's library by Charlotte included *Jane Eyre* and *Villette*.

In *Shirley* (Brontë, 1993), Anthony met characters with whom she shared a kindred spirit on many levels. Perhaps that is why she gave her niece a copy of the book. The two principal characters are Shirley and Caroline. Shirley is the stronger of the two and much more worldly than is Caroline. But some things they do share. Their close friendship might have reminded Susan of the friendship she shared with Mrs. Stanton. Shirley's love of nature and her distaste for the attitude of the man's world toward women certainly reflected that of Susan. When Charlotte writes in the story that "All men, taken singly, are more or less selfish, and taken in bodies, they are intensely so" (Brontë, 1993, p. 127), the author conveyed an attitude that Susan found reflected in her own feelings and experience.

The world of men that Anthony had come to know, with the exception of her father, was easily reflected in conversations between Shirley and Caroline in the novel. In the story Shirley says to Caroline, "Men, I believe, fancy women's minds something like those of children. Now, that is a mistake" (Brontë, 1993, p. 263). Susan had on many occasions had that same feeling when trying to work equally with men. Consistent with Shirley's views, Caroline genuinely believed that single women should have more to do, better opportunities for interesting and profitable professions, like those that men enjoyed, and that was a feeling that Susan had experienced time and time again.

Caroline had closely observed the gender relationships in her community with the same kind of concerns that Anthony harbored. She had noted the large differential between opportunities for her girlfriends when compared with those of their brothers. The young men had many activities to stimulate their lives while their sisters had virtually nothing, with the exception of household work and sewing, and no pleasures except for visiting each other. This stagnant state of things, in Caroline's view, made young women decline in health. To her mind, most women were never well, and their minds and views seemed to shrink to the small world they daily inhabited.

Shirley, like Susan B. Anthony, never looked at herself as being unequal to men in any fashion. To Caroline, she said, "I consider myself not unworthy to be the associate of the best of them, of gentlemen, I mean" (Brontë, 1993, p. 160). Like Susan too, Shirley doubted that marriage in a culture where women were not considered social equals could be happy or successful. To Caroline, she remarked, "Now, when I feel my company superfluous, I can comfortably fold my independence round me like a mantle and drop my pride like a veil and withdraw to solitude. If married, that could not be" (Brontë, 1993, p. 161).

Susan's love of nature was also represented in the character of Shirley. On any given day Shirley might spend a sunny afternoon lying quietly on the grass under a tree admiring the blue sky and many patterns of puffy white clouds high overhead. The sound of a bee buzzing and the whisper of a soft breeze, as it caressed the leaves on the trees, were soothing and satisfying to her spirit. Along with an identity in nature, Susan could also see in Shirley a bookish alter ego, a lover of reading. The author writes, "After tea Shirley reads, and she is just about as tenacious of her book as she is lax of her needle" (Brontë, 1993, p. 289).

By the end of the decade of the 1880s, Anthony had achieved the height of her powers as a woman's rights advocate, and with that, she enjoyed world acclaim. But women had still not achieved voting rights in the United States, so her work remained unfinished. In 1889 Susan heard through friends and contacts in Congress that a World's Fair honoring the four-hundredth anniversary of Columbus's discovery of America was planned for Chicago in 1893. Also known as the Columbian Exposition, Susan decided that women must have a prominent role in the event, an event that would draw people from around the world to Chicago. She quietly formed a committee of women to help persuade Congress to have women legally and rightfully involved. Again, she worked behind the scenes, drawing on her many friends and acquaintances in Washington for support. In March 1890, Congress passed a World's Fair bill that included a "board of lady managers." Having achieved her goal, Susan refused to accept any office in the organization but, rather, gave her moral support to those who were chosen to lead the group.

To make sure that women did participate in the exposition, Anthony spent much of the summer in Chicago. When the event finally opened, she became one of the most prominent and sought-after celebrities of the fair. Delegates from around the world knew her name and were well acquainted with her work. Whenever she entered a room, people cheered and asked to see more of her. If it were a meeting or a speech, the audience would not quiet down until Anthony was seated on the stage with those conducting the meeting. When she rose to speak, men and women climbed on their seats, threw hats and handkerchiefs into the air, and cheered until they were hoarse before she could utter a word.

The exposition became Susan's event. Every speaker in the many sessions paid tribute to her life and work. Women seemed to recognize that were it not for Miss Anthony they would not be participating at all. To her surprise she had become the most celebrated woman in the world. After a half-century of hard work, controversy, and abuse for her views, and still as financially poor as when she made her first speech, she had been elevated to a position of immortality (Dorr, 1928).

How did a person from a modest background and modest means achieve such international acclaim and adulation? Anthony's wide reading gave her a reservoir of knowledge that often commanded exceptional influence with others. Knowledge is power, and her power lifted her to the top of the woman's suffrage movement. She became the engine that powered the suffrage machine. Upon her seventieth birthday, she was honored at a gala event for her work in the movement. The chief speaker for the occasion was her close friend and long-time colleague, Mrs. Stanton. When speaking about her association with Anthony, Mrs. Stanton said that she had developed much more fully into a woman under the direction and influence of Susan than she could ever have been otherwise. Susan had fed her on "statute laws and constitutional amendments" where she might have been content to "read novels in an easy chair" (Anthony, 1954, p. 399).

Beginning while she was still a young girl, books and newspapers had always held an important place in Anthony's life. During 1897 to 1898 Mrs. Ida Husted Harper lived in the Anthony home to write a biography of Susan's life and work. Susan employed a secretary that she had known in Canajoharie, a Miss Hawley, to assist Mrs. Harper. Miss Hawley wrote to an aunt about her work in residence with the celebrated activist, stating that she found the home to be "nice and home-like and books all about" (Anthony, 1954, p. 446).

In her eightieth year, Anthony was taken seriously ill and remained weak and feeble for several weeks. During her period of convalescence, she found time, among other things, to "read a little." As she slipped deep into the twilight of her life, Anthony continued to rely on books as important companions and sources of mental and emotional enjoyment. Born into an average Quaker family that worked hard, she did not have the advantage of exposure to great minds and powerful people early in her life, but books made up the difference. Through the power of reading, Susan became one of the most celebrated persons of the nineteenth century. She died a quiet death in her own bed on March 13, 1906, at the age of eighty-six.

The Impact of Reading

Susan B. Anthony's early development as a reader helped to build a strong language foundation that served her well throughout a long and productive life. In a letter to her sister from her teaching post in New Rochelle, New York, her love of nature and ability with language would combine to produce a picturesque description of a scene she experienced while sailing with a friend on Long Island Sound. "The first glance of the eye beheld the broad expanse of waters and the far distant village, on Long Island, which seemed like specks in the distance." And a walk along the beach produced these lines: "The sun was passive toward the western horizon and all seemed calm and tranquil, save the momentary wash of the briny waters against the sandy beach and a gentle breeze from the water soothed our fatigued bodies, for we had walked, I think, nearly a mile and a half" (Barry, 1988, p. 34).

Anthony's reading produced an early maturity and a knowledge base that helped to define ideals about human relationships that would structure her life. She recognized early that the role of women in the world was very unlike that of men. Especially in marriage, she viewed an inequality that she could not accept. Being intelligent and well read on a wide range of subjects, Susan found the boys in her small world to be less than her equal. As she grew into womanhood, she received many proposals for marriage, but she could not accept a relationship in which men were deemed, solely on the basis of gender, to be more powerful and privileged than women. In her view, where unequal genders existed, equal relationships could never exist.

In Susan B. Anthony, books helped to create a person that was unique for the time and place in which she lived and worked. She was a self-defined and self-directed woman. Choosing to remain unmarried throughout her life, she had no significant other who could travel with her and share the daily grind of trying to rally others to the cause of women's rights. At the end of a long arduous day of campaigning through wilderness terrain, Susan found herself alone and lonely except for her books. Although she owned many friends and colleagues in the movement, she alone was the driving force, the engine in constant motion that kept the mission alive and viable. For her there was no separation of work and personal life. There was no hero or forerunner after whom she could model herself in leading her crusade. Like other natives of the Berkshire Hills that came before her, she was the first of a new breed of woman, a trailblazer for women's rights in a male dominated culture.

By the age of thirty-five Anthony had begun to realize the enormity of her task. She even began to wonder if the achievement of her goal might not be accomplished within the span of her lifetime (Barry, 1988). Future generations might have to complete something that she had merely been able to participate in building into a worthy objective. Knowing exactly what she wanted to achieve, Susan did become a model for the kind of woman she hoped to see emerge in the future, something she called a "new true woman." Through reading and experience in conducting her campaign, her perception of the reality of the time and conditions under which she had to pursue her mission made her fully aware of the choices and limitations with which she had to cope. With an unusual depth of insight, she shaped her life, made her choices, and was prepared to accept the outcomes.

By the time Anthony moved into her fifties, she had developed into a woman of such social strength and courage that one newspaper described her as one of the most remarkable women of the nineteenth century, a person who lived a life of purity, sincere in her views, and possessing an "indomitable courage with which she bears defeat and misfortune" (Dorr, 1928, p. 268). Susan had acquired a vision of what needed to be done to establish equality in the relationships of men and women. Without equality, she understood that women could never achieve a proper role in the life of the nation. Even though she did not live long enough to witness the outcome, Susan's dream was achieved.

Today, American women, and others in many parts of the world, are free individuals, free to make their own choices and pursue their own ambitions. Unlike Anthony's early life, women can now earn their own money, share in custody and control of their children, stand protected by law in possession of property, and most importantly, the thing that Anthony worked so hard to achieve, women can vote in public elections on an equal footing with men. Susan knew that all other rights evolved from the power of the ballot. When American women acquired voting rights in 1920, their lives began to change accordingly.

The scope of Susan's life and her vision of the future became the subject of a study by a reporter who once sat down to talk with her. She had been portrayed in some media as an obnoxious, hard-driven spinster who possessed a hatred for men and a distorted sense of the real world of everyday men and women. The reporter wanted to learn the truth about the lady for himself. After talking with her at length about her life and work, the reporter found her to be an ordinary woman who could chat on ordinary topics of the day. The solitary difference noted by the reporter was that Susan showed a wider scope of reflection and observation on all subjects than did most people he had interviewed (Barry, 1988, p. 219).

Anthony's vision and intellect lifted her above most of her contemporaries in understanding the relationships between people, governments and the need for human equality in life. In a speech on the right of all citizens to have the right to vote, a speech made in 1863 during the height of the Civil War, Anthony stated,

> The fundamental principle of democracy, [requires that] before our government can be placed on a lasting foundation, the civil and political rights of every citizen must be practically established ... [that being] a simple declaration of the fundamental truth of democracy proclaimed by our Revolutionary fathers [Harper, 1998, p.229].

Susan B. Anthony emerged from girlhood into a unique woman who served a special need in her time and place. Possessing a spirit and will that had been crafted through a strong heritage and extensive reading and supplemented by increasing exposure to a larger world, she made a profound impact on American life, an impact that eventually extended to other parts of the world. Her dedication and perseverance in the face of strong and hostile agitation allowed her to eventually bring about a change in the mind set of men about the place and role of women. Her legacy to the ages will place her as the everlasting symbol of women's emancipation from a status as second-rate citizens. The work she began continues in those countries where women still fight for equality with men. Her spirit is still at work around the globe.

Honors and Awards

Susan B. Anthony has been honored with numerous tributes and awards. Perhaps the most significant is the Nineteenth Amendment to the Constitution of the United States granting women the right to vote. The amendment was adopted and added to the Constitution in 1920. Because of the leading role that Anthony played in the movement that lead to its adoption, the Nineteenth

Amendment is also recognized by some sources as the Susan B. Anthony Amendment (Timeline, 2002).

One other honor deserves recognition here. In 1979, more than seventy years after her death, the United States honored Susan by choosing her image to appear on a one-dollar coin. She became the first woman to be represented on any form of United States currency. The Susan B. Anthony dollar was smaller than the traditional silver dollar and never became popularly used as money. It did, however, become a collector's coin and is still widely available through coin collector outlets.

Booker T. Washington

A BRIEF BIOGRAPHY

Booker T. Washington was born a slave in 1856. His place of birth was a small log cabin on a tobacco plantation owned by Jones Burroughs near Hales' Ford in Franklin County, Virginia. The cabin, a structure that measured twelve by sixteen feet, provided simple lodging for Washington, his mother, his sister, Amanda, and his brother, John. The mother was a slave who cooked for the Burroughs family and many of the slaves that worked the plantation. His father was reported to be a white man that lived on a nearby plantation. The alleged father was never identified to Washington (Washington, 1996).

The Washington family lived an impoverished existence. Their cabin had no windows and no floor, except the natural dirt it was built on. The children slept on the dirt floor with only old rags that their mother had piled together to protect them from the damp earth. The food they had to eat was simple, bland, and in short supply most of the time. Washington recalled years later occasions when his mother would wake her children in the middle of the night and feed them fresh cooked chicken. Where the chicken came from he did not know. He understood only that she was caring for them under very difficult conditions (Washington, 1901).

From meager beginnings in life, Washington set his course. He determined early that he would do all within his power and ability to become skilled and do as much good in the world as his abilities would support. He never wavered from that mission. At every point along the road of life, he looked for opportunities to get an education so as to lift his station from the impoverished condition into which he was born. While still a young boy, Booker had to work in the salt and coal mines of West Virginia. For a time he worked as a houseman for a wealthy family, all the while getting as much learning as he could wring out of the deprived conditions under which he lived.

At the age of sixteen Washington left his home, alone, and set out for Hampton, Virginia, in search of a new school for blacks that he had heard two men discussing in the mines. He had no idea where the school was located, how long it would take to reach it, and whether he would be admitted as a student if he could somehow get there. Undaunted, one day he set out to find the school with very little money or clothing to sustain him. He carried all of his possessions in a small satchel.

Transportation at that time was crude and limited. Unknown to him when he began the journey, he had to travel a distance of five hundred miles before he would reach his destination. The long journey began by stagecoach. Along the way he used any mode of travel that could be secured. He later wrote: "By walking, begging rides in wagons and in the cars, in some way, after a number of days, I reached the city of Richmond, Virginia" (Washington, 1996, p. 26). Arriving in Richmond late at night, tired, out of money and food, and with no place to sleep, he walked the streets until after midnight. The question of where to go and what to do haunted him. While walking he passed by food stands where fried chicken and half-moon apple pies were piled high, but he had no money with which to purchase anything. Finally, too hungry and exhausted to continue, he crawled under the planks of a boardwalk and slept on the ground through the night.

The next morning the hungry Washington found work on a ship where he assisted in unloading pig iron. He finally earned enough to buy food, but additional savings from his wages were very small. Booker remained with the job on the ship until he thought he had enough to get to Hampton. Thereupon, he left Richmond and completed the last leg of his long, challenging journey. When finally he saw the school that he had imagined for so long in his dreams, joy and relief swept over him. About his arrival, he has written: "The first sight of the large, three-story, brick school building seemed to have rewarded me for all that I had undergone in order to reach the place" (Washington, 1996, p. 28).

Washington had only arrived on the campus of Hampton Institute; he had not yet been admitted as a student. The exercise he endured to gain admission proved to be a forecast of the drive and determination to succeed that would characterize his life and work. Upon entering the school building, he went to the office and asked for admission. The head teacher, Miss Mackie, did not deny him admission but did not grant it either. Booker had to sit and wait. For what, he was not told, but he did not leave. He kept his seat and watched others enter and be accepted. He began to wonder. Perhaps his long hard days on the road, the hunger and strain he had endured, and his own, frail looking dress made him unacceptable. After some hours had passed, Miss Mackie, noting that he was still there, went to him and said she had a room that needed cleaning. She asked if he would clean it.

Booker recognized the opportunity to clean as a chance to prove his worth. He swept the room three times and dusted four. Every object in the room and in the closets was moved so as to remove every particle of dust. He cleaned until he was sure the room was spotless. He then went to Miss Mackie and told her the work was finished. She returned with him to the room and inspected from bottom to top. When she was satisfied there remained no dust anywhere in the room, she turned to Booker and said that he was acceptable to be admitted to the institute. With Miss Mackie's words Washington said, "I became one of the happiest souls on earth" (Washington, 1996, p. 29).

Washington's time as a student at Hampton was richly successful. He worked hard and took advantage of every opportunity to learn. When a teacher offered assistance, he accepted and endeavored to prove his ability to achieve. When presented with any opportunity, he displayed a willingness to cooperate with his teachers and administrators and to accept responsibility when it was offered. Washington's stature as a person and a student grew among the staff and his classmates as they saw more and more of his dedication to achieving success. When he completed the program of studies for his degree, his hard work paid dividends. He was delighted to learn that he was listed among the honor roll of commencement speakers.

After leaving Hampton with his degree, Washington did a number of things that advanced his career as an educator. He first returned to his home and taught school around Malden, West Virginia. While serving as a teacher he tried to reach as many students as he could, for there were many young people struggling in conditions similar to those he had endured as a young boy. Both day and night classes were offered and individual help given as much as his time permitted.

In 1878 Washington left Malden and entered Wayland Seminary in Washington, D.C. He studied there for a year, further developing his spiritual being. However, during his studies he determined that his true interest lay elsewhere. He returned to West Virginia and studied law for a time before ultimately deciding that his interest and future lay in being an educator. With the course of his future decided, he returned to Hampton as a teacher and worked there until he was offered an opportunity to develop a school at Tuskegee in the state of Alabama. The new school he would create would be patterned on the model developed at Hampton.

It was at Tuskegee that the world came to know about Booker T. Washington. His energy and leadership in building, from scratch, with very limited resources, a major institution for the educational training of ex-slaves and their children made his name known to the world. His influence and appeal was strong and far-reaching during a period when white and black relationships had to be handled with delicacy and tact. He knew what he wanted to achieve and what he must do to reach his goal. He was a friend to many of our nation's leading industrialists of his day. He was admired and accepted by American presidents at a time when such esteem for black citizens was not widely respected by whites. He is today recognized as one of the outstanding educators of his time.

For his life and work, Washington was widely honored with statues, memorials, gardens, and parks. How did such a man, born a slave, impoverished in youth, hampered in his pursuit of learning achieve national and international acclaim? The answer can be found in books, reading, and study.

READING IN EARLY LIFE

If ever there was a person who would bear any burden, suffer any hardship, or negotiate any arrangement to gain access to books and schooling, that person would have to be Booker T. Washington. To this author, the story of his pursuit of learning is one of the most inspiring stories in history. The obstacles he conquered in his quest for knowledge have few if any parallels in the chronicles of human achievement.

Washington received no schooling or educational experiences while he was a slave. His earliest memory of any awareness of books was as a young boy. On occasion he was assigned to walk to the white school carrying the books of the young daughters of his owner (Washington, 1996). The opportunity to hold and feel books created an image in his mind, a picture of many boys and girls engaged in study inside the school, an image that made him long for the same opportunity to learn. Knowing that such an opportunity was not open to him made his attraction to learning even stronger. Looking at schooling from the outside, he sensed that a chance to become a student himself would be equal to "getting into paradise" (Washington, 1996, p. 9).

Starting when he was still very young, Washington had a thirst for knowledge. In the absence of schooling and books, he availed himself of any means available to learn. During the Civil War, slaves, their families, and friends became creative in getting information about the progress of the war and its possible consequence for them. Even though most could neither read nor write, they collected news by way of what was known as the "grapevine telegraph." When slaves were sent into town or to the country store to deliver or pick up produce, they would listen to any bits of conversation they could find to learn what people were talking about. Much of what they heard was about the war. Each one would pass on what was learned to others in roadside talks or evening visits. Booker listened in the evenings as the adults sat around and talked in hushed tones about President Lincoln, the war and events they had heard discussed.

Young Washington also gathered news when he was required to stand at the dining table of the Burroughs family and operate a mechanical fan designed to keep flies away from the diners. He listened to their conversations regarding the progress of the war. With the information that all the slaves were able to gather, they came to believe that a northern victory would bring them freedom. When Booker complied all of the information from his sources, he gained a good sense of the significance of the war and its outcome.

Soon after the war ended, the Burroughs's slaves were called to the "big house" one morning for a meeting. All gathered around the porch where the family was seated. A Union officer proceeded to read the Emancipation Proclamation and told them they were now free. They could live and work wherever they chose. They were slaves no longer. Booker's mother bent down to her children and with tears streaming down her face, said to them, "Now my children, we are free" (Washington, 1901, p. 20).

With freedom now assured, the family set out for Malden, West Virginia, by horse and wagon to join Booker's stepfather. Booker later recalled the move as long and difficult. To the best of his memory the trip took about ten days. He remembered nights spent sleeping on the ground and sometimes in the wagon. One evening they stopped near an old abandoned house. The mother decided to put everyone down for the night inside to give a respite from the cold damp nights outside. Soon after starting a fire for cooking and warmth in the fireplace, a large snake came down the chimney. The house was quickly abandoned and they slept in the open as they had on previous nights (Washington, 1901, p. 21).

Upon reaching Malden, the family found Booker's stepfather. "Wash," as he was known, had escaped from slavery to Malden sometime before freedom came. He had settled in a poor, racially mixed community where filth, run-down shacks, noise, and frequent fights were a way of daily life. That is where Washington lived for the next several years. He did not like the setting, but was happy to be free and with his family.

The stepfather soon put Booker and his brother to work helping to pack salt in the mines. It was there that young Washington took his first small step in acquiring book knowledge. Each packer was assigned a number that was recorded on each barrel of salt. Booker's stepfather used the number *18*. Booker soon learned to recognize the number wherever it appeared. Soon thereafter, he learned to make the number himself. For some time that was all he could read. Reading that number wherever it appeared gave him enormous satisfaction because "from the time that I can remember having any thoughts about anything, I recall that I had an intense longing to learn to read" (Washington, 1996, p. 18). For young Booker, the number *18* was a beginning.

Washington's desire to learn to read grew more intense with each passing day. The desire burned so strongly in his body that he made a promise to himself that he would somehow learn to read well enough to read common books and newspapers. Even though his mother was illiterate, she supported his desire to learn. Booker finally prevailed upon her to secure a book for him from which he could begin to learn reading. From somewhere, he knew not where, his mother procured an old copy of Webster's *Blue-Back Speller*. The little book contained the alphabet as well as some phonetically regular nonsense syllables, like "ba," "da," and "ha."

Booker began learning as much about the reading code as he could decipher. Without help from anyone, he had learned most of the letters in a few weeks. Each small advance increased his desire to read even more. In town one day he saw a group of black people gathered around a young black man who was reading a newspaper to those assembled. The reader, a recent arrival in town, had come to Malden from Ohio. The sight of this young man reading to an audience fired Booker's desire to read so he could perform for an audience. But he still had not found anyone in his community who could help him.

Around this time the black people in the community began talk of creating a school for black youth. The discussion excited young Washington with the prospects that he might have an opportunity to attend school. Soon thereafter, another black man from Ohio arrived in town. He had been a soldier, and he could read. The black adults prevailed upon the man to start a school. The ex-soldier agreed, and a schedule was established for the start of the new school. Excited and delighted with such good news, Booker could hardly wait.

However, a major disappointment would intervene in his planned attendance in the school. His stepfather had found that Washington possessed economic value as a worker in the salt mines. When time came for Booker to enter school, the loss of his wages proved to be too much for the parent to accept. Booker's long-held dream of attending school was dashed. He later described that experience as one of the biggest disappointments of his life. To make his pain even more intense, he could see the happy children passing to and from school each day from his place of work. But, as noted earlier, Booker would overcome any setback or obstruction to achieve his dream of acquiring reading ability and book knowledge (Washington, 1996).

To overcome his disappointing setback, Washington worked out a plan with the teacher of the new school to give him lessons at night after work. The night lessons were very helpful, but he never gave up hope of attending day school with other children his age. With his mother's help, he was finally able to persuade his stepfather to allow him to get up early and do his work in the mine so that he could be free to attend day school. As agreed, Booker rose early and worked in the mine until nine o'clock. From the mine he would rush to school for the day. After school, he had to return to the mine and work another two hours. But a flaw in the arrangement was soon discovered.

School began at nine, and he could not leave the mine until nine. The school was located some distance from his workplace, resulting in his being late in reaching school. Because of the delay, he often missed early recitation lessons. To resolve this problem, Booker employed a bit of daring for a student so young. There was a huge clock in his workstation that was used by all workers to gage arrival and leaving time. In the early hours of the morning he would move the clock forward by one-half hour. This would permit him to leave at a real time of eight-thirty, giving him time to get to school by nine. This subterfuge worked for a time, but one day the furnace boss discovered that something was wrong with the clock's accuracy and locked it away in a cabinet.

Washington's first day at school produced an unexpected change that would remain with him for life. So far as he knew, he had only one name and that name was Booker. That was all that anyone had ever used to address him. When he heard the teacher asking his classmates for their names, every one had at least two names, and some gave three. When the teacher asked for his name, Booker quickly adopted the name of Washington for his last name. Later he learned that his mother had named him Booker Taliaferro at birth, but the name had been forgotten and never used. With that discovery, he revived the last name his mother had assigned and became for evermore Booker Taliaferro Washington. We, of course, know him today as Booker T. Washington.

Booker's joy in working out an arrangement that would allow him to attend day school proved to be short lived. Not long into the arrangement, his stepfather decided, again, that Booker's salary from the salt mine was too much in need for him to reduce the hours he worked in order to attend day school. Saddened, Booker left school and sought out teachers who could work with him at night. Desperate for help, he often walked several miles to get instruction from persons who knew little more than he did. His determination, however, never wavered. An education he would have despite the obstacles that kept surfacing to be surmounted.

After some time had been spent in the salt mine, Washington was sent to work in a coal mine. The coal mine was dark, deep, and scary. In spite of his dislike of the workplace, Booker never lost sight of his educational goal. He would take a book into the mine and, during spare minutes, read by the light of the little mining lamp that hung from his cap.

Always alert for any opportunity for learning, one Sunday morning an unexpected door opened. Booker and some children were playing marbles in the road by his house. A man came walking along on his way to Sunday school. The stranger asked Booker why he and the other children weren't going to Sunday studies. Booker had never heard of such a school and asked for information. After listening to a thorough explanation of the nature and purpose of Sunday school, Booker put away his marbles and followed the man to church. From that day forward he became a regular attendee. Later, he became a teacher in the school and, still later, its superintendent.

One day in the mine Washington overheard two men talking about a great school for black students somewhere in Virginia. He crept close to the voices to learn as much as he could about that school. As he listened, he learned it was Hampton Institute in Hampton, Virginia, they were discussing. When he heard that Hampton was a school where a black boy could study, earn his board through work for the school, and be taught how to work and appreciate the dignity of labor, exhilaration swept over him. He determined, then and there, to somehow, someday, reach that school.

After a few months in the coal mine, Booker found work in the home of General Lewis Ruffner, the owner of the mines in which he had been employed. In the Ruffner home his duties would be to serve as a house and errand person for Mrs. Viola Ruffner, the general's wife. Mrs. Ruffner had a bad reputation as a boss. No one had been able to work for her more than two or three weeks before leaving. Undaunted as always, Booker had confidence that he could measure up to her requirements. Besides, it would have to be awfully bad to be worse than the coal mine.

The general's wife was the daughter of a cabinetmaker in Arlington, Vermont. She had grown up in a large family of limited means and had gone to college and become a teacher. After many years as a classroom instructor, she had come to Malden to be a governess for the younger children of the general. The general's wife and the mother of his children had died. Not long after assuming her role, Viola became the wife of her employer and assumed complete responsibility for the operation of the home. Some acquaintances had described her as a beautiful woman with considerable intelligence, an austere disposition, and the granitelike qualities often associated with Vermonters (Washington, 1996).

After a short time with Mrs. Ruffner, Booker won her trust and confidence. She liked him and accepted him much like a student that she could train and mold into a useful citizen. Booker learned how to keep a house clean and neat, how to wash and dress himself to be in good company. She taught him how to go out into the community and sell the vegetables and fruits that she grew in her garden. Much later in his life, Booker assigned important educational value to the time he worked for the general's wife. He wrote, "The lessons that I learned in the home of Mrs. Ruffner were as valuable to me as any education I have ever gotten anywhere since. Even to this day I never see bits of paper scattered around a house or in the street that I do not want to pick them up at once" (Washington, 1996, p.25).

When he had completed his daily work in the Ruffner home, young Washington often looked for ways to use his spare time productively. One day Mrs. Ruffner offered to help with his reading, an offer he joyfully accepted. From that time forward he was permitted to keep a book available to read when he competed his work. She also gave him permission to attend day school for an hour each day during the winter months. Most of his studying had to be done at night when he was alone with no one to help him. Sometimes he would use a little of his small salary that his stepfather allowed him to keep to hire someone to help him with his lessons.

While living in the Ruffner home, Booker began his first personal library. He secured a dry-goods box, knocked out one side, and used it to hold the small number of books he had collected. Mrs. Ruffner often gave him books, slowly increasing the size of his collection. She became a strong supporter and encouraged his efforts to get an education.

The desire to attend the school that he had heard about in the mine never left Washington. One day he quit his job with the Ruffner family, said goodbye to his frail mother and his brother and sister, and set out for Hampton. He carried with him only a small satchel with a few items inside and a small amount of money that he had saved and a small amount his brother gave him from his meager earnings in the mine.

After a long and arduous journey Washington arrived on the campus of Hampton Institute with fifty cents in his pocket. Upon seeing the large school structure a new spirit of life rushed over him. In his words,

> It seemed to me to be the largest and most beautiful Building I had ever seen. The sight of it seemed to give me new life. I felt that a new kind of existence had begun — that life would now have a new meaning. I felt that I had reached the promise land [Washington, 1996, p. 28].

Reading as a Student

Hampton Institute was founded in 1868 by a former Union general who had trained and supervised black soldiers during the Civil War. General Samuel C. Armstrong had created a school for black adults that emphasized work, study, hygiene, morality, self-discipline, and self-reliance as the core of its philosophy and training. Booker knew little about the school upon his arrival. He simply believed that Hampton represented his best chance to become the person he wanted to be.

Upon being admitted as a work-study student, Washington devoted himself to a personal challenge of succeeding. He worked hard in his studies to overcome his limited academic background. Since he had proven his skills in cleaning, he was assigned a position of assistant janitor while pursing his studies, except for a short time when he worked on the school farm. His program of studies followed the standard literary and industrial program of the school. He participated in debating clubs, received private lessons in speaking from one of the Hampton teachers, and participated in discussion groups, all of which helped to prepare him well for speaking in public, something for which he would become famous later in his career.

At the end of his first year at Hampton, Washington had no money with which to go home on vacation. He decided to remain in the Hampton area and earn money for the next year's tuition. After a concentrated search for work, he found a job in a restaurant at Fortress Monroe. The wages covered little more than his meals. Between meals and in the evenings, he devoted his time to reading and studying. While he failed to save as much money as he had hoped, he did gain a wealth of knowledge from his books.

During his second year at Hampton, the determined student from Malden learned to read the Bible. With assistance from a Hampton teacher, Booker learned to enjoy his Bible reading and gained nourishment from the time he devoted to the spiritual book. In addition, he found enjoyment in biblical stories and events that he learned to read as literature. From that time forward, reading the Bible became a life-long habit. He also grew to enjoy debating and discussion groups, activities that he would use often after leaving Hampton.

After graduating from Hampton in the summer of 1875, Washington went to Saratoga Springs, New York, and worked as a waiter in a hotel for the summer. In the fall he returned to Malden and took a job as teacher in the school that he had periodically attended there. Three years of his life were devoted to the students in Malden, where he taught both day and night classes. An activity he had enjoyed so much at Hampton was continued when he organized debating societies that met other groups in competition in nearby towns.

In 1878 Booker left Malden and enrolled as a student at Wayland Seminary in Washington, D.C. While there he further enriched his religious development. Time in the seminary gave him an opportunity to observe and compare students from a more affluent and urban background with those of a poor and rural background that had been his experience. That opportunity gave him deep insight into the needs of the students that had been his peers at Hampton and in Malden. He would later draw on that insight when he was asked to create a new school for ex-slaves and their children in Alabama.

After a season at Wayland, Washington returned to West Virginia and began a period of reading and study in the law under the direction of a white Charleston attorney. While pursuing legal training, he slowly began to feel that his future should be that of an educator. He felt drawn to help those young men and women whose roots had been mired in the southern rural slave culture. A call one day from Hampton to return to the school as a member of the teaching staff and part-time graduate student made that choice firm and final. His career for life had been set. He would be an educator.

Always willing to be useful and to learn, at Hampton Booker accepted a unique challenge. He became a tutor and counselor to a large group of American Indian young men who had been admitted to Hampton. For both Booker and Hampton, the venture was new and untested. But Booker determined that he would not fail the young men. He lived in the cottage with the students and attended their needs and insecurities, for this was something new to them, too. Washington grew to like the Native Americans and acquired a wealth of insight into human nature that helped him as an educator. He concluded from the experience that, "The main thing any oppressed needed was a chance of the right kind, and they would cease to be savages" (Washington, 1901, p. 48).

At the end of his second year as a teacher at Hampton, Washington received a call that would give him the opportunity of a lifetime. The school principal at Hampton had received a letter from a little town in Alabama by the name of Tuskegee. A committee of citizens there wanted someone to come and serve as principal of a new school they were planning, a school that would be very much like Hampton. The Hampton leader recommended Booker, and he was hired. He soon resigned his position with Hampton and returned for a brief visit with his family in West Virginia. From Malden he traveled to Alabama to begin a new challenge.

READING AS LEADER OF TUSKEGEE INSTITUTE

The story of how Booker T. Washington, at the young age of twenty-five, built Tuskegee Institute from scratch into a highly regarded educational institution is an inspiring story indeed. When he arrived in the small town, he found no school, no land, no buildings, no students, and virtually no resources. The only existing asset with which to begin a school was a $2,000 appropriation for teacher salaries granted by the state legislature of Alabama. But Washington's past had prepared him for such a challenge. The young man who had been born into slavery, had worked and read by dim light in the mines, had traveled five hundred miles to reach a school he had only heard two men discussing, remained undaunted by what he faced in Tuskegee.

Washington quickly recognized that the task of creating a new school in Tuskegee would be great indeed. But nothing would stop him from fulfilling his duty. Work began, and progress was made. He found an old church and a little shanty in serious need of repair in which to begin classes. With much sweat and toil, he opened Tuskegee Institute on July 4, 1881, with thirty students (Washington, 1901).

In the weeks and months that followed, Washington applied all of the skills and knowledge he had ever acquired to the job of building Tuskegee. From the days he had stood by the dining table of his owner in Virginia listening to conversations about the war to the day he had arrived in the small town to build a new school, he had met every challenge successfully. The skills he had acquired along the way, through reading, training, and experience; his skills in planning and leadership; and his ability to speak convincingly and honestly to a group of people, won him scores of friends and supporters from all races in the region and across the country. He applied the philosophy of living and work that had evolved in his mind as he had studied the conditions of blacks in America, and especially in the lives of the ex-slaves that remained on the farmlands of the South. He had a purpose, and that purpose was to help those people whose lives of deprivation were rooted in a background of slavery.

Once the school at Tuskegee was launched, Booker began planning for its future. He combed the region and his acquaintances for money to buy a one-hundred-acre former plantation that lay dormant and covered in brush about a mile from town. If he could purchase that land, it would become the campus for his school. Through diligent work and pursuit, the money was found, and the land was purchased. Washington and his students promptly began clearing the brush away so that crops could be planted. New buildings were constructed, much of the work done by students. Money seemed to be always short, but he and the first teacher he employed traveled north and south bringing the message about Tuskegee to a national audience and soliciting contributions. As news of the new school and its program spread, donations became larger and more frequent. The school grew rapidly and gained a national reputation.

By the end of the fourteenth year of operation, Tuskegee had grown to an enrollment of 1,013 students with a teaching staff of 63 (Washington, 1901, p. 104). Scores of new buildings for dormitories and classrooms had been added to the campus, virtually all built by students under the direction of their teachers. In spite of his success, Washington lived through days and nights of sleeplessness and stress, always faced with the prospect that money could not be found to carry the school forward. A fear of failing his race constantly dogged his waking hours. Almost daily there were financial needs to be met, problems to be solved, and failures to be confronted. One of his most vexing problems proved to be his efforts to build a brick-making kiln on campus.

Washington wanted to construct a brick-making facility to be used for training students and to facilitate the need for brick in the rapidly growing construction program at Tuskegee. He and the brick-making instructors and their students searched the campus property for a good site to erect a kiln, one that would contain an adequate supply of good-quality clay. A site was chosen and a kiln was constructed. The first project produced 25,000 bricks that were placed in the kiln for burning. The kiln failed due to a flawed construction and destroyed the brick. Second and third kilns were constructed in an effort to get one that worked properly, but without success. The first three efforts had failed, and the money for construction was exhausted.

Undaunted as always, Washington searched for a source of money to try a fourth time. In searching his mind and resources, he remembered a nice watch that had somehow come into his possession some time in the past. He could not remember who gave him the watch. Seizing an opportunity for money, he took the watch to a pawnshop in Montgomery and placed it in hock for fifteen dollars. The money was then used to build a fourth kiln. That time the kiln worked, and brick-making became an important part of the training and student work program at Tuskegee. By the time he had enough money to retrieve his watch, the time allowed had elapsed, and he never saw it again. However, there were no regrets about what he had done.

As the profile of his work at Tuskegee illustrates, from the day Washington arrived in town, he was a very busy person. Time for reading and reflection was often difficult to find. But he did continue to read to learn and to keep informed about state and national events. Much of his focused reading was done while traveling on trains from one engagement to another. He was an avid newspaper reader. In an autobiography, he stated: "Newspapers are to me a constant source of delight and recreation. The only trouble is that I read too many of them" (Washington, 1996, p. 120).

Washington also continued to read books. He was most fond of biographies.

He read nearly every book and article written about the life of Abraham Lincoln. Books on the life of Frederick Douglass were favorites, some of which he read many times. He generally preferred reading about real people, especially the lives of great men. His fictional reading was limited to a few selections, principally only those novels he heard others talking about with deep interest.

During the course of his life, Washington absorbed a huge fund of knowledge about historical places, times, events, and people through the hundreds of books, magazines, and newspapers he read. When one reads his speeches and the hundreds of letters he wrote, it is clear that he had at his command an extensive knowledge base. His early desire to learn how to read proved to be his portal to self-fulfillment. Books helped to mold him into the person he so desperately wanted to become. Having begun life on the bottom rung of the social and economic ladder, Washington advanced to a level of high achievement, a man who served as friend and adviser to American presidents. He was a unique person, holding a unique experiential background, and was chosen for a unique job to be performed. He did the job admirably well with a uniqueness of talent, personality, heart, and character that defines him in history.

THE IMPACT OF READING

Booker T. Washington became one of the most famous and influential men of his day. As the nineteenth century slid into history and the new twentieth graced the calendar, Washington was approaching the height of his powers. He had become widely known throughout the United States and had acquired friends and influence among corporate and political leaders across the nation. With the publication of his autobiography *Up from Slavery*, he became internationally famous. The knowledge and skills he acquired from the day he first learned to read the number *18* on his stepfather's salt barrels in a West Virginia mine had prepared him to achieve a high station in life. While still a young man he defined his goal to be one of service to his people. He never deviated from that mission.

Without books in his life, Mr. Washington would have been a different kind of man. At the time he embarked on the task of building a school at Tuskegee, he had not traveled widely nor had he had exposure to a wide range of people. But through books he had acquired a knowledge base that firmly grounded him in the life and spirit of our nation. That knowledge helped him to create a vision of human potential and of how he could contribute to realizing that potential. Secure in his ability to meet a challenge, he arrived in Tuskegee ready to meet a human need. That need was a school for ex-slaves who had little to give them hope for a better life.

During his first year at Tuskegee, Washington traveled over the region on a wooden cart pulled by a mule. He met the people, ate and slept in their homes, and talked with them about the new school at Tuskegee. The depth of poverty and sense of defeat he witnessed deeply concerned him. But he had come to help them, and help them he would.

Washington became totally engrossed in building Tuskegee Institute. The school would focus on academic and manual arts training similar to that at Hampton. The central premise of the program would be to help ex-slaves in the South improve their lives through acquiring skills that would be so valuable to society that they could be sold for good wages. Once his race had achieved a high level of competence, they could compete with their former owners economically and in other ways required for social equality. As a black southern man speaking to black southern people, he believed their lives would improve more quickly if they remained in the South, a region with which they were familiar, a place where they could develop a work and economic base. That was the plan that he set about to develop through Tuskegee Institute.

Washington's acquired knowledge served as a useful guide as he set about to negotiate the delicate relations that he knew would be required to succeed in his mission. He began early to build good relations with both his black and his white neighbors in the town of Tuskegee. He then reached out to the people of Alabama and the citizens of the American north for support in his mission. He developed, himself, into an eloquent and entertaining speaker, using homilies and analogies that anyone could understand. White and black audiences turned out in large numbers to meet him and hear his speeches.

Washington made a speech in 1895 that lifted him to national prominence as a speaker and a leader of the black race. The speech was delivered before a predominantly white audience at the Cotton States and International Exposition in Atlanta, Georgia, on September 18. In his presentation, Washington made a plea for the white people of the South to incorporate their ex-slaves into the economic and labor structure of the region and work together to rebuild from its postwar economic slump. His point was simple and clear: the South could only be as strong and vibrant as were all of the people that lived and worked in the region. In part he said:

> Cast down your bucket where you are. Cast it down among the eight millions of Negroes whose habits you know, whose fidelity and love you have tested in days when to have proved treacherous meant the ruin of your firesides. Cast down your bucket among these people who have,

> without strikes and labour wars, tilled your fields, cleared your forests, built your railroads and cities, and brought forth treasures from the bowels of the earth, and helped make possible this magnificent representation of the progress of the South.... Casting down your bucket among my people ... you will find that they will buy your surplus land, make blossom the waste places in your fields, and run your factories [Washington, 1895, p. 2].

Delivered at a time when race relations in the nation were still raw and uncertain in the aftermath of the Civil War, the speech was widely reviewed and editorialized across the country. His common-sense, human appeal to all races made Washington's name known to virtually every household across the nation. One reviewer wrote that it was one of the most "notable speeches" ever delivered to a southern audience (Washington, 1996, p. 102). Similar comments were made in other reviews. President Grover Cleveland sent Washington a letter giving his praise for the hope and encouragement the address offered the nation's black citizens. The more recognition, praise, and support he garnered for his work, the more confident Washington became that he was using the correct approach to the southern black economic condition. The hearty support he received for his endeavors led him to observe that, "There is something in human nature which we cannot blot out, which makes one man, in the end, recognize and reward merit in another, regardless of colour or race" (Washington, 1996, p. 107).

Washington's commitment to his work at Tuskegee never wavered throughout his life. He was offered other positions that would have paid far more money than he made as an educator, but he rejected any enticements that would remove him from Tuskegee (Washington, 1901). His commitment to the institution remained firm and unbreakable. Rather than leaving, he continued to expand the reach of Tuskegee's services to black Americans.

In the summer of 1900, Washington organized the National Negro Business League and arranged its first meeting in Boston, Massachusetts. The league brought together, for the first time, a large number of black businessmen from across the country to discuss ways to help foster black enterprise. Thirty states were represented. An important outgrowth from that meeting was the creation of many state and local business leagues. Out of the expanding service and influence of Tuskegee across the country grew many forms of support and recognition for its work.

A big day for Washington and Tuskegee was December 16, 1898. President William McKinley, with Mrs. McKinley, paid a visit to Tuskegee Institute. The presidential couple was joined by all members of the president's cabinet except one, along with several generals from the military services. In addition, the

Alabama state legislature adjourned that day so that its members could attend the big day with the governor and other state officials. The students and townspeople of Tuskegee went all out to decorate the town and campus for the presidential visit. In his speech, President McKinley praised the people of the town and region for their work and progress at Tuskegee and Washington, in particular, for his work as an educational leader. In part the president stated:

> To speak of Tuskegee without paying special tribute to Booker T. Washington's genius and perseverance would be impossible. The inception of this noble enterprise was his, and he deserves high credit for it. His was the enthusiasm and enterprise which made its steady progress possible and established in the institution its present high standard of accomplishment" [Washington, 1901, p. 244].

The big day proved to be a crowning event for Washington.

Booker T. Washington died in 1915 at the age of fifty-nine. He had been the leader of the Tuskegee school for thirty-four years. His mission at the school he had created never wavered from his original design. The large vision and deep humanity he had developed through reading and study had made him a special man for a special mission at a special time in our nation's history. An important feature of his character was an absence of bitterness or prejudice. Even after he had achieved international fame he maintained a correspondence with members of the family of his former slave owner, the Burroughs family. He made every effort to accept and work with all people, regardless of their histories or past events. He once stated that, "I will let no man drag me down so low as to make me hate him" (Booker Monument, n.d.).

While Washington was widely accepted as an important leader among black Americans, there were some blacks that did not agree with his philosophy or approach to helping his race. Letters sent directly to him and newspaper editorials offered advice freely and consistently. Among many ideas offered were that he should expand his work beyond Tuskegee; that he ought to take his work to a bigger stage, such as Africa or the West Indies where blacks comprised a greater part of the population; that he should discuss political issues and policies that would give blacks more political influence; that his entire approach to helping blacks would keep them subservient to whites; and that he was too soft on southern whites when speaking to northern audiences. The Tuskegee leader considered all suggestions by assessing whether the advice was something he should adopt. In the end, he believed the course he had first chosen to follow would prove to be more helpful to his people. He, in effect, accepted the advice he had given to others in his Atlanta speech. He cast his bucket down among his own people.

In retrospect today, Washington stands out as a unique person in his time and place. Many of his critics did not seem to understand what he was all about. Unlike many of those who questioned his motives and approach, Washington was a southerner who grew up and was trained in the South. He had traveled the region, walked on southern farmlands and had spent time getting to know and understand the needs of the people. Most of his critics did not know the South as he knew it. They differed from him in leadership goals for blacks. No matter what position one might take regarding the debate of the time, it is clear that he stood tall as an influential leader.

Writing in the *Saturday Evening Post* in 1905, Thomas Dixon, Jr., wrote that Washington's life was a story with universal appeal. "His life is a romance which appeals to the heart of universal humanity, (a man that) saw a vision and followed it, until at last he presides over the richest and most powerful institution of harmony in the South, and sits down with crowned heads and Presidents, has no parallel in *The Tales of the Arabian Nights*" (Thornbrough, 1969, p. 99). The great industrialist, Andrew Carnegie, in 1907, said about Washington, "He is one of these extraordinary men who rise at rare intervals and work miracles" (Thornbrough, 1969, p. 90). Washington had achieved worldwide acclaim far beyond that of most other men and women of all races and creeds. In 1909 the *Nation Magazine* stated that Washington performs a "patriotic service which it would be hard to overestimate" (Thornbrough, 1969, p. 96).

Some writers have stated that Washington was a man for his time and place. Having entered upon the national stage of human endeavor at a time when social and political currents were swirling in many directions, where agreement and cooperation among groups were often hard to negotiate, and where fear and instability in racial and regional relations were deep, it would have been impossible for anyone to have pleased every group in the North and South. But Washington succeeded in his mission. He knew what he wanted to accomplish. His deep foundation of learning provided him the vision, confidence, and character to stay on course. Before his death, he built a great institution of learning for those who had virtually no other access. His greatest legacy may be his vision of education as the best guarantee of true individual freedom and achievement. For that he was widely honored and memorialized (Thornbrough, 1969).

HONORS AND AWARDS

Booker T. Washington received many honors and awards for service to his people and his country, far too many to be listed here. Perhaps, the one that gave him the biggest thrill was the awarding to him of an honorary degree by Harvard University. On June 24, 1896, Washington marched with President Charles Eliot of Harvard and other guests across the Harvard grounds to Sanders Theatre where the commencement was held and degrees conferred. When Washington's name was called, President Eliot conferred on him the degree, Master of Arts. Newspaper editorials were lavish in praise of the honoree from the South, making note of the applause and energized acknowledgement he received upon accepting the honor. Expressions such as "outburst of applause," "a glow covered the cheeks" of those in attendance who listened to Washington's speech that day. One editorial stated that the honor was conferred on him for "a genius and broad humanity which count for greatness in any man, whether his skin be black or white." Another stated that he had carried the "oratorical honors" of the day (Washington, 1901, p. 186).

Today, thousands of people annually visit many memorials and parks that have been erected and dedicated to Washington's legacy. His life is one that easily merits study and review. In this author's opinion, if the value of a life can be measured from the level of its beginning to the height of its end, the life of Washington stands with the best of lives ever lived on this earth.

Pearl S. Buck

A Brief Biography

Pearl S. Buck was born in Hillsboro, West Virginia, in 1892. Her parents, who were southern Presbyterian missionaries stationed in China, were on a furlough to the United States at the time of her birth. When only three months of age, she traveled to Chinkiang, China, with her parents and an older brother, Edwin, who was twelve years of age. For most of the next forty years, China served as her home.

Growing up in China as the daughter of American parents, Buck absorbed the language and culture of two countries. At home she learned to speak English and acquired a fundamental knowledge of her American heritage from her parents. Living in a Chinese community, she learned the Chinese language and culture as early as she did that of her heritage. She acquired reading skills in both English and Chinese at a very early age. Her first playmates were Chinese, and her earliest concept of society was that of China. In every respect, she thought of herself as Chinese, except when her Chinese friends reminded her that she was white with golden hair.

Buck received training in the English language from her mother. A Chinese tutor trained her in the Chinese language and schooled her in the ancient traditions of China. From "Teacher Kung," the name she used to address her tutor, Pearl learned the history, myths, and modes of thinking practiced by the Chinese. As she later recalled, the important lesson that Kung left with her was that a person who wants to be happy must not raise his or her head above that of the neighbors. Kung advised: "He who raises his head above the heads of others will sooner or later be decapitated" (Buck, 1954, p. 48). The lesson appeared to remain with Pearl for she was shy and reticent when it came to promoting herself to others, even after becoming a celebrated writer.

At the age of nine, Buck returned with her parents to the United States for a visit. While in the states she and her family lived with her grandparents in the West Virginia home in which she was born. While she was in America, she found the people she met to be so different from her Chinese friends that she was soon eager to return to her home in China. While the family was in the United States president William McKinley was assassinated while shaking hands with visitors at a public reception in Buffalo, New York. Pearl was very shaken by the assassination because it reminded her of revolutionary events that were beginning to unfold in China. Soon after reaching the age of ten, Pearl returned with her family to Chinkiang.

Buck's exposure to other peoples and cultures was far reaching while growing up in China. She played daily with Chinese children and talked freely with their parents and others on the streets where she walked and played. She absorbed the language and folkways of the people just as thoroughly as if she had been a native. She learned to enjoy Chinese food and came to think of herself as Chinese. She later wrote, "I lived among the Chinese people and spoke their tongue before I spoke my own, and their children were my first friends" (Buck, 1954, p. 19).

In addition to the Chinese, Buck had exposure to a wide range of nationalities in China. Although her home life was quite provincial, her individual initiative in meeting a mixture of nationalities gave her a cosmopolitan exposure. The adults that she got to know well included men and women from India, Japan, Korea, Thailand, Vietnam, France, England, Russia, and Italy. She lost no opportunity to learn about different cultures of the world.

Born with a strong curiosity, Buck would query anyone who could supply her with information to fill her thirst for knowledge. Her mother often stated, proudly so, that she was constantly drilled with a flow of questions from her daughter. Pearl wanted to know about those who came from other heritages, about what made them different in appearance and custom. In China her family physician was from India. Pearl pressed the doctor and his wife to tell her stories about the life and culture of India, and she begged to hear stories from their childhoods. A neighbor of Pearl's family was a Japanese woman married to an English husband. Pearl begged her for information and stories about Japan.

Buck's interest in people and cultures led her to decide that she wanted to become a writer of stories about people. From that time forward, she looked for ways to expand her knowledge and range of experience with all kinds of people. Walks about the town and countryside where she could casually meet and talk with new acquaintances became important. Any acquaintances of the family who might have had interesting adventures were solicited for what they could share with her. She learned about a Captain Swan and Mrs. Swan, a Scottish couple who lived on an old ship's hulk docked in the harbor. From the captain Pearl learned about Scotland. In addition, Captain Swan told stories about the days when he steered a boat up and down the China coast and skirmished with pirates.

Buck reached the age of eighteen in 1910. Her parents decided that she should return to America to attend college. Pearl wanted to attend Wellesley College in Massachusetts. However, with her parents having been born and reared as southerners and the Civil War and its aftermath still fresh in the emotions of most people, both north and south, relatives in the family prevailed upon her parents to send her to a southern school. The college chosen was Randolph-Macon Woman's College in Lynchburg, Virginia. The school had a strong program in intellectual development designed very much like those in all-male institutions. Moreover, the college appealed to her parents because their son, Edgar, a newspaper editor, was living in Lynchburg with his wife and two children.

At Randolph-Macon Pearl majored in psychology. Some studies she enjoyed and some she found boring. Although she was intelligent, well-read, and widely traveled, she did not compete for higher grades than her classmates. Perhaps her Chinese tutor had made competition unappealing to her with his statement regarding the raising of ones head higher than that of others. Upon graduation Pearl took a position as instructor in psychology at Randolph-Macon. In just a few months she received a letter from her father with sad news that her mother was seriously ill in China. Pearl resigned and promptly returned to her home in Chinkiang. Once she was settled into her parents' home again, she took a job as teacher in a school for boys and also supervised Chinese girls in training to work in local schools. The time remaining after her work was devoted to caring for her mother and to reading.

In the summer of 1917 Pearl met John Lossing Buck. He was an American and a young Cornell graduate who worked as an agricultural economist for the Presbyterian mission board in China. Within a few months they were married and took up residence in Nanhsuchou in rural Anhwei Province in North China where John worked. Pearl found life in the peasant village bleak and sparse. The people were poor and lived life close to the soil. To fill her time she learned to enjoy housekeeping, gardening, arranging and rearranging her simple furniture in the four small rooms of their Chinese home. Her marriage to John seemed to be missing some important attachments, but for many years she worked to make the best of what she increasingly viewed as a mistake in judgment on her part.

The year of 1921 was an eventful year in Buck's life. After many years of declining health, her mother died, and her father moved into the Buck home. A daughter, Carol, was born, tragically a victim of PKU (phenylketonuria), a condition that produces a metabolic inability to assimilate protein into the body. In those days the condition was not preventable or treatable, as it is today, and usually produced severe mental retardation in its victims. Such was the case with Carol. To further complicate an already devastating event in her life, during the delivery, Pearl's doctor discovered that she was carrying a uterine tumor. She immediately underwent a hysterectomy.

In 1929 Pearl returned to the United States for the purpose of putting her invalid daughter in a rest home where she would be safe from the revolutionary unrest that was then sweeping across China. After an extensive search she chose The Training School at Vineland in New Jersey. Pearl later wrote the story of her difficult decision to leave Carol in the states in a book titled *The Child Who Never Grew* (Buck, 1950). Before she returned to China, Pearl learned her first novel, *East Wind: West Wind* (Buck, 1930), had been accepted for publication by The John Day Company.

Back in China Buck missed her invalid daughter. To fill the void and the time that she had previously used in the care of her child, she began writing a novel that she had long carried in her head. The novel would become *The Good Earth* (Buck, 1931), published by The John Day Company. The theme of the book embraced the lives of the common people of China, people that Pearl had come to know intimately while living with and among them for many years. The novel lifted her from author obscurity to one of international fame. *The Good Earth* headed the bestseller list for months, sold nearly two million copies, and was translated into thirty languages. In addition, it inspired a Broadway play and a Hollywood film and won for Buck the Pulitzer Prize for literature (National Women's Hall of Fame, n.d.). After reading the novel, the famous American humorist Will Rogers was quoted in the *New York Times* as saying that the book was, "not only the greatest book about a people ever written but the best book of our generation" (Conn, 1996, p. 153).

By 1934 Buck's marriage to John was no more than a marriage on paper. Pearl decided to return to the United States and make it her permanent home. Several reasons prompted that decision. Her marriage had long ceased to function as a marriage, political conditions in China seemed to get worse rather than better, she wanted to be closer to her invalid daughter, and she and Richard Walsh, her publisher at The John Day Company, had fallen in love. Moreover, *The Good Earth* had become a big seller, and she was in demand back in the states.

Soon after her return to America Pearl and Richard were married in Nevada. She bought a farm and home in Bucks County in Pennsylvania and settled down with her husband and her adopted daughter, Janice, to live a quiet family life and to write more books. Over the next forty years, Buck adopted more children, enlarged the home on her Green Hills Farm, and created an adoption program that came to be called "Welcome House," the first international, interracial adoption program of its kind. In addition she wrote books, lots of books. By the time of her death in March 1973, Pearl Buck had authored more than eighty books in genres that included fiction, nonfiction and children's books.

READING IN EARLY LIFE

Pearl Buck has written that she does not remember exactly when she learned to read, but she does know that she read well by the age of four. Her time frame is based on a book that came as a gift. "On my fifth birthday I received a small book as a gift, entitled *Little Susie's Seven Birthdays*, and I envied Susie for having seven instead of five" (Buck, 1954, p. 356). Pearl must have learned to read quite early for she remembers word assignments being used as a form of corrective discipline. When she did something for which her mother thought she should be punished, one favorite task was to assign words to look up in the English dictionary and copy down their meanings.

The word task came as a result of a special circumstance within the Buck family. Pearl could be mischievous at times, and when given jobs to do for punishment, her Chinese nurse would feel sorry for her and do the jobs for Pearl. When the mother discovered what the nurse was doing, she admonished her to stop because she was undermining her efforts to properly train Pearl. But the help continued when the mother was not around to prevent it. As a partial remedy, the mother began using English word tasks in which the nurse, who was illiterate, could not relieve Pearl of the responsibility of completing the work herself.

From the time that Buck did learn to read, her love for books was strong and never diminished. Her young imagination was captivated by the visions that authors could create with letters and words on a printed page. She read the books in her parents' collection and then began to collect her own library of favorite stories. The children's books available for her reading were very limited, prompting her curious mind to turn to adult novels. By the age of ten, her adult novel reading had persuaded Pearl that she wanted to one day become a novelist. Both her Chinese tutor and her mother tried to convince Pearl that novel reading was for inferior minds, that content and information books by the great writers were far better reading for her intellectual development. Her mother even hid the novels in the family library from Pearl to keep her from spending so much time with fiction. Undaunted, Pearl found them and continued reading, never discussing it with her mother. Pearl always believed her mother knew, but neither ever raised the issue with the other.

At a very young age Pearl began reading the works of Charles Dickens. Reading became a way for her to gain close connections to people. By nature and circumstance she was a solitary type of person. Casual friends she had, but she was not very close to anyone. Pearl's lifelong passion for reading and her inner sense of self-reliance were rooted in her childhood loneliness where her father was consumed with his missionary work and her mother was often sad and lonely for her family back in America. While she was emotionally attached to her Chinese nurse, the nurse could neither read nor write English and, therefore, could not be an intellectual companion. Pearl fulfilled that need with books. She read many books, some many times.

Dickens stirred Buck's young imagination and created wonder about human beings. She read *Oliver Twist*, a book she read twice without stopping. From that selection she moved to other Dickens books contained in a dark blue, cloth-bound set kept on a shelf in the family parlor. Her mother became alarmed at Pearl's interest in Dickens, for she saw him as a writer of course material concerned primarily with those who lived on the low end of the economic scale of life. But Pearl had no trouble enjoying his books. Over a period of ten years she read many Dickens books from cover to cover, among them the *Pickwick Papers* and *Hard Times*. She remembered stealing away into a sunny corner of the south veranda of their Chinese home and spending many winter afternoons reading alone, periodically consuming oranges and peanuts for refreshment. She sometimes irritated her younger sister, Grace, by keeping the light on in the bedroom they shared, while she read far into the night (Buck, 1954).

As a part of her educational training, Pearl was tutored in the classical Chinese language by Mr. Kung and in English by her mother. By the age of seven she was reading both Chinese and English literature. The Chinese texts used included selections from Confucius, Mencius, and some of the major Chinese poets. The English books used included Fox's *Book of Martyrs*, Plutarch's *Lives*, the Bible, the poems of Tennyson and Browning, and the novels of Scott and Thackeray.

When China rebelled against foreign intervention and war began in the region where Pearl lived, the family had to flee for safety. Pearl could take only a few of her books. The others she could enjoy only through memory, and memory was all she could take of a big Chinese elm tree that she had so often climbed to sit on its branches and look down on a garden bench under a tall bamboo where she had so often had gone to sit and read.

With increasing age Buck began to think more about the few months she had spent in America on visits. Those memories prodded her to seek knowledge about her homeland. She began reading whatever she could find about America and the Western world. As the revolts and revolutions became more frequent across China, she knew that someday she would probably have to return to live in America. She wanted to know as much as possible about the land and people of her heritage. The longer the time interval since her last visit, the more difficult it was for her to recall the look, feel, and texture of her homeland. About her memories she said:

> I remembered certain hours, such and such an event, rather than consecutive time, and in an effort to hold what I had, I read incessantly. I had always read but now I read to search for and find my own world, the Western world, to which some day I would return, and must return, when the gates of Asia closed against me and my kind [Buck, 1954, p. 62].

Buck's search for books to read about life in America proved to be more difficult than she would have liked. In her Chinese environment a large number of the books written in English were more likely to be authored by British rather than American writers. Her family did own some Mark Twain books, but her mother considered Twain's writing to be slightly coarse and encouraged other works. Even so, Pearl did read *Tom Sawyer* and *Huckleberry Finn*. In Twain's books she met an America that was totally unreal to her. She had never seen Americans like those he described. Years later, when she had returned to America and was guiding the teenage development of her adopted sons, she realized that Mark Twain had captured something uniquely American in his writing. While her sons were growing up, she reread *Tom Sawyer* once each year to help her better understand the boyish behaviors that frequently left her puzzled.

In Shanghai, Pearl had access to a Kelly and Walsh Bookshop that carried a good stock of novels by British authors from which the family could order books. They acquired sets of Dickens, Thackeray, George Eliot, and Walter Scott. They also had most of the English poets and a fine edition of Shakespeare. Those books were an important part of her childhood reading. Her family also subscribed to *The Delineator* and her father took *The Century* magazine. To keep the children in touch with young people and events back in the states, the family subscribed to *St. Nicholas* and *The Youth's Companion*.

In 1909 at the age of seventeen, Pearl was enrolled in a boarding school in Shanghai for the purpose of meeting Western girls her own age and, through that association, developing the kind of social skills that were more American and less Chinese. Soon after starting school she and her two roommates engaged in prolonged discussions about Chinese customs and religions. Pearl's views on the Chinese, their culture, and their religion were favorable, and she told the roommates her honest views. It was not the best choice of an audience before which to speak positively about non–Christian religious practices. Christian missionaries were in China for the express purpose of converting the Chinese to the Christian religion, and the boarding school was created principally to serve the daughters of missionaries. The roommates tattled on Pearl to the school director that Pearl's views on non–Christian religions made her a heretic. To keep Pearl from corrupting her two roommates, the director moved her to a small private room where she would be alone. Pearl found the change to be much to her liking. She no longer had to contend with two narrow-minded roommates, and late at night she could read in her room after the lights had been turned off elsewhere in the school (Buck, 1954).

In 1910, at the age of eighteen, Pearl's parents decided that she should attend an American college. She and her family planned a trip to the states that would take them by land across China and through Russia to Europe and across the Atlantic to America. Normally they would have traveled to Shanghai and taken a ship across the Pacific to the west coast of the United States. But her mother was prone to seasickness and wanted to avoid that difficulty on such a long sea voyage. As they worked out the plans for the long trip, it would be an educational tour for Pearl so that she might learn more about the European continent before she entered college.

To get the most educational value from the trip, Pearl's mother stocked a large trunk full of books about the European countries they expected to pass through or visit. While traveling, principally by train, the mother and daughter read and discussed the many books in their collection. Through reading, discussion, and observations made while traveling through the several countries, Pearl acquired a wealth of knowledge on the characteristics and achievements of the peoples of Europe. Both she and her parents were alarmed at the depth of poverty they observed in the Russian countryside. Pearl especially liked England and the English people, finding them to be much more civil than the English she had known in China (Buck, 1954).

While Buck was a student at Randolph-Macon College, she wasted little time on subjects she did not enjoy. Instead, she spent hours away from her assigned reading, shut away in the campus library reading books she had long wanted to read, ones to which she had not previously had access. She later wrote, "I read prodigiously, extravagantly and greedily, in season and out, and certainly lowered my general level of grades thereby" (Buck, 1954, p. 95). Among the many books read while secluded were the works of American writers Theodore Dreiser and Sinclair Lewis. Years later when she had become a famous author herself, she happened to sit beside Lewis at a dinner one evening. Pearl made a casual attempt to minimize her writing, but Lewis would not hear of it. He told her that she must do more because a novelist does noble work and must be proud of what is produced. She must learn to ignore the negative remarks made by those who tried to belittle her work. "You must not minimize yourself.... You must write many novels ... and let people have their little say! They have nothing else to say, damn them!" (Buck, 1954, p. 78).

During her senior year in college Buck found that she needed extra money to meet incidental expenses and to help her live as a true American in a culture where money reigned important. She looked for ways to earn extra cash without having to go to her family. In searching, she discovered two college contests, both of which paid money to the winner. One was for the best short story of the year and the other for the best poem. She entered and won both contests.

Not long after graduation, Buck returned to China and took a job as a teacher in a local school not affiliated with missionary work. She also accepted a few social invitations from American young men working for an American firm in China. Threatened with censure if she maintained a social life outside the missionary circle, she quit accepting social invitations and filled her free time with reading and studying Chinese books. Some of each day was spent in reading. To add to her knowledge, she also traveled widely through and around China. Still an unmarried young woman, Pearl's life would soon change, but not her love of reading.

Reading During an Unhappy Marriage

In the summer of 1917 Pearl met John Lossing Buck in the mountains of China. He was an American and a young Cornell University graduate who worked as an agricultural economist for the Presbyterian mission board in China. Pearl was ready for marriage, and John seemed to her the best prospective husband she had met. After seeing each other only four times, they announced their engagement to be married. Pearl's parents liked John well enough but believed the two were too far apart in their intellectual interests and temperaments to create a compatible marriage. They believed John had little interest in reading and things of the mind, while Pearl was always with a book. Unfortunately, Pearl disregarded her parents' advice, reasoning that John would begin reading when she could create a proper opportunity and atmosphere. In addition, she wanted to believe there would be other interests they could share.

Pearl and John were married in the summer of 1917 and moved immediately to a rural province in North China where John worked as a farming advisor to local farmers. Pearl often traveled with her new husband out to farms and villages where she enjoyed meeting the rural people and tried to be helpful to her husband. She spoke the language fluently and was easily accepted by the Chinese people in the region. The couple set up residence in the village of Nanhsuchou where she developed new hobbies in which to invest some of her free time. She learned to keep bees for honey and experimented with a variety of jams and jellies made from local products like dates and dark red haws, a cross between damson plum and crab apple. A long-held interest that she continued to indulge was reading. She even designed and built bookshelves for her books. An American living in the village at the time said of Pearl, "She is pretty and attractive, reads a good deal, and thinks about what she reads" (Conn, 1996, p. 64). While living in Nanhsuchou she collected most of the material that would later appear in her big novel, *The Good Earth*.

During the approximately three years the Bucks lived in Nanhsuchou, the marriage relationship grew distant and lacked emotion. Pearl began to realize that their lack of common interests appeared to be far greater than she had ever imagined. The marriage had become a serious mismatch. In addition, John grew increasingly frustrated with his efforts to help improve Chinese farming. He found his American training to be inappropriate for the kind of farming he found practiced in that region. He looked for a way out.

In 1920 he accepted a teaching position on the faculty at Nanking University in the College of Agriculture and Forestry. The couple moved to Nanking and settled in to a lifestyle centered around John's work at the university. Pearl enjoyed living in Nanking and thought the city and countryside quite beautiful and appealing. She began dabbling in writing, something she had long planned to do but had delayed starting until she felt sufficiently mature and informed to be a good writer.

Pearl's marriage to John had not gone well, and writing was one way to fill the void she felt in the relationship. By the time they moved to Nanking she had come to accept the reality that she and her husband were incompatible as mates. His intellectual training and interest were too distant from hers for them to build a meaningful bond. But thoughts of divorce in a close-knit missionary community of the kind to which her family belonged created enormous conflicts with which she was ill prepared to cope. In addition to writing and some work in teaching, Pearl dug evermore deeply into reading to fill her need for companionship. While John built his life around work at the university, Pearl spent her evenings with books.

During Buck's years in China, revolution and an unstable government brought many cultural changes. Among the more significant alterations was the appearance of books written in the common spoken language of the people.

Previously, books were written in Wen-li, the classical written language that only the well educated could read. With the introduction of a written common language, called Pei Hua (Harris, 1970), Chinese authors began to plagiarize Western novels in the new printable language, usually claiming them as their own work (Buck, 1954). The novels became hugely popular among Chinese readers. Once their popularity was firmly established, Chinese authors began producing new and original short novels written about common Chinese people in their daily lives. Pearl read hundreds of these novels to better understand what forces were influencing the lust for change that became so evident among the Chinese people. She wrote, "Publishing houses sprang up and the bookstalls in my city were crowded with the cheap little paper-backed volumes. I could buy a basketful for a dollar or so and read for days, and this generous fare has made me impatient ever since of expensive books" (Buck, 1954, p.179).

When Pearl, her husband, and child returned to America for his one-year sabbatical leave, he taught at Cornell University, and she worked on her masters' degree. While there, she entered and won an essay contest that awarded a prize of $200. To assist their financial needs even further, she sold a second story to *Asia Magazine*. With the money she earned, Pearl paid her school bills and living expenses, bought a new coat, and took some items back to China for her family and some gifts for friends (Buck, 1954).

While at Cornell, Buck continued to read avidly. At night, when her child was asleep and her husband had retired to his study, Pearl walked to the university library, where she spent many happy hours reading as many books as her time would allow. In her memoir she recalled those happy hours in seclusion: "The joys of that library! I worked alone in the stacks, free to read as many books as I liked, free to think and to write" (Buck, 1954, p. 201). When the hour grew very late, she would leave and walk by lantern light back to her small home. Before they returned to China, she and John adopted a baby daughter that they named Janice.

Buck's deep thirst for books is illustrated by an incident that occurred in China when another revolutionary conflict between rival forces erupted. She and her two children had to leave Nanking and retreat to Shanghai. Under hurried and stressful conditions they boarded a ship that would take them to safety. As the ship sailed down river toward their destination, most of the passengers were taken ill with food poisoning, a result of bad food served aboard that ship. Pearl was one of the few who did not get sick. After she helped all the others as best she could and all were settled down for the night, Pearl longed for something to read, something that would take her mind off the dreadful conditions of the moment, but no books were in sight. Some unknown intuition caused her to reach under her berth, and there in an open canvas bag she felt the outline of a book. Out it came, and she discovered in her hand a copy of *Moby Dick*, a book she had never read. The newly found treasure held her enchanted for the remainder of the night.

In retreat from the dangers of revolution in China, Pearl read deeply into the history of revolutions, trying to gain insight and perspective into what was happening to the country she considered her home. Existing in a state of limbo, unsure whether she could ever be safe and secure living in China again, her reading helped to give her a better sense of the uncertainty that faced the China she had known. Her reading developed within her an intellectual perspective that would finally produce a resolve to leave China permanently. But that day was still some time away.

On a visit to America in 1932 Buck became so disturbed by the treatment of minority citizens by the white majority that she returned to China and began reading everything she could find on the subject of race and racial behavior in the states. Before departing, though, she visited the campus of Yale University, where she stayed in the home of the president. While there, she discovered his personal library housed in a big living room. So fascinated was she with the range of his book collection that she spent much of the evening scanning and discussing rare books she discovered. In some of her host's books she found autographs of many of her favorite English authors, such as Dickens, Browning, Thackeray, Lord Byron, and George Eliot.

Any opportunity to touch the places and things her favorite writers had touched always excited Buck. On a trip to England, she spent some time in London walking the streets that she had read about in the writings of Dickens when she was a young girl growing up in China. Pearl found on one street Ye Olde Curiosity Shoppe that Dickens had described in a book. She was pleased to find that the shop looked just the way she had imagined it while reading the book. And on a trip to Stockholm, Sweden, she found that she enjoyed reading the books of Swedish author Selma Lagerlof, an author she met while in Sweden to receive the Nobel Prize in 1938.

By 1933 Buck had virtually decided to leave China to establish a permanent residence in the United States. Before leaving the country in which she had lived for most of her forty years, she decided to take one more trip through that part of the world and get to know more about the people that inhabited those regions she had not yet seen. The trip began with a tour through the beautiful province of Kukien in South China and the province of Kwangtung. From there she went southward to Canton where she walked the ancient narrow streets of the old city where ivory dealers, jade lapidaries, gold and silversmiths worked in their one-story shops. Next she crossed through Vietnam, Cambodia, and Laos, then known in the West as Indo-China. From there she traveled to Bangkok in present day Thailand.

From Thailand Buck traveled to India, a country she knew something about from her many Indian acquaintances in China. From India she proceeded through the jungles of present-day Indonesia and found that she was not a jungle devotee. She then returned to China and prepared to leave for the United States.

In 1934 Buck left her husband, John, in China and returned with her adopted daughter to live in America. She spent her first year in New York promoting her book, *The Good Earth*, and being promoted as a successful new author. During the year, after refusing proposals of marriage for many months from Richard Walsh, her publisher, she finally accepted. She traveled to Reno, Nevada, and lived with her future mother-in-law long enough to qualify for a divorce from John. While living in Reno, she bought a car, and the two women traveled around the state exploring old ghost towns. They visited the site of Virginia City, famous in Western lore, by then deserted. From such trips Pearl acquired an extensive knowledge of the history of the American West. When the day of her divorce arrived, Richard, who was by that day already divorced, arrived in Reno. After receiving a decree of freedom from her marriage to John, Pearl and Richard were wed within the hour in Reno.

Reading During a Successful Marriage

Buck found that getting adjusted to a new culture, a new marriage, and celebrity as a popular writer a challenge. Many characteristics of American society she found to be new, and some were deeply troubling. An image of America that she had obtained from books and the few Americans she had known in China proved to be inaccurate. The thing that most astounded her was the economic and social gap that existed between blacks and whites. A visit to an exhibition of black art opened her eyes even more. In the paintings she saw lynching, charred remains of black homes, children burned, poverty and poverty-stricken black faces who could not help themselves. She prevailed upon the artists to tell her about the paintings and the reality they portrayed. In the words of a biographer, "She was appalled to discover that this brutal form of murder continued to be a common feature of American life" (Conn, 1996, p. 165).

So disturbed was Buck by what she learned about human behavior in a country that she had imagined to be so perfect that she began reading all she could find on human relations. Her observations of American society made her think more deeply about the way Asians were treated by Westerners in Asian countries. In her mind the murder of many whites by Chinese rebels during the Chinese Revolution had resulted from the superior attitude of Westerners toward the Chinese. She knew the Chinese to be good and gentle people, but the Western world did not know them as she did.

After living for one year in New York, Buck decided that if she were to ever become a true American in mind and spirit, she must establish a home in a place where American roots and traditions were deep. After a brief search she found what she was looking for, a farm that included a stone house at Perkasie in Bucks County, Pennsylvania. She named her new home Green Hills Farm. With her new husband and adopted daughter, Pearl moved to Green Hills and began building a home life, improved the farm and house, and created a writing environment in which she would produce scores of new books.

In her new setting, Buck's reading continued. One reading theme revolved around her farm. She had learned from the Chinese that land is a sacred possession. To her dismay, the farm she had purchased had been in a state of neglect for years. One of her early projects was to rebuild the farm into a productive property. Upon analysis, the scope of the job to be done in restoring her property convinced Pearl that she had much to learn to restore the place the way she wanted. To properly prepare her for the task at hand, she spent two years reading, talking, observing, and acquiring all the knowledge she could absorb to direct the restoration. Indeed, she read and discussed so much with her neighbors and helpers that they one day asked, "Be you goin' to do real farmin' or book farmin'?" (Buck, 1954, p. 384).

With her settlement in America happily completed, Pearl made a decision to make family and writing her life. For the next thirty-five years, she turned out book after book, so fast in fact that her publisher and readers were having trouble keeping up with her pace. At one point she had so many books on bookstore shelves that her advisers worried she would lose some of her audience, that she was saturating her market. For that reason she wrote five novels under the pen name "John Sedges." *The Townsman* was the most popular of her Sedges books (Harris, 1970). Additionally, Pearl wanted to prove that she could write successful books on subjects other than her Chinese experiences. *The Townsman* became a bestseller, proving that she could, indeed.

After Pearl and Richard were settled into their new life together, she devoted some of her time to assisting him in his publishing business at The John Day Company. She worked in the company office, wrote articles and produced book reviews for *Asia Magazine*, which her husband edited. In addition to her writing during this period of her life, Pearl engaged in an extraordinary amount of reading to find good books she believed to be worthy of written reviews, sometimes as many as seven per month. Two Chinese novels that she especially liked were *The Dream of the Red Chamber* and *Three Kingdoms*.

A book she read and reviewed on radio was Edgar Snow's *Red Star over China*, a book based on a series of interviews with a rising Communist leader in China. That leader was Mao Tse-tung, the leader who later ruled China for several decades. When the Japanese were trying to gain control of China through war, Pearl read books and reports on the war and produced several articles for publication. When she read a book about the war in those parts of China in which she had lived, she felt the conflict and devastation more deeply than did the authors of most of what she read. *Wheat and Soldiers* was one such book written by a Japanese soldier who had fought in China.

As an editorial advisor at John Day, Pearl read hundreds of manuscripts in search of the next great book that the company could publish. About that search she once observed:

> Of these hundreds of manuscripts I read many are surprisingly well written, some are also well conceived and intelligently developed. But that is the best that can be said and it is not enough.... Whatever they are, these pages are for me always an exciting possibility until I have scanned them and laid them regretfully on the heap of manuscripts to be rejected [Harris, 1970, p. 176].

During the first half of 1939 Buck read as many as thirty novel manuscripts for consideration for publication by John Day (Conn, 1996). At the same time she maintained a heavy writing and speaking schedule, all the while maintaining a home in New York and Green Hills Farm and helping Richard raise and direct their children that had increased to five through adoptions.

A particular theme that guided a large amount of Buck's reading was that having to do with the problems women faced in male-dominated cultures. One such book Pearl read in 1940 was *Restless Wave*. The book was an autobiography by a Japanese woman named Haru Matsui. In the book the author describes her frustration after being educated in the United States and, upon returning to Japan, not being accepted as a person with an educated mind. She had to resort to the traditional role of subservience expected of women in the Japan of that day. Such treatment of women by men reflected the status of women that Pearl had known in China and even in her own home, where her father believed that women should be wives and mothers and not much more.

Another issue that drew Buck into much reading through the 1940s was a condition she saw as a distortion of truth between American democracy and the world's perception of American democracy. She read a book by Charles Ferguson, *A Little Democracy Is a Dangerous Thing*, in which the author drew attention to weaknesses in our democratic system. The author presented the point of view that in American life, only the whites enjoyed a true democratic presence. Pearl had made a similar observation after becoming an American resident. It was a view about which she had been speaking and writing for a number of years. In the early 1940s her reading turned increasingly toward social and political topics about which she wanted to write and speak.

In the late 1940s Buck trended back to reading the kind of fiction that she had so enjoyed in her early reading life. She read several novels by Edith Wharton, among them *The Age of Innocence* and *A Backward Glance*. By the mid–1950s her reading turned strongly to her identity as a woman and the place of women in the world. Among many books she read on the subject were *The Second Sex* by Simone de Beauvoir, *Music and Women* by Sophie Drinker, and *The Natural Superiority of Woman* by Ashley Montagu. Her reading and study of women's issues lead to a new novel by Pearl published in 1956.

In her novel *Imperial Woman*, Buck fictionalized a recreation of China's dowager empress who rose from serving as a concubine to the emperor to become ruler herself upon his death. The story draws attention to a woman who had the strength and power to rule a vast nation, a woman who had risen from the social basement to the penthouse of political power against all odds to rule China for forty years. The life of the empress proved to Pearl that women were equal to men, even in the most powerful positions the world had to offer.

At the age of forty-nine, Buck complained in her diary that she had not found a really good book to read during the summer. "Yes," she wrote, "I have read one good book—*The Fortunes of Richard Mahoney*—a great book, and one I should have liked to have written" (Harris, 1970, p. 288). Her search for good books remained never ending. When she reached the age of fifty, although she was somewhat tired from the large volume of writing she had produced, she was able to say that she still enjoyed "sky and land and children, good books and fine and simple music is as strong as ever" (Harris, 1970, p. 296).

In the late 1950s Buck began reading books and literature on scientific and political issues related to the use of nuclear power. As with most of the people in the world, the atomic bombs dropped on Japan ending World War II had left a haunting memory with her. Pearl read widely, interviewed many scientists, and visited scientific laboratories in an effort to sort out the bad and good uses of nuclear power. The reading and research led her to write a three-act play titled *A Desert Incident*. When produced on Broadway, the play had very limited public appeal and ended with a short run.

During the 1960s Buck became an elder stateswoman among American female authors. On issues and roles related to women, her advice was frequently sought. One such instance occurred when the publisher of a book by Betty Friedan, *The Feminine Mystique*, asked Pearl to read the proofs and submit her opinion. Pearl read the manuscript and liked it. The book represented her own views regarding the plight of women in a male-controlled culture, no matter what the name and location of the country.

During the last decade of her life, Buck devoted increased attention to bringing foreign children that were fathered by American servicemen to America. Each trip made to those countries where such children lived in poverty and rejection compelled her even more to do her utmost to resolve a condition that left such children degraded and outcast in their native cultures. She read and studied any material that would be useful in persuading Americans of the truth and need behind her effort. A book read at the time was *Man's Most Dangerous Myth: The Fallacy of Race* by Ashley Montagu. The author pressed the point that mixtures of alloys, plant life, and even human life showed more desirable qualities and characteristics than so-called pure stock. That was the same view that Pearl had been promoting for years.

In the end, Pearl Buck's life represented many dimensions. The most outstanding and far-reaching trait was that of reading. She remained an avid reader until the end. Upon her death, her two libraries at Green Hills Farm contained about 5,000 books (Conn, 1996). Her reading life had made her a highly literate person whose mind had traveled millions of miles with the minds of the authors she had read. Her mental excursions had produced within her a vast reservoir of knowledge, vision, and compassion that made her one of the most courageous and productive persons of the twentieth century. The power of reading is clearly exemplified in her life.

THE IMPACT OF READING

Once having learned to read, Pearl Buck read with a passion, a passion for learning and to fill a chronic loneliness. As a young American girl growing up in China, she was not close to anyone. She loved her Chinese nurse, who could neither read nor write and, therefore, could not share in Pearl's intellectual interest. Her mother and father were both busy with their activities, her father being away from the house much of his time involved in his missionary work. That left books to fill the loneliness Pearl felt. Recalling those days, she has said that she "lived mostly in books" (Harris, 1970, p. 95). In addition to filling her need for companionship, Pearl saw in books the accumulated wisdom of the human race, and she wanted to absorb as much of that wisdom as possible (Buck, 1954).

An early reading ability led Buck to develop a thirst for knowledge. The world of knowledge would lead her to become a writer. In addition to her mother, an early influence on her desire to be a writer were the novels of Charles Dickens. She has stated that Dickens, after her mother, had the greatest influence on her desire to write (Harris, 1970, p. 86). Dickens's influence must have been strong for she had her first article published at the young age of six in a Louisville, Kentucky, newspaper.

While growing up in China, Buck read deeply into both Chinese and American literature. That reading led her to see a cultural gap between the two societies, a difference that would become important in her life. She had gained a powerful understanding of Chinese history and culture through reading their books and traveling through their country. When she chose writing as a career, it was only natural for her to write about that which she most knew and understood. Her knowledge of China and its people she used for material in many of the books she wrote. Her novels and nonfiction works educated thousands of Western readers about a people and continent that most knew little about. She made China and Asian cultures significant to Western readers. In that effort, Buck became a bridge between two peoples that would become increasingly important to each other as time moved forward.

No one was better positioned to introduce China to Western readers than was Buck. She had become so thoroughly a part of both cultures that she felt at home in both but not completely a part of either (Buck, 1954). She read so many Chinese books that she became thoroughly immersed in their patterns of thinking and cultural ideals. In 1930 Pearl published an article on the Chinese novel titled "China in the Mirror of Her Fiction." The premise of her theme was that the intellectuals in China had never considered fiction as acceptable literature. Pearl had read their fiction and knew that it had wide appeal to the common people. In her article she sought to bring respect to Chinese fiction because it represented the stories of the people, interesting stories that had been passed down orally from one generation to another. She knew the stories to be important to the common people, and once they learned to read the common language, the stories would be cherished and important to their common heritage.

Buck also learned that what is written about a people can be biased and distorted by those who do the writing. She learned from reading both Chinese and Western authors that the two cultures held very different views of each other. Historians from the two regions gave different versions, not only of the same events but also very different views of the same culture. Based on her reading, she judged that each despised the other as a lesser breed, although neither knew enough about the other to know what the other actually was all about (Buck, 1954).

Reading in Buck's life gave her a domain of comfort within the dual social context in which she had to live. Books helped her to move mentally and socially beyond the parochial environment into which she was born. Her depth of knowledge opened a broad view of human existence that helped her to see that all people are important and that no level of society should have advantage over another. She read many books about China and the influence of the educated class that read the classical language, but she delighted in reading the novels of the common people written in the language they spoke. The great vision and wealth of understanding she acquired, both through reading and personal experience, helped her to understand and appreciate the goodness in productive and simple living. After she was comfortably settled in America and had become a successful writer with a loving family life, she was able to write in her diary at age forty-nine: "life itself is the great good — not love, not ambition ... only life. Sleep at night ... getting up to the world ... eating ... work ... reading ... play ... good enough!" (Harris, 1970, p. 286).

Perhaps the biggest impact of Buck's reading was to infuse her with a deep awareness that the perceived differences between Asian and Western cultures was basically irrelevant. She believed that Chinese and Americans were more alike than they were different. If only each could get to know the other, everyone would recognize that the two societies possessed so much that could bring them together in friendship. Her concern was that the treatment of the Chinese by Westerners in China would make enemies of the two peoples. Her writing and humanitarian work were both devoted to bringing the two cultures together in friendship so as to avoid conflicts that could lead to senseless wars.

Across the twentieth century, Buck's vast reading, along with travel and research, turned her into a premier authority on China and the Chinese people. No other American could match her depth of understanding of that culture. On so many issues, time proved her judgment to be correct. Her expectation that Americans and Chinese would some day become more socially and economically interlocked has arrived. Her counsel that the two nations would need each other has been realized. Buck's influence on American thought regarding China can be said to be substantial.

Honors and Awards

Pearl Buck received too many awards and honors for her work to include a complete list in this book. Honors came to her both during her life and after her death. Perhaps the most significant was the Nobel Prize for Literature awarded in 1938. In the words of the Nobel Foundation, Buck received the honor for her, "rich and truly epic descriptions of peasant life in China and for her biographical masterpieces" (The Nobel Foundation, 2002). In the year of her death, 1973, she was inducted into the National Women's Hall of Fame, located in Seneca Falls, New York. In 1985, twelve years after her death, a commemorative United States postage stamp was issued in Pearl's honor.

Louis L'Amour

A Brief Biography

Louis L'Amour was born in Jamestown, North Dakota, March 22, 1908. The youngest of seven children, he was the son of Louis Charles LaMoore and Emily Lavisa Dearborn LaMoore. The spelling of the family name went through periodic revisions. In an interview, Louis once said that the original spelling was L'Amour (Phillips, 1989). His father changed the orthography because too many people spelled the original version incorrectly. Years later, when Louis became a published author, he adopted L'Amour again.

The family heritage into which L'Amour was born was rich in frontier history. His father told stories of his own boyhood, of time spent in the woods harvesting lumber, keeping a pet bear and a deer, and of a friendship with a Huron Indian boy with whom he played as a youngster. His mother told stories of her girlhood and family while growing up in Minnesota. Both grandfathers served in the Union army during the Civil War. L'Amour's maternal great-grandfather was scalped by the Sioux Indians while serving as a member of the Sibley Expedition in Minnesota. A maternal ancestor had been a writer, having published about six books, only one of which Louis was ever able to find. There were two uncles who had worked on western ranches for many years. A strong heritage of men taming the American frontier provided young Louis with an early exposure to western ranch life and the cultures of historical frontiers where clashes and battles were frequently fought for control of the land and for human survival.

When Louis was very young his maternal grandfather came to live in a little house just in back of the LaMoore home. The grandfather told Louis story after story of the great battles in history and of his own experiences as a soldier in both the Civil and Indian wars. The grandfather taught the grandson military tactics by drawing on a blackboard battle plans that he had learned while fighting, along with great battles in history he had studied. Years later Louis could draw diagrams of the Battle of Canaan, even before he ever studied the battle on his own. That exposure to western lore and military tactics developed in Louis an early interest in the world beyond Jamestown, an interest that would later explode into an unquenchable thirst for books and travel.

By the time L'Amour reached the age of fifteen, economic conditions had grown difficult for the LaMoore family in North Dakota. The parents decided to sell their property in Jamestown and move to the southwest in search of better economic opportunities. In December 1923 the family left Jamestown and traveled southwestwardly in search of a place in which to earn a living. Not wanting to be an economic burden on his parents, Louis left both school and his parents and set out on his own. As a result, he lost contact with his parents for several years.

Alone and completely on his own at the age of fifteen, L'Amour began a life of wandering and working at any odd job he could find to keep from starving. He hopped freight trains and eventually found his way to Texas where he took a job skinning dead cattle, cattle that had been dead for weeks and stank horribly. He earned three dollars per day while helping his boss skin 925 carcasses (L'Amour, 1989).

The next few years became years of wanderlust and many jobs for Louis, none that lasted very long. A short stint at baling hay was performed in the Pecos Valley of New Mexico, across the road from the grave of the western outlaw Billy the Kid. While in the area Louis visited the home where Billy was killed and talked to the woman who offered the outlaw his last meal. Further wanderings around the western regions of the country brought him into contact with about thirty former gunfighters, rangers, and outlaws. Louis thoroughly enjoyed meeting the products of the western frontier and was fascinated by their many stories. He regretted that he could not have met more of that legendary breed, for they helped him to shape a concept of the Old West that would mold his writing years later.

During the course of his travels L'Amour held a job with the Hagenbeck-Wallace Circus, where he was assigned to care for the elephants. After only a few weeks he quit and moved on. He worked in a mine in Arizona and in the sawmills and lumberyards of Oregon and Washington. At times he participated as an amateur in exhibition prizefights in small towns across the southwest to earn money for food. Later, he fought professionally as a light heavyweight, winning 51 of 59 fights and knocking out 34 of his opponents during a relatively brief career (Phillips, 1989). Some reference versions have put the number of victories at 54 instead of 51 (Gale, 1985).

L'Amour eventually worked his way to the beach at San Pedro in California, where he hung out and did odd jobs while waiting to secure a job on a merchant ship. His days at San Pedro were hard and hungry times. For every job that became available, there were at least ten others waiting for work. Virtually all men waiting to ship out to sea had no money and had to take any odd jobs they could find to make money for food. Louis accepted work as a painter and rivets handler in the shipyard nearby. Sometimes he would find a day's work on a ship at dock and while on board would beg for a meal.

One night L'Amour was browsing in the Seaman's Institute, checking the lists to see what ships were due to arrive and what their destinations would be, when a stranger came in looking for a seaman who could ship out immediately. He jumped at the offer, grabbed his bag, and went aboard. His new home was a freighter bound for the Far East. The voyage took him to ports in Japan, China, Hong Kong, Singapore, and many others in the Far East. The unusual adventures he encountered there included one in which he fought pirate invaders with nothing but a broken oar. In China he witnessed the horror of criminals being beheaded. On a side trip he walked through the Tibetan mountains where he had to negotiate a space only three inches wide, with a drop of up to two hundred feet (Phillips, 1989).

As he wandered in and around the ports of the world, L'Amour met a wide range of strange and interesting characters. Many of them would appear years later as fictional characters in his short stories. He saw in those foreign men of raw adventure a similarity to the hoboes and wanderers he had known back in the states. But one difference seemed to distinguish the two groups. The hobos and rail riders of the states, those men of the American frontier, seemed to be always looking for a place where they could eventually put down roots and build something to call their own. The foreign adventurers seemed only interested in getting rich quick.

L'Amour's days as a wanderer of the world were often spent without money and no means of acquiring food. On at least three occasions, he went for four days without eating anything. But the upside to his hardship was reading. During his years of wanderlust he read hundreds of books. His reading began to create an interest in writing as a career. Initially he tried writing poetry and managed to get a few published. But the meager returns soon prodded him to try writing short stories. In 1935, after receiving hundreds of rejection slips, Louis sold his first manuscript to *True Gang Life* magazine, a story titled "Anything for a Pal" for the sum of $6.60 (Phillips, 1989, p. 81).

In late summer of 1942, L'Amour was drafted into the United States Army. After completing basic training he attended Officer's Candidate School and earned the rank of second lieutenant. Upon graduation he served in a number of roles, one of which was as instructor in winter survival techniques, an assignment for which he was well prepared after years of wanderlust where he often had to sleep outside on the ground or on stacked lumber, whatever he could find. Soon thereafter he was assigned to the European theater of war. While in Europe he served in France and Germany with the transportation corps. When time and conditions permitted he traveled through several countries. He was promoted to first lieutenant before the war ended.

After the war L'Amour moved to Los Angeles to continue his writing career. He was advised by an acquaintance in the industry to write western stories. He accepted the suggestion and adopted the pen name "Jim Mayo" which appears on approximately one-third of his work (Weinberg, 1992). In 1950 his first full-length western novel, *Westward the Tide*, was published in England. The novel was not published in the United States until 1977.

During the early 1950s L'Amour wrote four Hopalong Cassidy novels as work-for-hire for Doubleday Books under the pen name "Tex Burns." Two novels were also published under his Jim Mayo pen name. During this period he wrote and sold many short stories for small fees, but financial success and fame still eluded him. As he struggled for wider recognition as a writer, he turned increasingly to western and American frontier novels as his preferred genre.

In 1952 a short story published in *Collier's* magazine would dramatically boost Louis L'Amour's writing career. "The Gift of Cochise" was read and liked by the movie actor John Wayne. Wayne bought the screen rights for $4,000 and made plans for his new production company to turn the story into a movie. While the movie was in production, Louis expanded the short story into a novel that he titled *Hondo*. The book and the movie, titled with the same name, were released on the same day in 1953. Both quickly became hits, and Louis signed a contract to write more western novels. With the success of Hondo, he was soon recognized as an established writer, and success was assured.

With his name now established in western fiction, L'Amour became America's most prolific western and frontier writer. During a career that spanned sixty-two years, he published more than 400 short stories, over 100 novels, wrote 65 television scripts, and sold more than 30 stories to the motion picture industry (Great Plains Software, Inc., n.d.). Shortly before his death in 1988, he was notified that sales of his books had topped the 200 million mark. Since his death over 80 million copies of his books have been sold (Louis L'Amour Enterprises, Inc., 2000). He is easily one of the best selling authors of all time.

READING IN EARLY LIFE

Louis L'Amour was born into a family that valued books and learning. The family home in Jamestown, North Dakota, contained a library of several hundred books, with important works by writers that included Longfellow, Whittier, Lowell, Emerson, Poe, and the Stoddard lectures on travel. In his memoir, *Education of a Wandering Man* (L'Amour, 1989), Louis wrote that he did not remember the number of books in the home library. However, one source has estimated the number to be approximately three hundred (Gale, 1985). In addition, a public library was located within easy reach of the home. All of this proved to be grist for the reading mill of a small boy born with a prodding curiosity and burning desire to learn. At a very early age he bugged his older sister to read to him when she was trying to read for herself. To stop his pestering, she taught Louis how to read. Once he learned, there was no stopping his insatiable thirst for books.

Young L'Amour began reading with children's books. But he soon moved past those to books like *Treasure Island* by Robert Louis Stevenson. His reading interest grew and expanded quickly. His father soon recognized his son's need to learn. When Louis was in the fifth grade, his father gave him a three-volume edition of *History of the World*, books that had come to the home as a premium with a subscription to *Collier's* magazine. For the next several months, Louis sat on his father's lap each evening and told what he had learned from the books during that day. Quickly he moved on to more serious reading. At the age of twelve he read a book on philosophy called *The Genius of Solitude*, the subject of which was some of the world's leading thinkers.

During his middle boyhood years, Louis did not enjoy the books he was supposed to read in school. His interest had grown well beyond the subjects of his schoolbooks, and his reading choices followed that expanded interest. Thus, he read scores of books outside the school's textbook collection. Among his choices were at least a dozen novels by G. A. Henty, a British author; a dozen novels by Horatio Alger; and virtually all of the well-known youth stories of the time, such as *Black Beauty*.

As Louis grew more disenchanted with what he was required to read in school, he began to see the world of books beyond the school's walls as his principal route to the kind of knowledge he most wanted to acquire. He spent much time in the public library reading books on such subjects as kite flying, hot air balloons, gliders, submarine experiments, botany, geology, and mineralogy to name just a few. He later wrote that a good education is easily available to anyone within reach of a library (L'Amour, 1989).

The young North Dakota reader possessed a gnawing hunger for all kinds of literature, for he harbored a broad eclectic interest. The more he read, however, the more discerning his taste became. Gradually he became drawn to those books that have been recognized through time as important and noteworthy contributions to the world's literature.

While working as a messenger boy for Western Union, young Louis was introduced to pulp adventure magazines. Those materials included stories by writers like Edgar Rice Burroughs. About the same time he discovered a magazine called *Science and Invention*, a publication that initially covered material on various aspects of science but later began to include science fiction. Those articles and stories led him to read books about the planet Mars, books written by Percival Lowell, a professor who was engaged in a serious study of the planet. In his early teen years he added to his reading program such well-known works as *Lorna Doone*, *Ben Hur*, *The Count of Monte Cristo*, and *The Three Musketeers*.

When L'Amour quit school at the age of fifteen and began a life of wanderlust, completely alone and on his own, books became his friends and companions. Having determined that he could learn more on his own than in school, he carried books with him always. Even when working at the many odd jobs he picked up along the way, he read when he had free time. For the remainder of his life, he read on buses, trains, planes, while waiting in restaurants, dentist's offices, any place where he had to wait for an appointment, to be helped, to be served, or to reach a destination.

READING DURING WANDERLUST YEARS

The years that L'Amour spent wandering the globe were years in which he read with a passion. While hopping a freight train out of El Paso, Texas, he was introduced by another hobo to Little Blue Books. Little Blue Books were small books, slightly bigger than playing cards that fit neatly into one's pants or coat pockets. With approximately three thousand titles in print, Louis began carrying ten to fifteen of the small books in his pockets, reading whenever and wherever he could. When riding the rails looking for work, hobo style, Louis would often be discovered by train detectives and ejected from the train, often in out-of-the-way places. While waiting for another train to hop, he would spend the time reading. Included among the titles available were stories by famous names like De Maupassant, Edgar Allan Poe, Jack London, Gogal, Gorky, Kipling, Gautier, Henry James, and Balzac. The range of subjects available covered everything from music to electricity. In time, Louis read several hundred of the Little Blue Books.

Even though L'Amour preferred books that were recognized as important literature, he would read whatever he could get. His interest began and remained random and eclectic. In his travels he encountered and read a set of books called The Rover Boys and a series by Joseph A. Altsheler on the Civil and Revolutionary wars. During much of the time that he was involved in boxing, he was an avid reader of a weekly fight magazine named *Boxing Blade*.

Reading for the wandering L'Amour became a way to live many lives. He found in fiction, biography, and history many adventures that were exciting to read and enriching to his own life. Hundreds of lessons were gained from reading about what others had learned and experienced. While still a young man he grew to be so widely read he could often use books as a link to a new acquaintance or friend. While hitchhiking in Arizona, he was picked up by a driver who quickly took a liking to Louis. In the course of conversation they discovered that both had read Porter's *Scottish Chiefs* and Scott's *Marmion*. That connection led the driver to buy his hungry and broke passenger breakfast so that he could hear more of the vast collection of stories Louis had amassed from his reading and travels.

While working as a dead cattle skinner on the plains of west Texas, Louis would read by firelight after a long hard day of work. One of the books he read at this time was *Gil Blas*, a book he had found in the laundry room of a tourist court where he had spent the night in Plainview, Texas. When the skinning job was completed and he had collected his wages, Louis rented a room in a small hotel where he took three showers a day to remove the smell from his body and, between showers, went to the local library and read. One book consumed was John Matley's *The Rise of the Dutch Republic*.

When employed to do assessment and serve as caretaker of a copper mine in Arizona, L'Amour found abandoned in the cottage where he bunked a large collection of boxed books that had been left by his predecessor, a teacher who left unexpectedly. Louis read most of the books during the three months he worked the mine. Most notable among the collection of books were *Don Quixote*, the *Iliad* and the *Odyssey*, the short stories of O Henry, a complete volume of Shakespeare's plays, Robert Burton's *The Anatomy of Melancholy*, and *The Autobiography of Joseph Jefferson*, a volume on the theater in the time of Elizabethan England. Louis also read some books and magazines left by other occupants of the cottage. These included several volumes by Charles Mumford, who wrote the Hopalong Cassidy series, Zane Grey novels of the Old West, novels by James Oliver Curwood and Harold Bell Wright, and a collection from several years of the *Saturday Evening Post*.

As Louis read those many works in the lonely quiet of isolated mountains, they opened vistas to him of things he did not previously know. He learned the names of scholars, historians, and political leaders that were new to him. Where other caretakers had only lasted a week or so because they could not handle the isolation and loneliness, Louis thrived. He was seldom lonely. For companionship he enjoyed Hopalong Cassidy, Hamlet, Sancho Panza, and Ulysses hanging out with him on the pages of the books he had discovered. He developed a satisfying routine in which he would work for a while, take a break, drink coffee, and read. He was so hungry to devour the cache of books that he read several at a time, anxious to get the flavor of many before reading a single book to completion.

Why did L'Amour read with such hunger and passion? Every book contained new adventure in places and with people he had not previously known. Moreover, his reading raised questions to which he wanted to find answers. The more he read the more questions that surfaced to which he wanted answers. He burned inside to fill the void in his knowledge matrix. His reading flooded him with questions to which he needed answers. He had to know what people in all ages had thought and believed. He wrote, "I was a young man in a hurry, wanting to know all that had been thought, pondered, speculated upon" (L'Amour, 1989, p. 44). That need drove his passion for books.

While working a five-day stint on a prospective manganese mine, Louis also found many hours to read. The desert heat was too intense to work during most of the daylight hours. He spent that time inside reading and saved his work for the early morning, late evening, and night hours. Two books read during this job were Edith Wharton's *Ethan Frome* and Donn Byrne's *Messer Marco Polo*. After completing the job, he traveled to Los Angeles, where he rented a room near a library and split his time for several days between reading in the library and browsing in nearby secondhand bookstores. When browsing, he discovered many books that he merely sampled but would search for and read many years later.

While waiting in San Pedro to sign on with a merchant ship, Louis spent his free time in a library in the Seaman's Institute reading and scanning books he had not seen before. Some books read during this time were *Call of the Wild* by Jack London, *The Expedition of Humphrey Clinker* by Tobias Smollett, *The Bar Sinister* by Richard Harding Davids, and *The Life of Samuel Johnson* by Boswell. After completing the Boswell book he considered it to be one of the greatest biographies in the English language. So captivated was he with the content that he read it slowly, often returning to reread parts of the life of Johnson. Louis later acquired a complete set of Boswell's papers for his personal library and referred to them from time to time when he wanted to get a good description of London's taverns and inns from that period.

At San Pedro L'Amour read a book about the sea titled *Knight on Seamanship*. Most importantly, he read a book titled *Memoirs of Vincent Nolte*, a work that enriched his appreciation of first-person memoirs written by travelers, soldiers, sailors, and merchants. He discovered that such books gave him an excellent real-life portrayal of the life and times in which the authors lived, a device he would later use freely in his own writing. About four o'clock one morning, he unexpectedly was offered a job on a ship bound for the Far East, an offer he quickly accepted and was soon out to sea. The departure was so sudden that he had to leave two books he had been reading at the seaman's library unfinished.

A long-held fascination that L'Amour had with Asia was met when his ship left San Pedro going to the Far East. He could not account for his interest in that region of the world except it could have sprung from reading a version of *The Arabian Nights* when he was a child (L'Amour, 1989). Years later, when he acquired a full set of the stories in a Sir Richard Burton translation, he believed that he had obtained the best version. Burton's knowledge of the Arabic language, of the customs and mores of people in the region in which the stories were set, gave Louis confidence in the comments and notes that depicted the real life of the people there.

During the next few years, L'Amour spent most of his time at sea and in foreign ports, always in the hunt for books to read. New places and new opportunities to read and learn were never lost on him. While sailing to England on a merchant ship, he read Jack London's *The Sea Wolf*, along with *The Ivory Child* by H. Rider Haggard and Arthur Conan Doyle's *The White Company*. Byron's *Don Juan* he read on an Arab dhow sailing north from Aden up the Red Sea to Port Tewfik on the Suez Canal.

All of the browsing in bookshops that L'Amour enjoyed was not lost time for which nothing was gained. When he later had money and came across a book that he had previously sampled and liked, he became a book collector. For example, while in Singapore he began reading *The Annals and Antiquities of Rajasthan* by James Tod, a book he found in a British library for sailors. Before he could finish, his ship went to sea, and he had to leave the book unfinished. Years later he came across the book in a secondhand bookstore in Greenwich Village in New York. He bought the copy and kept it thereafter in his personal library.

Books often seemed to gravitate toward L'Amour in uncanny ways and places. When his ship took on a new sailor in Shanghai, books proved to be a connection to a new friendship and to his personal book collection. The new sailor saw a couple of volumes on Louis's bunk and asked if he liked books. Louis answered that he did. The sailor responded that he would bring Louis some books. The works in question had belonged to a woman the sailor had been caring for but who had recently died. The new acquaintance brought Louis fourteen books from her collection to keep as his own. Among the titles were *Lavengro* and *Romany Rye* by George Barrow, two volumes that covered accounts of the author's long time spent among gypsies and what he had learned from that association, books that Louis found fascinating. Included also were *The Harvester* by Gene Stratton Porter, Mary Johnston's *To Have and to Hold*, and *Lord Jim* by Joseph Conrad. Louis later wrote that Conrad's book was "one I have read several times since, and which for me was a real discovery" (L'Amour, 1989, p. 79).

While traveling in foreign countries L'Amour would often hire students to read aloud in English from books in foreign languages he could not read for himself. Those sessions would take place on a riverbank, in a coffee shop, or in a teahouse. Virtually always, such sessions attracted an interested audience. On one occasion, an Asian was reading to Louis when a bystander who had been quietly looking on and listening corrected the reader in the translation of a word. An argument ensued, and the two almost came to blows. At that point the intruder walked away and when out of sight, the reader looked at Louis and said, "He may be right at that" (L'Amour, 1989, p. 83).

While traversing through Asia and the Middle East L'Amour sojourned in Iran (formerly Persia) and made inquiries regarding books on the local history of the region. Upon overhearing his inquiry, a young man, a native of the area, but one who spoke English very well, walked up and recommended *Shah-nama*, Iran's great *Book of Kings*. The entire epic contains much of the history of Iran, and Persia before Iran, including some of its rich folktales. Years later Louis kept in his personal library the Reuben Levy translation of the book, an edition he came to believe to be the best on the subject. In his personal memoir (L'Amour, 1989), he indicated that the *Shah-nama* tales are still told along the caravan trails of the Middle East, albeit, with some variations.

L'Amour enjoyed some of the fiction of China. Among those he has recommended is *Hung Lou Menq* by Tso Hsueh-Chin. Known in English as *Dream of the Red Chamber*, the novel gives a good picture of Chinese life and society from that period. A work of Chinese fiction that Louis found to be exciting was *Outlaws of the Marsh*, written about twelfth-century events and translated by Pearl Buck in a shortened version under the title, *All Men Are Brothers* (L'Amour, 1989).

During his wanderings across the American West, L'Amour sometimes met people who had difficulty placing him in proper perspective. He dressed like a hobo but spoke with the knowledge of a university professor. There were always books puffing up his pockets, raising curiosity among those who did not know him. When hitchhiking he once secured a ride with a professor from a small college. The professor noted that Louis carried in his coat pocket a Modern Library edition that contained Nietzsche's "Ecce Homo" and "The Birth of Tragedy." The professor could not understand why a hitchhiking hobo would be reading such a sophisticated level of material. Indeed, he wondered if Louis could even read and understand literature of the kind that Nietzsche wrote. Louis did not try to justify himself to the professor.

L'Amour did read serious books, many of them. While working in a sawmill in Klamath Falls, Oregon, he read *Crime and Punishment* by the Russian author Dostoevsky. He added *The Moonstone* by Wilkie Collins and *Kim* and *Plain Tales from the Hills*, both by Rudyard Kipling. While working in a wood veneer plant in Portland, Oregon, during the Great Depression, Louis, for a time, lived on one sandwich per day so he could buy three books for which he had read reviews. They were: *Marriage and Morals* by Bertrand Russell, Roger Baldwin's *Liberty under the Soviets* and Stuart Chase's *Men and Machines*. Such titles indicate the breadth of his interest and reading at that time. While living in Portland, Louis rented a room in a hotel near a public library where he spent most of his free time for several months. Often he went in at ten in the morning and stayed until ten at night. While there he read many books on philosophy and plays by the most famous playwrights (L'Amour, 1989).

One day in the Portland library an elderly gentleman stopped by to chat with L'Amour. They had both spent many hours in common in the library but had never spoken to each other. The older man looked at what Louis was reading and saw that it was *Soliloquies* by Friedrich Schleiermacher. The man looked at L'Amour and remarked that he rarely saw a young man reading philosophy. But he did read philosophy and many kinds of books containing serious content.

The avid reader from North Dakota never let idle time go to waste. Every opportunity to read and learn was occupied. While traveling through Texas on a bus he read Jack London's *Burning Daylight*. While he was in the army he read *Taras Bulba* by Gogal one bitterly cold night in Paris, France, while sitting in an enclosed Jeep waiting for orders to move out. On a trip from Oregon to Oklahoma with his parents he read Theodor Mommsen's *History of Rome* during nightly stopovers for food and sleep. As they crossed the landscape by day, Louis studied the western country, getting a full sense of the history and the topography that would one day appear in his novels and short stories.

While living with his parents in Oklahoma Louis stumbled upon a source of books that he had not previously read. During a stroll one day along a country road near his residence, he came upon a neighbor whom he had not previously met. While chatting they each learned that the other was an avid reader. The neighbor invited Louis into his home, where he witnessed an extensive library. When the two men became better acquainted, the neighbor opened his library to L'Amour. Among the books he borrowed and read were the *History of the Intellectual Development of Europe* by John W. Draper, *The History of Civilization in*

England by Henry Buckle, and *The Decline and Fall of the Roman Empire* by Edward Gibbon.

Throughout his wandering years, Louis read with a passion. That he made reading the principal focus of those years there can be no doubt. He began keeping lists of the books he read each year so as to go back and review any that he later found he wanted to revisit. However, the lists made during his early years were lost during his frequent moves and extensive traveling. The lists that survived cover the years from 1930 to 1935 and the year 1937. Those lists show that he read 115 books in 1930, 120 in 1931, 120 in 1932, 105 in 1933, 114 in 1934, 73 in 1935 and 84 in 1937 (L'Amour, 1989).

In addition to fiction and nonfiction books, L'Amour also enjoyed reading and reciting poetry. During the days of the hobo when he was a young wanderer, poetry was important to men like Louis. In his book, *The Hobo* (1923), Nels Anderson writes about the importance of poetry and songs to the hobo culture.

> His ballads of the road and his battle songs of protest induce a unanimity of sentiment and attitudes, the strongest form of group solidarity in the hobo world. Through the universal language of poetry the homeless man bridges the chasm of isolation that separates him from his fellows [Anderson, 1923, p. 214].

Like wandering men in general, Louis read and listened to poetry. Among his favorite poets were Stephen Vincent Benet who wrote two poems that he liked very much: "The Ballad of William Sycamore" and "American Names" (L'Amour, 1989). He also enjoyed reciting poetry on occasion when it filled a void or need for entertainment. When standing lookout in a ship's bow, he often passed the time by reciting poetry to himself. When grouped around campfires or in bunkhouses with other wanderers, he often recited poetry for himself and those who wanted to listen. A favorite was "Mr. Flood's Party" by Edwin Arlington Robinson. Hobo audiences were usually appreciative of his efforts and would often request poems they wished him to recite. Poems by Wordsworth, Byron, or Tennyson were favorites.

L'Amour never seriously considered the possibility of studying for a trade or profession. During his wanderlust years his sole interest was in reading and travel to gather knowledge and experience that would one day be useful to him as a writer. A professional writer was what he most wanted to be, and only reading and travel could prepare him as he wanted for that role in life. But writing would not interrupt his reading. When the day arrived for him to cease wandering and begin writing, he continued to read, but with a somewhat different emphasis.

Reading During a Career as a Writer

Once L'Amour turned to writing full time, his reading interest turned more to materials that would enrich his writing. Early in his career he received a long series of rejection slips for his short stories. Puzzled as to why others were being published and he was not, he endeavored to read a host of stories by such well-established writers as O Henry, Guy de Maupassant, Jack London, Conan Doyle, Maxim Gorky, and Robert Louis Stevenson for the purpose of determining why they were so successful and how his work differed from theirs. He found that the stories of those famous writers began with the heart of the story and pulled the reader right into the crux of the issue from the beginning. He concluded from those authors that story action should begin on the first page. He adopted that approach, and his stories began to sell with much greater frequency.

In *The Iron Marshal* (L'Amour, 1979b), L'Amour opens the story on page one with, "A brutal kick in the ribs jolted him from a sound sleep and he lunged to his feet" (p. 1). Who would not want to read further to find out what happened and why? In *The Broken Gun* (L'Amour, 1966), he creates a mystery for the beginning with the following line: "He lay sprawled upon the concrete pavement of the alley in the darkening stain of his own blood, a man I had never seen before" (p. 1). Sometimes L'Amour began with a tragedy as in *The Mountain Valley War* (L'Amour, 1978) with this opening, "Smoke lifted from the charred timbers where once the house had stood" (p. 1). Louis developed a style for presenting his material that embraced a straightforward, fast-moving action that was short on interior monologues and space-filling descriptive passages.

In the year 1931, L'Amour read widely while trying to improve his writing and while searching for avenues through which he could be published and get his name before the public. One tactic he used was reading books and writing reviews for newspapers and magazines. He wrote reviews for twenty-two of the books he read during the year. His reading, writing, and search for publishers continued until he was drafted into the army.

After leaving the army at the end of World War II, L'Amour began to evolve in his mind the framework for a series of novels that would be set in the period of exploration and settlement of the American West by white Europeans and eastern Americans. To prepare himself for the venture, he began reading books, both fiction and nonfiction, that gave him a depth of knowledge about the vast migration of peoples from east to west. Among the books he read at this time were *Log of a Cowboy* by Andy Adams, *Tales of the Mustangs* and *A Vaquero of the Brush Country* by J. Frank Dobie, and *The Overland Route to California* by Andrew Child.

His passion for learning about the life and times of the early West was so great that Louis never passed up an opportunity to acquire more knowledge. On one occasion he and a companion were driving across west central Texas when they stopped at a ranch where the companion had once worked as a cowboy. The host invited both to spend the night, an invitation they eagerly accepted. In the bedroom to which Louis was assigned he discovered a copy of *The Life of Billy Dixon* by Olive R. Dixon, Billy's wife. The book was then out of print and difficult to find. Louis knew something of the story of Billy and desperately wanted to read the book.

Billy Dixon was a famous buffalo hunter and had been involved in some of the most famous battles between whites and Indians in the West. Afraid he would not come across another copy of the book, and even though he was very tired from daylong traveling, Louis began reading and stayed up all through the night. He was able to finish the book just as the sun began to creep above the horizon the next morning.

The more involved L'Amour became with the western frontier through his writing, the more he searched for books and materials on that period in America's development. He wanted his writing to be as realistic and true to the period as possible. He, therefore, felt a compelling need to read all he could find regarding the western frontier. He once wrote: "A writer's brain is like a magician's hat. If you're going to get anything out you have to put something in" (L'Amour, 1989, p. 75).

Increasingly he found his favorite reading to be in western diaries, journals, newspapers, history books, and essays, all of which gave him ideas and settings for the many stories he would write. But he continued to read a wide selection of books on western subjects. During the period he reread *The Log of a Cowboy* by Andy Adams, who had been over the cattle trails driving cattle. He read *The Trail Drives of Texas* and *Tales of the Mustangs*. During the same year he read thirty-two books on various aspects of western history, including biographies of Bill Tilghman, Captain Bill McDonald, Dave Cook, Wild Bill Hickok, and *The Last of the Bandit Riders* by Matt Warner, a cowboy who had ridden with Butch Cassidy (L'Amour, 1989).

Through his reading L'Amour found that the Old West enveloped many features and phases of change and development. Among many identified by him (L'Amour, 1989) were the exploring, the trading and trapping, the wagon trains carrying new settlers westward, the big Gold rush, buffalo hunting, the cattle drives, ranching, the stage-coach era, bandits and outlaws, sod-house settlers, the Indian fighters, silver mining, and the so-called bone pickers, those people who collected and sold the bones of buffalo that were left behind by hunters.

As L'Amour read more deeply into the records and literature of the Old West, he acquired a deeper appreciation for the region, its history, and the people who occupied the land. He found the region to be rich with interesting people and stories. Those who had occupied the land were brave souls who possessed special qualities and characteristics. They were pioneers who chose to break with the customs and traditions of the regions and cultures they had known and venture into an unknown land that confronted them with an unknown future and fate. To leave all behind and accept a high level of risk made them special people in his eyes (L'Amour, 1989).

L'Amour enjoyed reading books and other sources that enriched his knowledge of the great westward migration and its affiliated developments. Among the sources he read for this information were Josiah Gregg's *Commerce of the Prairies*, a book he considered to be one of the basic books on the westward movement, and Henry Inman's *The Great Salt Lake Trail*. A source that gave him good insight into the westward migration and its people was *Pioneers of the San Juan*, a collection of stories assembled by the Daughters of the American Revolution. The stories were a compilation of spontaneous recollections by pioneers from the southwest corner of Colorado. His continuing search for the diaries and journals kept by those who had lived in the period and participated in the events was never ending and a complete joy for the famous writer.

Louis found in his research that court trials were important events for socializing in the early West. The absence of recreational activity in towns and villages made the drama that was entwined in trials interesting to watch unfold and to discuss after completion. When he found occasion to include trials in his stories Louis read many sources on the law and court proceedings. Among the volumes read were two histories of American law by Blackstone, four volumes of the history of English law by John Reeves, and four volumes of *Commentaries* by Frank Kent.

By the time L'Amour had given up his wanderlust and settled down to become a serious writer, he had traveled many roads, stopped in many ports of call and met hundreds of interesting and unusual people. When reading he often saw a commonality among the characters or people he met in books and those he met while traversing the globe. While reading the *Odyssey* by Homer, a book written many centuries ago, Louis thought that many of the people Homer described were like some of the people he had met. The observation led him to conclude that there existed a kind of kinship between people who live in different periods and places in human history (L'Amour, 1989).

Once he settled down in Los Angeles, L'Amour became a collector of those books and materials he wanted to have always available in his personal library. Rather than wander about the world, he changed his wandering to the pages of the books he continued to collect. At his death he owned a personal collection of more than 10,000 books (Henry-Mead, 1989, p. 4). Those were books that he had come to treasure for what they could reveal, for what they could teach. As he once wrote, "A parent or teacher has only his [or her] lifetime; a good book can teach forever" (L'Amour, 1989, p. 195). "Upon the shelves of our libraries, the world's greatest teachers await our questions" (L'Amour, 1989, p. 192). L'Amour was a product of the teaching found in books, and he became a teacher through the books he wrote, books in which he shared his storehouse of knowledge with his millions of reader the world over.

THE IMPACT OF READING

During his early reading L'Amour learned many characteristics of stories and story construction that would later impact his own life and his writing. One of the more influential was an awareness on his part that he enjoyed story lines in which the characters were placed in an authentic setting for the time and place of the story. For example, he didn't care for a story set in the eighteenth century but written with a twentieth century point of view. When he began writing stories himself, he took time to visit the places and landmarks that would mark the setting of his work. Books like Josiah Gregg's *Commerce of the Prairies* and Henry Inman's *The Great Salt Lake Trail* were works that helped Louis to form a framework for the kind of stories that he would turn into best-selling novels years later.

As a writer L'Amour created stories that were rich in historical detail. His long years of reading, on-site research, and first-hand observation brought to life on his printed pages times and places that had ceased to exist in real life. But the stories, diaries, and logs of those who lived that history gave him a view of the Old West as they saw and lived it. He read so widely into the records he found that he became a part of the Old West himself. He came to feel the fears of those who peopled the region, their loneliness and the courage they had to muster to keep from turning back. Through the brochures, booklets, and newspapers he collected in small towns across the region, he found ideas for many stories he would write. His stories often examined the brutal effects that the encroaching white culture had on Native Americans. His heroes consistently dramatized a healthy regard for the environment, a stand for truth and justice as it was understood in their time and place, and a willingness to fight for their values and ideals regardless of the odds against them.

Perhaps the greatest impact that reading had on L'Amour was to implant within him a deep knowledge of the broad sweep of human history. His depth of knowledge is revealed in his work and adds a historical dimension to time, place and people in history. In his novel *Jubal Sackett*, the principal character, Jubal, is speaking to a Cherokee friend named Ni'Kwana. Ni'Kwana is worried about rumors that foreign warriors will be coming to displace the Indian. Jubal attempts to put the rumor in a meaningful historical context for the elderly Indian with the following explanation.

> Those who come will not go further than what they see. They will buy some land but will take more. They do not believe this is wrong, for they, too, believe they are The People, and it has been the way of the world for men, animals, and plants to move in wherever there is opportunity and where they can survive [L'Amour, 1985, p. 33].

Then Jubal explained that his father had come to the New World from England where similar movements had displaced people who had occupied the land.

> In the land where my father dwelt there were a people called Picts, then Celts moved in, and after them, Romans. When the Romans moved out the Angles, Saxons, and Danes moved in, each new people taking the land and pushing the others out or making slaves of them. Then the Normans came and dispossessed all the others, and their king took all the land for his own, giving it to those who served him best [p. 33].

The author's historical perspective often added depth and context to stories like *Jubal Sackett*, giving the reader a rich historical tapestry as the story unfolded.

Forever a reader himself, L'Amour often used his stories and characters to promote reading to his readers. Many of his story characters are poorly educated. But he lets them know that they can gain wisdom by reading books. In *The Daybreakers* (L'Amour, 1960), Orrin Sackett is taught to read and write by Tom Sunday and is inspired by stories of Davy Crockett and Andrew Jackson. In *To Tame a Land* (L'Amour, 1955), a well-read adult character gives his surrogate son a book and urges him to read it several times, advising that he will like it better each time. The book was *Lives* by Plutarch, a volume that L'Amour had once read. *Bendigo Shafter* (L'Amour, 1979a) is cited by Gale (Gale, 1985) as the L'Amour novel that grants the most attention to books and reading in its characters and storyline. In that work Ruth Mackin takes a library of fifty volumes west beyond the Dakotas. The library includes books that L'Amour had read, authors that included Washington Irving and Henry David Thoreau.

Another reading influence apparent in L'Amour's novels is his thorough knowledge of the history of the American West. From reading, extensive travel and research, Louis had come to know the story of westward migration and its clash with Indian cultures as no other writer. He often took advantage of opportunities to share that knowledge with his readers. One technique used was to identify early real-life explorers in the regions where his stories were set. Opportunities to let his characters reveal information about the inhabitants of a region at the time of the story were frequently woven into the fabric of the story line.

In *Over on the Dry Side* (L'Amour, 1976) a character named Owen Chantry gives a lesson to a reluctant listener on the Ute Indians in the region and also discusses the nearby Navajos. Chantry describes in detail the forts and small towns as they once existed in the locale of the story. Information on subjects ranging from anthropology to sailing and saloons is often provided within the context of L'Amour's story material. He took great pride in his wealth of knowledge and enjoyed sharing it with his readers.

Through his written works L'Amour created worlds that no longer existed in real life. But those worlds had been created in his mind through reading, and he transferred them to paper for others to read and enjoy. Through his extensive travel around the world and the thousands of books he had read, he knew the places and people about which he wrote. Louis could sit at his typewriter, close his eyes, and transport himself to that time and place he had chosen to recreate on paper. Those experiences merged in his mind and imagination to form the stories that millions of readers have found entertaining. The dual experiences of travel and reading produced the writer, Louis L'Amour.

That Louis L'Amour was a product of books seems self-evident to this author. No one could have read thousands of books with the passion that he committed to the venture without being seriously influenced by what he read. Louis acknowledged as much when he once wrote: "Of the value of books I am myself my best example. If it were not for books, I should never have been more than a common laborer, perhaps killed in a mine disaster, as some of my friends were" (L'Amour, 1989, p. 104). Reading and writing were his life, the two forces that defined his identity as a person. Aside from his family, nothing else seemed as stimulating or meaningful to him. L'Amour used reading to lift himself from the rank of a common laborer to a man of wealth and fame, one with an international legion of fans. By the end of his life, he had been widely honored for his contributions to the history and literature of the early American West.

HONORS AND AWARDS

Louis L'Amour has received scores of honors for his body of work in American literature. A complete list would comprise a lengthy accounting that is beyond the scope of this book. However, two are so significant that they should be recognized in this discussion of his life and work. In 1982 the U.S. Congress awarded him its National Gold Medal, an award that was presented by President Ronald Reagan. The medal was awarded in recognition of his distinguished career as an author and for contributions to literature through his historically based writing. He was the first novelist to ever receive the honor.

In 1984 L'Amour was awarded the U.S. government's highest civilian honor, the Medal of Freedom. The award, again presented by President Ronald Reagan, recognized that through his western novels, "Louis L'Amour has played a leading role in shaping our national identity. His writings portrayed the rugged individual and the deep-seated values of those who conquered the American frontier" (Medal of Freedom, 1996–2002, p. 1). The citation went on to say that L'Amour's descriptions of America and Americans had added to a national understanding of our past and reaffirmed our potential as an "exploring, pioneering, and free people" (p. 1).

Nelson Mandela

A Brief Biography

Nelson Mandela was born in a small village in the Transkei province in the eastern cape of South Africa on July 18, 1918. At birth his mother gave him the name Rolihlahla Mandela. Upon entering a Christian school at the age of seven, his teacher gave him the first name of Nelson. That would be the name by which the world would come to know him.

Mandela was born of a royal African heritage. His great-grandfather was a Thembu king, well known, according to legend, for his skill in settling disputes among the diverse Thembu clans (Meredith, 1997). The clan to which Mandela belonged was the Mandiba clan. Throughout his life friends and relatives often addressed him as Mandiba in honor of his clan name. Although his royal birthright was in a minor branch of royalty and did not carry a right to one day succeed to the kingship, Mandela did profit from his royal lineage. His heritage represented a strong tradition in which laws, education, and courtesy were held to be important customs for personal conduct. As his life was to demonstrate, Mandela never forgot his place of birth or his heritage.

When Mandela was nine years of age, his father died unexpectedly. Through a preplanned arrangement, the regent of the Thembu people, a man who functioned as a regional king, adopted Nelson as his own son. The regent also had a son, Justice, who was slightly older than Nelson. The two young boys shared a bedroom and grew up playing and working together like true brothers.

Nelson loved his new home. He found that living with the regent and his family put him in the center of tribe activity. When clan leaders came to hold discussions with the regent, Nelson listened to the stories told by the elder clansman, stories about the great African heroes who fought against white subjugation during the history of European conquests in Africa. Nelson remembered those stories and would adopt many of the heroes as role models for his life and career.

In addition to learning the history of his people during those clan sessions with the regent, Mandela acquired knowledge that would later serve him well. As issues such as drought, the culling of cattle, new policies decreed by the white ruling government, or new laws that would impact their lives were discussed, he looked and listened. He observed how speakers were alike and different. Some seemed to ramble and never get to the point of the debate. Others came to the point of an issue quickly and with clarity. Some used emotion and dramatic language to move an audience and win a discussion. Most importantly, Mandela noted how the regent would listen to all sides and points of view before voicing his own judgment. He noted how decisions were usually made through reaching a consensus rather than by majority vote.

By the time both Mandela and Justice reached adulthood their father was getting old and losing his health. He wanted to see both young men married and settled down before his death. Unknown to Nelson and Justice, the regent arranged marriages for both. When the father announced the marriage plans to the two sons, they both rejected the idea, but their father insisted. To escape a marriage that neither son was willing to accept, Mandela and his brother left their home with the regent and ran away to Johannesburg. There both found work with a mining company. Nelson soon left the job at the mine and began working in a law firm where he worked and learned law through both practice and study. Interest in the practice of law grew with experience.

Upon learning about the work of the African National Congress (ANC) for ethnic equality, Mandela joined the congress and became a dedicated servant of its work. He held many positions in the organization and traveled widely about the country promoting its objectives and drawing in new members. He proved to be so successful in promoting the fight for equality that he became a target for the white apartheid government. After several arrests and trials for actions the police declared illegal, Mandela was sentenced to prison for life and sent to prison on Robben Island in 1964.

For twenty-seven years Mandela remained confined at Robben Island and other prisons in South Africa. During captivity he never allowed himself to believe that he would not one day be free to play an important role in the future of South Africa. In prison he continued to study and keep himself physically fit so that he would be ready when an opportunity arose for him to help his nation. His life in prison ultimately changed him into a different person. He became less angry and more compassionate as he evolved a point of view that South Africa must become a multiracial nation in which all ethnic groups shared in its government and resources.

Mandela's dream did come true. In 1990, domestic violence and international pressure forced the government to release Mandela from prison and begin talks to create a new democratic government that would include all the people of South Africa. An agreement was finally reached to form a new government under a new constitution. Elections were scheduled for 1994. Mandela ran for president and won, defeating F. W. de Klerk, the president who had freed him from prison. The inauguration of South Africa's first president to be elected in a free and open election and its first native ethnic president took place on May 10, 1994. Martin Meredith (1997) described the event as the "greatest celebration ever seen in South Africa" (p. 519).

What fashioned Mandela's meteoric rise from a rural boy who herded cattle to become recognized today as one of the most celebrated and compassionate political leaders of the twentieth century? Many factors contributed to his development. However, one element stands out as paramount. That feature was his passion for reading.

READING IN EARLY LIFE

Nelson Mandela's reading life began when he entered the English language Methodist mission school not far from his home. There he studied English, Xhosa (his native language), history, and geography. He learned to read from Chamber's *English Reader*. A young boy whose mother and father could neither read or write, Mandela made reading and language usage an important tool in his personal development.

In 1934, when he was sixteen years of age, Mandela was sent to a boarding school at Clarkesbury, a school that had been founded in 1825 by Methodist missionaries. The school was about an hour's drive from his home. Entering a new and much larger school with a small-school and village background was a dramatic change for him. He had to read a lot and study hard to keep up with his classmates. But he accepted the challenge and proved that he was a very capable student. According to Guiloineau (1998/2002), Mandela earned a diploma at Clarkesbury in two years rather than the normal three.

In 1937 at the age of nineteen, Mandela entered Healdtown, a secondary school operated by the Methodist church. Healdtown offered a Christian and liberal arts education based on an English model. By the time he entered school at Healdtown, reading had become a dominant part of his life. There he was required to read and study in class from 8:00 in the morning until 12:45 P.M. After lunch, studies were continued until 5:00 P.M. After the evening meal, studies continued from 7:00 to 9:00. Lights were turned off at 9:30. He became recognized as a serious student, one who succeeded in his studies.

In 1939 at the age of twenty-one Mandela continued schooling at Fort Hare University, a school for higher education located about twenty miles east of Healdtown. There he studied the English language, anthropology, political science, history, law, and native administration. Native administration dealt with laws relating to native Africans. In addition to the reading required in his courses of study, Mandela also read deeply into the history of the native tribes of the eastern cape, drawing for information on government reports recorded in the late nineteenth century. While a student he also read *The Transkei in the Making*, a booklet by Govan Mbeki, a person with whom he would work in the ANC's struggle for political freedom. After two years of study he left school after a disagreement with the school's director. He would later take courses through correspondence and graduate from Fort Hare in 1943 with a Bachelor of Arts degree.

In 1943 Mandela enrolled at the University of the Witwatersrand to study for a degree in law. There he attended classes with white students, a new kind of environment for the young man from the native African veldt. He was the only black student in his law classes. At the university he met a wide variety of people and made many friends, people who would later work by his side in the struggle for racial freedom in South Africa. A small close-knit group of his friends frequently met in the evenings in the apartment of one member and studied, talked, and even danced until the early hours of the next day. Life at the university awakened Mandela even more to a wider world far removed from the simple village life he had known as a young boy.

While working as a law clerk in Johannesburg, Mandela took correspondence classes with the University of South Africa to complete requirements for his degree at Fort Hare that was never finalized after his dispute with the school's director. He worked hard as a law clerk by day and studied with concentration by night. A part of his meager salary was spent to buy candles so that he could read his books at night, as no electricity was available where he lived.

During the period he worked as a law clerk, Mandela developed a friendship with a man named Gaur, who acquainted him with the African National Congress. Gaur explained to Nelson how the ANC had long been working to bring about political rights and equality for black Africans. Gaur provided books for him to read about the subject. When time permitted, Mandela enjoyed spending quiet evenings at home with his wife and baby son, bathing him, feeding him, and playing with him until the baby went to sleep. Then he spent hours in reading for his legal work and his law studies and learning about the work and operations of the ANC.

READING AS A FREEDOM FIGHTER

Mandela became a member of the ANC in 1943 and began to focus much of his attention on the work of the organization. Within the ANC he began to meet a wide variety of people who were working to bring racial and ethnic equality to South Africa. There were white members, many of whom were also members of the South African Communist Party. While he had entered the organization believing that the fight for freedom was basically a black struggle against the white apartheid government, the Communists he met gave him a different perspective on the struggle for freedom. Mandela realized he knew very little about the ideology that supported Communism.

To be better informed, Mandela acquired the complete works of Marx and Engels, which he read along with works by and about Communist leaders like Lenin, Stalin, Mao Tse-tung, and many other leaders and writers. He later wrote that he was stimulated upon reading the *Communist Manifesto* but was exhausted by *Das Kapital*, both written by Karl Marx (Mandela, 1994, v. 1, p. 172.) In reading about Communism, he was attracted to the concept of a classless society that supported their ideology. He believed it to be similar to the traditional African culture that he had known in his youth. There he had experienced life in an equally shared communal setting.

According to Sampson (1999), during the early 1950s Mandela read voraciously "with a concentration which amazed his friends, marking passages, taking notes, making comparisons" (p. 65). He read the works of many Western philosophers, among them, Harold Laski, Bertrand Russell, and Bernard Shaw. His reading also included the writings of South African liberals like Edgar Brookes and Julius Lewin. The publications of the Institute of Race Relations in Johannesburg he read with deep interest. Accounts of liberation struggles in other areas of Africa were also read, among them, those by Nnamdi Azikiwe of Nigeria, Kwame Nkrumah of Ghana, and George Padmore of Jamaica. Included were the biographies of South African Marxist writers like Sidney Bunting and Bill Andrews.

In 1961 Mandela went into hiding to avoid confrontations with police and arrest for his antigovernment work. From his many "underground" locations he promoted a wide array of antigovernment protests and confrontations. He moved about the country disguised as a common laborer or a chauffeur. The police were in constant search for his whereabouts, but he remained elusive. The inability of the apartheid officials to capture Mandela gave rise to a powerful mystique.

Newspaper around the world reported the intrigue, and in so doing, created a high level of interest in Mandela, the freedom fighter, as well as interest in the plight of nonwhites in South Africa. He wrote letters and magazine articles, supplemented with calls to reporters, in which he gave assessments of conditions and proposed solutions to the troubles in South Africa. His words and messages revealed a depth of historical knowledge about people and events so thorough that his reputation as a canny and savvy operative seemed to lift his work and his image to a heroic level among those who tried to follow events. Even a British newspaper referred to Mandela as "enormously well read" (Sampson, 1999, p. 146).

His growing involvement in the work of the ANC led Mandela to read more deeply into the diversity of people and cultures that made up South African society. Newspapers from all areas of the country were read to build his understanding of the biases and perceptions of both those who produced the papers as well as those who read them. As a freedom fighter he found the information useful in planning and executing tactics.

In 1956 Mandela, along with many other freedom fighters, was arrested and charged with treason against the government for allegedly inciting protest and violence. The treason trial absorbed most of his time for the next four years. While he was held in jail during the trial, many friends came to visit and talk. Some brought him books that he read with enjoyment. While confined he also was allowed to read newspapers, a privilege for which he was grateful. From the papers Mandela learned about the protests and demonstrations being conducted across South Africa and in many parts of the world as a result of his and many of his coworkers' arrests.

When the treason trial got underway, Mandela daily brought to court a book or legal briefs to read during the long and tedious sessions. Sometimes he and his codefendants would be admonished to pay attention to the proceedings. The books and newspapers would disappear. After some time had elapsed and the legal maneuvering grew tiresome again, the books and papers would reappear, and reading would continue until he was admonished to put the material away again. In the end, the court found Mandela and his codefendants not guilty of treason.

After the treason trial was over Mandela grew increasingly involved in the work of the ANC. The obligation he felt to help the victims of the apartheid government grew strong and led him to look more deeply into what would be required to achieve freedom and a multiracial government in South Africa. To extend his understanding of what his country faced, he read about people in other countries who had been subjected to colonial expansion by European nations. One such country was India. He read into the life and works of Jawaharlal Nehru. He learned how the Indian leader and others had conducted anti–British campaigns to rid India of colonial rule. Mandela admired the Indian leader and once used a line from Nehru's writing to title a speech he prepared to be presented to a conference of the ANC. The speech, "No Easy Walk to Freedom" (Mandela, 1994, v.1, p. 231), had to be read to the conference for him. By the time of the ANC conference, the government had banned him from participating in ANC activities.

In addition to Nehru, Mandela read into the lives of Franklin Roosevelt, Winston Churchill, Joseph Stalin, and Mahatma Ghandi. On the walls of his home in Johannesburg he displayed pictures of the four leaders along with a picture of the storming of the Winter Palace in St. Petersburg, Russia, in 1917 (Mandela, 1994, v. 1). The pictures were used to explain to his two sons how those men, each in his own way, had achieved a kind of freedom from rulers who would subjugate and deny freedom to those they ruled. To Mandela their lives demonstrated why the struggle for liberation in South Africa must be fought. He helped his sons to understand that the white leaders of South Africa represented something very different.

In June 1961 Mandela was appointed commander of a new militant arm of the ANC. Known as "MK," the new organization would launch an aggressive and overt campaign against the apartheid government in an effort to force it to negotiate for a democratic government. As commander of a new militarylike operation, Mandela had very little knowledge of guerrilla warfare or sabotage tactics that would be required for an effective campaign. Recognizing his lack of knowledge, he immediately embarked on a plan of reading while he also made plans and preparations for an armed struggle against the government. He read widely into books and other materials on how to organize and conduct disruptive acts. Literature on how to attract and train guerrilla fighters proved to be of great interest. Works about the Cuban Communist revolution by Che Guevara and Fidel Castro were read. He read the report of Blas Roca on the application of guerrilla tactics during the revolution in Cuba. In *Commando*, by Deneys Reitz, he read and studied the tactics used by Boer generals during the Anglo-Boer War in South Africa. The writings of Mao Tse-tung on the Chinese Communist revolution proved to be interesting reading for his mission. A book titled, *Red Star of China*, by Edgar Snow, added to his knowledge on how Tse-tung applied nontraditional ideas and thought to achieve victory in China.

In books on revolutions and guerrilla wars closer to his own country, Mandela read The Revolt by Menachem Begin of Israel. Begin had conducted a guerrilla force in a region that offered neither mountains nor forests, conditions Mandela would have to work with in South Africa. He read into revolutions in the many African nations that had waged wars of liberation against European conquerors: Ethiopia against Mussolini of Italy and the guerrilla armies of Kenya, Algeria, and the Cameroon against European conquerors. He studied the wars that had been waged by Africans against Africans, Africans against whites, and whites against whites. To better plan the operations he would have to direct against the apartheid government, Mandela read about the industrial makeup of South Africa.

At the suggestion of a close friend who had fought in North Africa and Italy during World War II, Mandela read a book titled *On War*, written by a Prussian general named Karl Von Clausewitz. The book characterized war as a continuation of diplomacy by a different means, something that Mandela viewed as his task in South Africa. Other works read on war included Louis Taruc's book on the guerrilla war in the Philippines titled *Born of the People*. While directing the MK operation from underground, he hid out for two months in the flat of a friend who secured books from the local library for him to read. To avoid the police, he spent the daylight hours inside with the blinds drawn and read. At night he would slip out dressed in a disguise and meet with his fellow soldiers in the MK.

A portion of Mandela's underground time was spent hiding out in a cottage on an isolated farm known as Lilliesleaf Farm, located in an area known as Rivonia. While there, he dressed and pretended to work as an employee of the white owner to conceal his identity. During that period he had many quiet hours to read, think, and plan. He fully understood that he would have to be well informed in order to be an effective leader. Consequently, he read deeply to learn the requirements for being a liberation soldier. To acquire a deeper sense of the lives and drama of his own people, whom he would have to rely on for help and support, he read works by the African poet Ingrid Jonker.

In early 1962 the ANC decided it needed help from outside South Africa in its struggle to bring democracy to the nation. Mandela was sent on a mission to several African countries to solicit money and military support. He was still operating from underground and, therefore, had to leave South Africa secretly and illegally. While visiting other African nations he made several speeches in which he vividly described the rapidly deteriorating racial conditions under apartheid. Upon reaching a new country he would usually spend the first day in a hotel room reading and learning about that country's policies, history, and leadership. Upon leaving Africa he traveled to London, where he spent several days sightseeing and meeting with members of the government. While there, he acquired literature on guerrilla warfare that he read whenever he had a break in his busy schedule.

In 1962 Mandela returned to South Africa after an absence of six months from his country. While driving to Johannesburg dressed as a chauffeur, he was overtaken by police and arrested. His life as an underground freedom fighter came to an abrupt end. Authorities charged him with inciting workers to illegally go on strike, with promoting work stoppage campaigns against South African factories (both of which he had been involved in before leaving the country), and with leaving the country illegally. While in jail awaiting trial, Mandela received a visit by a clergyman. When the clergyman asked what he could do, Mandela asked for some books. During his days in and out of court sessions he read works that included *A Short History of Africa* by Roland Oliver and J.D. Fage, *A History of Europe* by H. A. L. Fisher, and *Anatomy of Britain* by Anthony Sampson. Mandela was tried, convicted, and sentenced to five years in prison. After serving only nine months of the sentence, he was returned to court to face another set of charges that were far more serious than any he had faced before.

In October 1963 Mandela and several others were charged with sabotage, planning guerilla warfare, and attempting to overthrow the apartheid government. The new trial became known as the Rivonia trial because most of those arrested and charged had participated in meetings in an area known as Rivonia. Documents and records of plans and preparations for guerrilla warfare were confiscated at Rivonia. Many of the documents directly implicated Mandela. Prosecutors offered into evidence copies of handwritten notes made by him that included quotes from books on freedom fighting. Among them were selections from a book about Irgun, the Israeli terrorist group, and notes about the Philippine revolutionary army called Hukbalahap. Included were notes from readings about Frederick the Great, Field Marshall Montgomery, and President Harry S. Truman. There were notes from Stalin's *The Foundation of Leninism* and notes on a pamphlet by the Chinese Communist Liu Shao-chi on "How to Be a Good Communist" (Sampson, 1999, p. 189). The notes easily demonstrated that Mandela had been a tireless reader and that his material covered a wide range of cultures and ideologies.

The trial lasted for eight months. Mandela acknowledged in court that he had read some Communist literature. His judgment was that Communists held the parliamentary systems of the West to be undemocratic. He did not accept that interpretation. Instead, he had, through reading, come to admire such systems of government (Mandela, 1994, v. 2). In addition, he stated that he had read many books, both pro and con, about socialism and socialist countries. According to Meredith (1997), Mandela displayed such a depth of knowledge and understanding of events and history, both inside and outside South Africa, that even his prosecutors were impressed.

Near the end of the Rivonia trial Mandela admitted his role in fighting the apartheid government. He delivered a dramatic speech in court about his work underground and why he chose to risk his life as he had. His motive was to help his people gain freedom from a hated and ruthless government that had held his people in a kind of racial bondage that he could not and would not accept. His plea for liberation of all nonwhites in South Africa was reported around the world and gained him an international audience and reputation as a compassionate man who was willing to sacrifice himself for the liberation of others. When the trial ended in June 1964, Mandela and six others were found guilty as charged and sentenced to life in prison. He was forty-six years of age. After saying goodbye to his wife, he was promptly whisked away and returned to prison. He spent six months in the Pretoria prison and was then returned to the prison on Robben Island, where he had previously spent a few months.

Reading in Prison for Twenty-Seven Years

Prison life on Robben Island for Nelson Mandela throughout the latter half of the 1960s was harsh and cruel. The wardens made conditions deliberately difficult as a part of his punishment for fighting the government. Mandela was assigned to a seven-foot-square cell that had a barred window looking out onto a cement courtyard. Beyond that he could see a high wall patrolled by guards. The cell was damp and barren, furnished only with a mat on which to sleep, three thin blankets to protect him against sometimes severely cold temperatures, a toilet bucket, and a plastic bottle of water.

Breakfast was served from a barrel filled with porridge, a concoction that Mandela found difficult to swallow. Prisoners were required to wash and shave from iron buckets filled with cold water. The day was spent outside in a cold courtyard hammering large stones into gravel. Always under constant watch by guards, talking among the prisoners was seldom permitted.

Evening hours were equally drab and depressing, and reading and writing were often restricted. A bare forty-watt light bulb burned in each cell through the night while a guard paced the corridor outside the cells to ensure complete compliance with the rules. Prisoners complained often about the harsh treatment and bad food but garnered little to no improvement.

No matter the harsh conditions with which Mandela had to endure on Robben Island, he made every effort to use any privilege to achieve something positive. He soon realized that he could improve his conditions and prison privileges by getting to know and understand the white guards who were, in effect, agents of the apartheid government. To achieve that goal, he undertook a study of the Afrikaner language. (Afrikaans was the language of the white ruling party). Mandela learned to read and speak the language and used it when talking with his guards. He read and studied Afrikaner history and culture. He learned how they lived, how they thought, and in what their ideals and beliefs were vested. He discovered that he could teach his guards to talk with him and treat him with the respect that every person should receive from another. Once he learned that he could gain respect and acceptance as a man from the very people who held him captive, he then projected that ability into a future application. If he could bring about human respect between guards and a prisoner, why couldn't he do the same with all the different groups that made up the nation of South Africa?

Toward the end of the 1960s the continuing pleas by Mandela and others for improved prison conditions slowly began to show some results. Authorities began to allow some sport activities, such as football on Saturday mornings. Other sports, like rugby and cricket, replaced long dreary weekends locked in cells. The new activities and better prison atmosphere made prison life more endurable. Prisoners felt a reduction of tensions and worries about home, family, and their personal survival in prison.

Beginning in the early 1970s a new prison administrator came in and began to significantly improve prison life. The International Red Cross applied pressure with some success. Younger guards arrived that were more easily influenced by intelligent prisoners like Mandela. The work assignments became more relaxed and varied. The food improved, even allowing for special diets. While collecting seaweed that would be converted into fertilizer, prisoners found new joy in collecting mussels and clams, fish and crayfish, which they used to mix seafood stews. Games like tennis on an improvised court were added to their recreational choices.

On Robben Island books and newspapers became ever more important to Mandela when he could get them. Although the prison library was limited in its selection, he read what was available. He even resorted to learning some songs from a book. Some of the selections he taught to a fellow prisoner who needed his spirits lifted. Mandela often drew on his wide reading experience to discuss and debate issues with fellow inmates. He and his friends read and discussed Shakespeare, going so far as to identify to each other favorite passages. At one point he and others debated whether George Bernard Shaw or Shakespeare was the better playwright. According to Sampson (1999), Shakespeare almost provided a common culture among the incarcerated colleagues. Another activity involved Mandela and some friends in the reading and dramatization of the play *Antigone* by Sophocles.

For many years Mandela and his prison mates were not allowed to receive newspapers or books from outside the prison. Therefore, reading material was often limited, especially current news reading. The prisoners would do anything they could dream up to get their hands on current newspapers. They bribed the guards, stole newspapers from visiting priests, and retrieved papers from rubbish cans that had been used to wrap the guards' sandwiches. The papers were hidden under their shirts until they could return to their rooms and hide them until they were safe to read.

Sometimes the prisoners would buy papers from nonpolitical prisoners who found ways to steal them from the guards. At times they were able to buy papers from smugglers, or they could bribe the guards to conveniently forget to take papers they were reading with them when they departed for the day. Such papers were treasured and read from cover to cover. Some current information was read in a censored version of the *Economist* magazine that was allowed in the prison for use by those engaged in economic studies. Using all of the wit and chicanery they could muster to secure newspapers and books, many of the prisoners, and especially Mandela, became better informed than were most of those from the outside who came for visits (Bam, 1999).

After some time had passed on Robben Island, Mandela was allowed to continue correspondence studies for a law degree at London University. The task of getting the needed reading materials at times proved to be both frustrating and humorous. Prison officials were always suspicious of what prisoners were reading and planning. Mandela once wrote a letter to authorities requesting permission to purchase a copy of *The Law of Torts*, a book required in his studies. The officials were ignorant of legal terms and thought that he was trying to get a book on how to make torches. Such were the obstacles he had to overcome to achieve his goal of an LLB degree. He also worked an arrangement in which books were sent to him through the British embassy, books in which he spent long hours reading. Many hours were also spent reading in the *International Journal of Law*.

In addition to reading for his legal preparation, Mandela read for enjoyment and interaction with others. He discovered and read a Victorian poem titled "Invictus" by W. E. Henley. In the poem he discovered lines that read, "I am the master of my fate; I am the captain of my soul" (Sampson, 1999, p. 212), lines that were both inspirational and gratifying. Lines like that gave him a delineation of his own bold leap into the political turmoil in South Africa. Mandela remarked to a friend, "When you read words of that nature you become encouraged. It puts life in you" (Sampson, 1999, p. 212).

Mandela never overlooked an opportunity to develop new areas of interest while incarcerated. On Robben Island he worked for several years in the lime quarry, digging and loading lime onto trucks. Having a rural background, he took an interest in the elements of nature that were around him. In the quarry he studied rock formations and became interested in any archaeological artifacts he uncovered while digging. That interest led him to read everything he could find in the limited prison library on rocks and archaeology.

When Mandela had read all of the books and newspapers he could find, he enjoyed puttering in a small prison garden that he planted. However, the garden did not come to him easily. After asking again and again for several years, he finally gained permission to start a garden in the prison courtyard. Wanting to prove that the privilege granted to him was well placed, he read the books on gardening and horticultural he found in the library and then began his garden. He took great pride in the vegetables he was able to grow along the inside of a prison wall. The garden almost became an obsession since he had already read everything he could find inside the prison.

When a potential opportunity to secure new books arose, Mandela would make his move. While being visited in prison by the South African minister of justice, he asked for a copy of the collected works of Opperman, an Afrikaner poet. Soon thereafter the prison library received the complete works of the poet from the publisher. Mandela wrote a letter thanking the publisher, a letter that was printed in full in an Afrikaner newspaper.

In 1977 the required manual labor by prisoners on Robben Island was discontinued. That left Mandela with much time for reading. Reading was the activity that most energized and sustained him during a long imprisonment. A fellow inmate who arrived on the island in 1980 described Mandela's tiny cell as always neat with legal documents piled high and boxes of books under his bed (Sampson, 1999, p. 279). Among the books in his cell collection were The New English Bible, *Great Stories of Mystery and Suspense*, and a book on the economic history of Europe. There were times, however, when he would not be permitted to read or study because of conflicts with the guards about conditions or restrictions. But when he was free to read and could get books and newspapers, he read voraciously.

With more freedom to read, Mandela dipped into books he had not previously included in his reading interests. There were novels, mysteries, and detective stories that he found enjoyable. Many novels were about South Africa or were written by South African writers. Those he read included some novels by South African writer Nadine Gordimer, one of which was a 1979 novel titled *Burger's Daughter*. Mandela enjoyed political novels and books set in white South Africa when he could get them. Books authored by white writers from his own country and books about the white culture there helped him to better understand the mindset and attitudes of those who controlled the government and institutions of his country. He read an authorized biography of John Vorster, prime minister of South Africa and principal architect of apartheid, a book that further developed his understanding of Afrikaner thinking.

The man who had grown up in the quiet landscape of the Transkei enjoyed books that taught him about conditions and behaviors in other cultures. He read many American novels, including John Steinbeck's *The Grapes of Wrath*, a book that made him aware of many similarities in the conditions of migrant workers in America and his own people in South Africa who did most of the manual labor while living in crowded and depressing conditions. He especially enjoyed *War and Peace* by Leo Tolstoy, a story that presented a portrait of the fictional General Kutuzov. The general appealed to Mandela because he represented to the freedom fighter, in a compelling way, the principle that to lead people, a leader must truly know and understand those whom one proposes to lead.

As the prison atmosphere became more relaxed and Mandela developed better relations with the guards, he was able to secure a greater variety of books. There were books by Daphne du Maurier. Along with Tolstoy's works, he enjoyed the famous Russian novels by writers that included Fyodor Dostoyevsky. To educate himself in the faith of Islam, he read the Holy book of Islam, the Qur'an, in an English version, along with other books about that religious faith.

The greater part of Mandela's reading was in the English language and included scores of English writers. Among them were books by Charles Dickens and the poets Wordsworth, Tennyson, and Shelley. Included also were the war memoirs of Winston Churchill and biographies of John F. Kennedy, Abraham Lincoln, and George Washington of the United States. Other biographies included Benjamin Disraeli, a prime minister of England. A biography of Napoleon III of France was read with much enjoyment. His interest in French history led him to Alexander Worth's *History of France 1919–1958*.

With so much of his reading done in the English language, Mandela became more adept with that language than any other and kept a copy of *The Oxford Book of English Verse* by his bedside. But perhaps his favorite reading was the Xhosa poets whose words gave him a nostalgic longing for his Transkei homeland and its people.

Beginning in September 1980, prisoners were permitted to receive outside newspapers legally. In time Mandela and others were able to read censored versions of the *Cape Times*, the *Afrikaans Die Burger*, the *Johannesburg Star*, the *Rand Daily Mail*, and the *Johannesburg Sunday Times*. Even though heavily censored, Mandela found some editorials and featured articles to be fairly objective and informative on the events and conditions in South Africa. Daily newspaper reading was a delight for the prisoner, and he encouraged his children to follow his example. When his oldest daughter, Maki, decided to go to school and train for a profession, he was delighted with the news and advised her to read at least two newspapers each day.

Richard Stengel (1999), a writer who worked with Mandela on his autobiography after his release from prison, told a story that illustrates Mandela's love of newspapers. The two were on a plane crossing the Natal. The former prisoner was reading a newspaper when he paused and looked out the plane's window. He noticed that the propeller on his side had stopped turning. Mandela looked over to Stengel and told him he might want to tell the pilot the propeller had stopped turning. Then, calmly, Mandela returned to his newspaper. When the plane finally landed safely, he did admit that he was scared when he discovered the plane's problem.

After being transferred from Robben Island to the prison at Pollsmoor on the mainland in 1982, Mandela's avid reading continued. He had four volumes of J. D. Bernal's *Science in History*, Schapera's *Government and Politics*, Schurmann and Schell's *Republican China*, and Samir Amin's *Neo-Colonialism in West Africa*. Along with those he read Tom Lodge's *Black Politics in South Africa Since 1945*, Eddie Roux's *Time Longer Than Rope*, Karis and Carter's *From Protest to Challenge*. He was allowed to receive a wide range of newspapers and magazines, among them *Time* and the *Guardian Weekly* from London. Every edition he read from cover to cover.

For many years Mandela accumulated and read materials that would help him in the role he expected to one day play in the future of South Africa. In the latter part of his imprisonment, he collected books from many sources, but one source in particular seemed to delight him. One day in 1986 he received a visit in prison from the aging widow of an early friend in the freedom struggle. To his delight, she brought to him what he referred to as "an entire library" (Sampson, 1999, p. 350).

Near the end of his long years in prison, when he was scheduled to meet with President Botha about the future of the nation, the now-famous prisoner read all the recent newspapers and publications he could get his hands on so as to be well informed on current conditions in South Africa. Reading material was his lifeline to the knowledge he required to lead his nation out of the chaotic conditions that had evolved under the apartheid government. He collected and used all that was accessible in his often-restricted environment. By the time he left prison, after twenty-seven years of incarceration, he had amassed enough books and papers to fill more than a dozen boxes and crates.

That Mandela was a man who both used and enjoyed reading, both before and during his twenty-seven years in prison, there can be no doubt. Reading impacted his life and his work in profound ways. In letters to friends on the outside of prison, he revealed that his reading and reflection had led him to a vision, a vision in which he would play a key role in shaping the future of South Africa. He did not believe that he would remain in prison forever as his sentence suggested, but rather, he would one day be freed to help form a new democratic nation in his homeland. In his mind, his imprisonment had not ended his usefulness to his country; it had merely been delayed, for he would one day be freed to continue his work. In a letter written in 1985 to a friend, he reflected on the long-delayed struggle to bring freedom to all South Africans. He stated, "the harvest has merely been delayed, but far from destroyed. It is out there, our rich and well-watered fields, even though the actual task of gathering it, has proved far more testing than we ever thought" (Meer, 1999, p. 5).

Nelson Mandela's dream did come true. He walked out of prison on February 11, 1990. His release became headline news around the world. In 1994 he ran for president of a new nation under a new democratic constitution and won. Through the five years of his presidency he became one of the most easily recognized names and faces the world has yet produced. Leaders of other nations welcomed him to their capitals. At the close of his five-year term in 1999, he left public life and retired to the home he had built in the Transkei near where he had spent his boyhood. His achievements and special qualities as a person made of him one of the genuine heroes of the twentieth century.

THE IMPACT OF READING

As a schoolboy, Nelson Mandela read Macaulay's history and other nineteenth-century English textbooks. That reading helped him to begin early developing a big view of the world. Through attending English-language schools and using English textbooks, Mandela became intrigued with things that were English. During World War II, he often listen to the radio speeches of Winston Churchill (Stengel, 1999). He came to look upon London as a great city, perhaps the center of the world. He admired the English gentlemen and accepted their decorum as proper conduct for a well-bred man. That early introduction to the English model for personal conduct molded Mandela, and he was always a gentleman in the presence of others.

Upon becoming a member of the ANC, Mandela's life began to change, and his reading interest also changed. The goal of the ANC was to rid South Africa of the hated apartheid government. He recognized that the struggle would be long and difficult. To be as useful to that goal as he could be, Mandela worked hard to inform himself about the conditions the people faced. He read many books for the purpose of learning how struggles for freedom had been conducted in other times and other countries. He learned from reading about the work of Nehru and Gandhi in India how a campaign for liberation could be structured to defeat foreign conquerors through a disciplined mass movement.

The membership of the ANC presented another reason for Mandela to read more deeply. Prior to joining that organization, he had believed that the struggle for freedom in South Africa was a task for only native black South Africans. But he found that the ANC embraced a multiracial membership. There were not only African natives but also European whites, Indians, and many members of racial mixtures called "Coloureds." He undertook a program of reading to better prepare for judging the proper makeup of the ANC. After reading many books, especially on Communism, he amended his views and decided he could accept Communists and other non–Africans as members, even though he would not become a Communist himself.

A new view of the liberation struggle emerged in Mandela. He came to believe that all South Africans who were working to rid the country of the hated apartheid regime had more to unite than divide them. From that time he held that the future of South Africa must be multiracial with all groups living there having a voice in the government and culture of the nation.

Mandela's long participation in the struggle to bring freedom and democracy to all people in his country was nourished and guided principally by his avid reading. During his trials for promoting protests and disruptions against the government, he spoke about why he fought. His reading had developed within him an understanding of wars of liberation in history. He understood how repressive regimes could build conflict in people between their conscience and the repressive laws of such regimes. He was acquainted with how Bertrand Russell in England had been sentenced to jail for protesting against the construction and use of nuclear weapons. Through political literature from many cultures and political systems, he had gained a good command of the foundations underlying political thought. When questioned during his last trial about alleged Communist connections, he replied,

> From my reading of Marxist literature and from conversations with Marxists, I have gained the impression that communists regard the parliamentary system of the West as undemocratic and reactionary. But, on the contrary, I am an admirer of such a system. The Magna Carta, the Petition of Rights and the Bill of Rights are documents which are held in veneration by democrats throughout the world [Mandela, 1994, v. 2, p. 52].

Mandela's reading made an impact on what he believed, why he believed, and what he must stand for as a man. As his court trials came to a close he completed his message to the court and to the world with the words, "I have cherished the ideal of a democratic and free society in which all persons live together in harmony and with equal opportunities. It is an ideal which I hope to live for and to achieve. But if needs be, it is an ideal for which I am prepared to die" (Mandela, 1994, v. 2, p. 54).

When his last court trial ended in which he received a sentence of life in prison, Mandela never lost hope that he would one day be set free. He believed that he would one day play a role in shaping the destiny of South Africa. In prison he read and studied with total commitment, acquiring knowledge that would be useful to him. Never losing hope, he planned and prepared to participate in a politically free nation, one in which all South Africans would have to be trained for participation in an economically and socially liberated society. The more he read of the civilizations in history and the great leaders who had helped to create and define their structures, the more he became infused with a sense of his own destiny as a contributor to the future of South Africa (Bam, 1999).

During his long confinement on Robben Island, Mandela matured and changed as a person. He grew from a headstrong activist into a reflective, contemplative, and self-disciplined man. His reading, study, and reflection helped him to build a broader perspective of the time and the place that had become his life. The change in him created a man with a deep ideological core, a core that became a guiding force in his life. The need for social change that he saw in his country was never far from his mind, but he had to put his dreams in perspective. He learned to set his goals in the far distant future to a time that he could not specify. His reading generated ideas for political and social change that drove him to read and study even more. A friend who was in prison with Mandela for ten of his twenty-seven years has stated that Mandela anticipated a role in the future of South Africa. "He certainly knew that he had a role to play given his position within the ANC. Then he seriously prepared himself for that. He studied very hard, and the sort of things he studied were things which were obviously going to be of assistance in the future South Africa" (Bam, 1999, p. 3). But just how and when he could pursue those dreams remained beyond his conception. He believed that learning the language of the Afrikaner people and reading their books would be helpful to him, but just how it would help remained undefined. Once he learned to work with the guards and win their respect and acceptance, his dream became one of someday extending that success to all of South Africa.

The knowledge gained through reading continued to shape and remold Mandela throughout his long prison confinement. He gained personal strength from the ideals he discovered in books, ideals that sustained him through difficult years. Always eager to learn, he took advantage of any opportunity. The Greek plays he read helped him to develop an understanding and appreciation of character development. He grew to understand that character is measured "by facing up to difficult situations and that a hero was a man who would not break down even under the most trying circumstances" (Mandela, 1994, v. 2, p. 182). In a letter from his prison cell to a friend, he wrote, "A few years ago I was browsing hurriedly through a review of the works of Euripedes, Sophocles, and other Greek scholars when I came across a statement that one of the basic tenets we have inherited from classical Greek philosophy was that a real man was one who could stand firmly on his feet and never bend his knees even when dealing with the divine" (Meer, 1988, p. 409). That philosophy gained through his reading of the ancient Greeks gave Mandela strength and nourishment when he had to negotiate with the apartheid leaders of South Africa for the formation of a new democratic government in that country.

Reading helped Mandela to build a spirit of compassion and acceptance of differences that had not been so easy for him when he was a young man. Through both reading and life experiences, he grew in self-confidence and the knowledge required in accepting people for who they were, even when he did not agree with their ideals and beliefs. He had worked with Communists in South Africa and had read much of their literature. He never became a Communist, but he could discuss objectively their ideologies. He believed that certain features of the Communist doctrine did fit the conditions in his country. On one occasion he read a document written by a Chinese theoretician named Liu Shao Chi. In a discussion of the document with a friend, the friend maintained that such literature was not relevant or understandable to an African audience. Mandela responded by noting that useful ideas, such as a spirit of community, could be made relevant. To prove his point, he rewrote the document showing how useful ideas in Communist literature could be made relevant to the needs and interest of an African mass audience (Mandela, 1994, v. 2).

Alone in his cell for long periods of time, deprived of interaction with large audiences and television and without having any authority or responsibility, Mandela was able to define his beliefs and values. He evolved a wider view of the long struggle that he saw ahead for his country. He came to accept people in the struggle that he had formerly rejected. They were all fighting for the same objective and should work together. But such a movement needed strong leadership. He would make himself be one of those that became strong and powerful. A vision of the leader that was needed evolved in his mind, and he would prepare himself for such a role. Of his twenty-seven years in prison, Mandela once stated about what he had learned: "It is possible that if I had not gone to jail and been able to read and to listen to the stories of many people, I might not have learned these things" (Battersby, 2000, p. 6).

What Mandela did learn was a vision and compassion for his country and his fellow human beings. He learned how to use what he had gained in knowledge to help others. In prison he taught classes for those who had limited educational training. For several years he taught a course in political economy.

Finally, the day that Mandela had long dreamed of arrived. Serious discussions with the government about a new government and society began. His wide knowledge made it possible for him to hold his own and even prevail in talks about the future South Africa. He demonstrated a depth of knowledge about his country and its history that far exceeded that of most officials with whom he held discussions. That knowledge proved to the apartheid representatives that they were not dealing with just an ordinary native African who knew little about South Africa or the world beyond its borders. Mandela revealed a deeper knowledge of the white Afrikaner people and their history than that held by many Afrikaners. His vast storehouse of knowledge so impressed them that a congenial atmosphere for discussion emerged. In the end, Mandela's ability to command the respect and admiration of his adversaries led to agreements for meetings with government leaders. After numerous delays and frustrations, he got what he had long worked for: talks that lead to a new democratic government in South Africa.

Mandela's long-held commitment to reading and study led him to a vision that he confirmed in a conviction. The only way all of the people in his country could live in peace was for all the ethnic groups and cultures to unite in freedom and create a truly democratic country. Every party would have to hold a legitimate voice in the affairs of the nation. And, too, he came to see that he would probably have to be the person who would provide the leadership to create that kind of nation. In the end, his acquired knowledge helped him to project onto the people of his nation the only avenue available to them for a peaceful future. South Africa must become a multiracial society that promoted unity and compassion for all. In his demeanor and as the voice of his people, Mandela came to personify what South Africa would become as a new nation.

Upon his release from prison Mandela began sharing with the world his compassionate demeanor and his voice for a new South Africa. As a free man traveling across his country and throughout the world, he demonstrated time and again the impact that reading had made in his life. One such event occurred while he was traveling from the United States to Ireland. On a stopover for refueling at Goose Bay in Canada, he left the plane for a walk along the tarmac. Next to a fence, at the border of the airport, he spotted some people standing and looking out to him. Seizing an opportunity to meet new people, he walked over and greeted the bystanders. To his delight he discovered they were young Eskimos who had watched his release from prison on television. They knew who he was, knew much about his life, and were familiar with events in South Africa. Having read about Eskimos and Eskimo life when he was still a growing boy, he was able to discuss with them their life and culture. His early reading had left him believing that Eskimos were a backward people, but in his conversation with them there by the fence, he discovered a bright and informed group of young people. That was a thrill for the former prisoner, a man who had waited endless years for opportunities to learn firsthand about a world he had only read about (Mandela, 1994, v. 2).

Another opportunity to demonstrate the influence of reading in his life occurred when Mandela's close friend and former law partner, Oliver Tambo, passed away. Mandela was asked to speak at the funeral. In part, he said, "In Plato's allegory of the metals, the philosopher classifies men into groups of gold, silver and lead. Oliver was pure gold" (Mandela, 1994, v. 2, p. 414).

Perhaps the most profound impact that reading had on Mandela is the way in which he changed from a fiery, angry young man into one who could show love and compassion to his worst enemies. There were other important influences in his life in addition to reading. Along with reading Mandela has identified religion, the development of a discipline required for survival in prison, his legal training, and the personal discipline required in his daily exercise program as factors in his transformation. But his deep reading gave him the spiritual core that made it possible for him to love and respect those who had been his toughest opponents in life. Through reading the biographies of the great leaders of the century he came to realize that problems can make some people stronger while others might be destroyed (Battersby, 2000). The obstacles and setbacks he experienced along life's journey would have destroyed many people. But he grew stronger and rose above all who would have denied him his birthright as a man. His life represents what can be achieved through dedication to personal development and commitment to freedom and human compassion.

HONORS, AWARDS AND MONUMENTS

Nelson Mandela's life has earned for him hundreds of honors and awards for his contributions in pursuit of human freedoms and his personal traits as a man. They include honorary degrees from scores of colleges and universities around the world, honorary citizenship awards in numerous cities, honorary memberships in many clubs, and an untold number of streets and roads named in his honor. There have been far too many peace and human rights awards to list in this work. Statues have been erected to honor him, and others are planned. His life of achievement and his stature in history have made him one of the most honored people of the twentieth century.

Bibliography and References

Anderson, Nels. (1923). *The Hobo.* Chicago: The University of Chicago Press.
Anthony, Katharine. (1954). *Susan B. Anthony—Her Personal History and Her Era.* Garden City: Doubleday and Company, Inc.
Armstrong, William H. (1974). *The Education of Abraham Lincoln.* New York: Coward, McCann and Geoghegan, Inc.
Baldwin, Stanley. (1932). "Books." *Men and Books*, edited by Malcolm S. MacLean and Elizabeth K. Holmes. New York: Ray Long and Richard R. Smith, Inc.
Bam, Fikile. (1999). "The Long Walk of Nelson Mandela—Interview." Retrieved June 10, 2003, from http://www.pbs.org/wgbh/pages/frontline/shows/mandela/interviews/bam.html.
Barry, Kathleen. (1988). *Susan B. Anthony—A Biography of a Singular Feminist.* New York: Ballantine Books.
Bartlett, John. (1955). *Bartlett's Familiar Quotations.* 13th ed. Boston: Little, Brown and Company.
Battersby, John. (2000). "Nelson Mandela—Interview." *The Christian Science Monitor.* February 10, 2000. Retrieved June 9, 2003, from http://csmweb2.emcweb.com/durable/2000/02/10/p15s1.htm.
Booker T. Washington Monument. (n.d.). Retrieved April 4, 2002, from http://svmc107.tusk.edu/tu/historic/monument.html.
Brontë, Charlotte. (1993). *Shirley.* Hertfordshire: Wordsworth Edition Ltd.
Buck, Pearl S. (1930). *East Wind: West Wind.* New York: The John Day Company.
_____. (1931). *The Good Earth.* New York: The John Day Company.
_____. (1950). *The Child Who Never Grew.* New York: The John Day Company.
_____. (1954). *My Several Worlds.* New York: The John Day Company.
Conn, Peter. (1996). *Pearl S. Buck—A Cultural Biography.* New York: Cambridge University Press.
De La Mare, Pierre. (1997). *An Industry Is Born.* Electronic edition. Retrieved June 13, 2002, from http://www.dotprint.com/fgen/histroy1.htm.
Dorr, Rheta Childe. (1928). *Susan B. Anthony—The Woman Who Changed the Mind of a Nation.* New York: Frederick A. Stokes Company.

Douglass, Frederick. (1846). "Reception Speech at Finsbury Chapel, Moorsfield, England." Electronic text. Retrieved October 31, 2003, from http://www.online-literature.com/frederick-douglass/bondage-freedom/26.

_____. (1852). "The Hypocrisy of American Slavery." Electronic text. Retrieved October 31, 2003, from http://www.historyplace.com/speeches/douglas.htm.

_____. (1855). *My Bondage and My Freedom.* Electronic edition. Retrieved October 28, 2003, from http://docsouth.unc.edu/neh/douglass55.html.

_____. (1860). "A Plea for Free Speech in Boston." Electronic text. Retrieved October 31, 2003, from http://douglassarchives.org/doug-a68.htm.

_____. (1867). "An Appeal to Congress for Impartial Suffrage." Electronic text. Retrieved October 31, 2003, from http://etext.lib.virginia.edu/etcbin/browse-mixed-new?id=douappe&tag=public&images=images/modeng&data=/te.../parse.

_____. (1881). *Life and Times of Frederick Douglass.* Electronic edition. Retrieved October 31, 2003, from http://docsouth.unc.edu/douglasslife/douglass.html.

_____. (1982). *Narrative of the Life of Frederick Douglass — An American Slave.* New York: Penguin Books.

Franklin, Benjamin. (1793). *The Autobiography of Benjamin Franklin.* Electronic edition. Retrieved October 29, 2002, from http://www.earlyamerica.com/lives/franklin/index.html.

Franklin Memorial. (1976). "The Benjamin Franklin National Memorial." Electronic text. Retrieved October 29, 2002, from http://sln.fi.edu/tf./exhibits/memorial.html.

Gale, Robert L. (1985). *Louis L'Amour.* Boston: Twayne Publishers.

Great Plains Software, Inc. (n.d.). Retrieved April 16, 2002, from http://www.greatplains.com/pioneer_spirit/rider/lamour.htm.

Guiloineau, Jean. (1998). *The Early Life of Rolihlahla Madiba — Nelson Mandela.* Translated by Joseph Rowe, 2002. Berkeley, California: North Atlantic Books.

Hanebutt-Benz, Eva-Maria. (n.d.). *The Time of Gutenberg.* Electronic edition. Retrieved June 13, 2002, from http://www.gutenberg.de/english/zeitgum.htm.

Harper, Ida Husted. (1998). *Life and Work of Susan B. Anthony.* Vol. 1. North Stratford: Ayer Company Publishers, Inc.

Harris, Theodore F. (1970). *Pearl S. Buck — A Biography.* London: Methuen and Company Ltd.

Henry-Mead, Jean. (1989). "An Interview with Louis L'Amour." Retrieved April 16, 2002, from http://www.readthewest.com/interviewlouislamour.html.

Herndon, William H., and Jesse W. Weik (1949). *Herndon's Life of Lincoln.* Edited by Paul M. Angle. New York: The World Publishing Company.

Jefferson, Thomas. (1944). *The Life and Selected Writings of Thomas Jefferson.* Edited by Adrienne Koch and William E. Peden. New York: Random House, Inc.

L'Amour, Louis. (1955). *To Tame a Land.* New York: Bantam Books.

_____. (1960). *The Daybreakers.* New York: Bantam Books.

_____. (1966). *The Broken Gun.* New York: Bantam Books.

_____. (1976). *Over on the Dry Side.* New York: Bantam Books.

_____. (1978). *The Mountain Valley War.* New York: Bantam Books.

_____. (1979a). *Bendigo Shafter.* New York: Bantam Books.

_____. (1979b). *The Iron Marshal.* New York: Bantam Books.

_____. (1985). *Jubal Sackett.* New York: Bantam Books.

———. (1989). *Education of a Wandering Man*. New York: Bantam Books.
Lincoln, Abraham. (1859). *Abraham Lincoln — A Short Biography — 1859*. Electronic edition. Retrieved November 11, 2003, from http://www.historyplace.com/lincoln/autobi-1.htm.
———. (2003). "Address to the Senate of New Jersey." Electronic text. Retrieved November 11, 2003, from http://lincoln.lib.niu.edu/cgi-bin/getobject-?c.2083:1./lib35/artfl1/databases/sources/IMAGE.
Lincoln Memorial. (2003). Electronic text. Retrieved November 5, 2003, from http://www.nps.gov/linc/home.htm.
Linder, Doug. (2001). "The Trial of Susan B. Anthony for Illegal Voting." Electronic text. Retrieved July 1, 2001, from http://www.law.umkc.edu/faculty/projects/ftrials/anthony/sbaaccount.html.
Louis L'Amour Enterprises, Inc. (2000). "The Official Louis L'Amour Website." Retrieved April 16, 2002, from http://www.louislamour.com/aboutlouis/biography6.htm.
Malone, Dumas. (1948). *Jefferson the Virginian*. Boston: Little, Brown and Company.
———. (1981). *Jefferson and His Time — The Sage of Monticello*. Boston: Little, Brown and Company.
Mandela, Nelson. (1994). *Long Walk to Freedom*. Vol. 1, 1918–1962. Great Britain: Abacus.
———. (1994). *Long Walk to Freedom*. Vol. 2, 1962–1994. Great Britain: Abacus.
McFeely, William S. (1991). *Frederick Douglass*. New York: W.W. Norton and Company.
Medal of Freedom. (1996–2002). "Medal of Freedom — Louis L'Amour." Electronic text. Retrieved November 12, 2002, from http://www.medaloffreedom.com/louislamour.htm.
Meer, Fatima. (1988). *Higher Than Hope — The Authorized Biography of Nelson Mandela*. New York: Harper and Rowe.
———. (1999). "The Long Walk of Nelson Mandela — Interview." Electronic text. Retrieved June 12, 2003, from http://www.pbs.org/wgbh/pages/frontline/shows/mandela/interviews/meer.html.
Meredith, Martin. (1997). *Nelson Mandela — A Biography*. New York: St. Martin's Griffin.
Mitchell, Suzanne, and Maiken Baird, producers. (1999). *Biography of the Millennium*. (Television Documentaries). A & E Television Networks. New York: New Video Group.
National Women's Hall of Fame. (n.d.). Retrieved January 7, 2003, from http://www.greatwomen.org/women.php.
The Nobel Foundation. (2002). "The Nobel Prize in Literature 1938." Electronic text. Retrieved January 7, 2003, from http://www.nobel.se/literature/laureates/1938/press.html.
Oates, Stephen B. (1977). *With Malice Toward None — The Life of Abraham Lincoln*. New York: Harper and Rowe, Publishers.
Phillips, Robert. (1989). *Louis L'Amour — His Life and Trails*. New York: Paperjacks.
Quarles, Benjamin, ed. (1968). *Frederick Douglass — Great Lives Observed*. Englewood Cliffs: Prentice-Hall, Inc.
Randall, Willard Sterne. (1993). *Thomas Jefferson — A Life*. New York: Henry Holt and Company.
Randolph, Sarah N. (1978). *The Domestic Life of Thomas Jefferson*. Charlottesville: The University Press of Virginia.

Riley, James. (1965). *Sufferings in Africa: Captain Riley's Narrative—An Authentic Narrative of the Loss of the American Brig* Commerce. New York: Clarkson N. Potter, Inc.

Russell, Phillips. (1926). *Benjamin Franklin—The First Civilized American.* New York: Brentano's Publishers.

Sampson, Anthony. (1999). *Mandela—The Authorized Biography.* New York: Vintage Books.

Sandburg, Carl. (1954). *Abraham Lincoln.* Vol. 1, *The Prairie Years.* New York: Dell Publishing Company.

Schlesinger, Arthur M., Jr. (1946). *The Age of Jackson.* Boston: Little, Brown and Company.

Sedges, John. (1945). *The Townsman.* New York: The John Day Company.

Stengel, Richard. (1999). "The Long Walk of Nelson Mandela—Interview." Electronic text. Retrieved June 12, 2003, from http:www.pbs.org/wgbh/pages/frontline/shows/Mandela/interviews/stengel.html.

Tarbell, Ida M. (1974). *The Early Life of Abraham Lincoln.* New York: A. S. Barnes and Company.

The Nobel Foundation. (2002). "The Nobel Prize in Literature 1938." Electronic text. Retrieved January 7, 2003, from http://www.nobel.se/literature/laureates/1938/press.html.

Thomas, Sandra. (n.d.). *Frederick Douglass—Abolitionist/Editor.* Electronic edition. Retrieved April 23, 2002, from http://www.history.rochester.edu/class/douglass/home.html.

Thornbrough, E. L., ed. (1969). *Booker T. Washington—Great Lives Observed.* Englewood Cliffs: Prentice-Hall, Inc.

Timeline. (2002). "Susan B. Anthony Timeline." Retrieved July 1, 2002, from http://www.susanbanthonyhouse.org/timeline.html.

Tourtellot, Arthur Bernon. (1977). *Benjamin Franklin—The Shaping of Genius.* Garden City, New York: Doubleday and Company, Inc.

Van Doren, Carl. (1938). *Benjamin Franklin.* New York: The Viking Press.

Washington, Booker T. (1895). "Booker T. Washington Delivers the 1895 Atlanta Compromise Speech." Electronic text. Retrieved April 4, 2002, from http"//historymatters.gmu.edu/d/39/.

_____. (1901). *An Autobiography—The Story of My Life and Work.* Atlanta: J.L. Nichols and Company. Electronic edition. Retrieved April 5, 2002, from http://docsouth.unc.edu/washstory/washing.html.

_____. (1996). *Up from Slavery.* Edited by William L. Andrews. New York: W.W. Norton and Company.

Weinberg, Robert. (1992). "The Official Louis L'Amour." Electronic text. Retrieved November 12, 2002, from http://www.randomhouse.com/features/louislamour/biography.html.

Wilson, Douglas L. (1996). *Jefferson's Books.* Charlottesville: Thomas Jefferson Memorial Foundation.

Index

Abolition of slavery 100
Adams, John 28, 29, 39, 41, 42, 46
Adams, Mrs. John 37
Adams, John Quincy 78
African National Congress (ANC) 172, 174, 175, 177, 178, 186, 187
American Anti-Slavery Society 79, 98
American Equal Rights Association 101
American Philosophical Society 18
Anglo-Boer War 177
Anthony, Aaron 71
Anthony, Guelma 95, 96
Anthony, Susan B. 91–110; Canajoharie Academy 93, 97; Daughters of Temperance 93; Moulson's Seminary for Females 95; Sons of Temperance 93; Woman's State Temperance Society 94; Women's Rights 98, 99, 100, 105, 108; Women's Suffrage 101; Worcester Hydropathic Institute 98
Armstrong, Samuel C. 120
Assing, Ottilia 83, 88
Auld, Hugh 72
Auld, Lucretia 72
Auld, Sophia 72, 74
Auld, Thomas 72, 77

Bailey, Betsy 71
Bailey, Harriet 71
Battle of Canaan 152
Begin, Menachem 177
Berry, William F. 57
Bland, Richard 34
Booth, John Wilkes 52
Bowen, Sam 95
Brown, John 83, 84
Buck, Carol 133, 134
Buck, Edgar 133
Buck, Grace 136
Buck, Janice 134, 141
Buck, John Lossing 133, 139, 143
Buck, Pearl 131–150, 160; Green Hills Farm 134, 144, 147; "John Sedges" 144; National Women's Hall of Fame 150; Nobel Prize for Literature 150; Randolph-Macon Woman's College 133, 138; Teacher Kung 131, 136; The Training School 134; Welcome House 135
Burroughs, Jones 111

Carnegie, Andrew 128
Carr, Dabney 31, 34
Carr, Peter 44
Castro, Fidel 177
Chicago World's Fair 105
Churchill, Winston 177, 184, 186
Civil War 51, 63, 66, 97, 99, 100, 109, 114, 126, 133, 151
Cleveland, Grover 126

Congressional Library 40
Covey, Edward 72, 73
Crawford, Andrew 54

Declaration of Independence 28, 36
de Klerk, F. W. 173
Dixon, Thomas, Jr. 128
Dorsey, Azel 54
Douglas, Stephen 51, 65
Douglass, Frederick 71–90, 93, 124; abolition and abolitionist 76, 77, 79, 81, 89; menial jobs 79; Minister to Haiti 87; publishes Frederick Douglass' papers 82; publishes the *North Star* 81, 82; purchases Cedar Hill 86; Sabbath Schools 78; Sage of Anacostia 90; visits Great Britian 80, 84

Eliot, Charles 129
Emancipation Proclamation 85, 100, 115
Eppes, Francis 42

Fifteenth Amendment 102
Fillmore, Millard 103
Foster, Rachel 104
Fourteenth Amendment 102
Franklin, Benjamin 5–25, 29; authors "Silence Dogood" articles 14; becomes newspaper publisher 14; becomes printer's apprentice 11; builds Franklin stove 19; Colonial

Index

Representative to France 21; electrical experiments 19; honors and monuments 25; inventions 19; leaves Boston for Philadelphia 14; travels to London 15
Franklin, James 6, 14
Franklin, Sarah 8
Franklin, William 7

Garfield, James A. 86
Ghandi, Mahatma 177, 187
Griffiths, Julia 81, 82, 83
Guevara, Che 177

Hampton Institute 120
Hanks, Dennis 50, 54
Hanks, John 56
Harper, Ida Husted 106
Harpers Ferry 84
Harrison, Benjamin 87
Hayes, Rutherford B. 86
Henry, Patrick 32
Herndon, William H. 64
Holmes Hill Farm 71

Institute of Race Relations 175
International Red Cross 181

Jackson, Andrew 66
Jefferson, Jane 33
Jefferson, Maria 38
Jefferson, Peter 27, 30
Jefferson, Thomas 27–47, 89; appointed Secretary of State 29, 36; builds University of Virginia 30; College of William and Mary 27, 31; "commonplace books" 31; elected president 21; elected vice-president 29; financial quandary 40; Lewis and Clark Expedition 29; library 30, 31, 33, 34, 35, 36, 39, 40, 46; Louisiana Purchase 29; Monticello 28, 30, 34, 38, 39, 46; Poplar Forest 39, 41; Reverend James Maury School 27, 30; Sage of Monticello 41, 46; Shadwell estate 27, 30, 33; United States Minister to France 29; wrote *Notes on Virginia* 29

John Day Company 134, 144
Johnston, John 56

Keimer's Print Shop 6, 14
Kennedy, John F. 184

Lagerlof, Selma 142
LaMoore, Emily Lavisa Dearborn 151
LaMoore, Louis Charles 151
L'Amour, Louis 151–169; Medal of Freedom 169; National Gold Medal 169; Old West 166
Lincoln, Abraham 43, 49–70, 83, 85, 87, 90, 100, 115, 124, 184; assassinated 52, 66, 85; "blab school" 52; Black Hawk War 51; House Divided speech 65; Illinois House of Representatives 51, 59; jobs performed 58; lawyer 51; New Orleans 56; New Salem 51, 56; Offutt's General Store 58; patented invention 64; postmaster 51, 58; president of the U.S. 51, 65; Sam Hill's General Store 58; surveyor 51, 59; U.S. House of Representatives 51, 62
Lincoln, Mary Todd 51, 85
Lincoln, Nancy 49, 50
Lincoln, Robert Todd 51
Lincoln, Sara 50, 52, 53
Lincoln, Sara Bush Johnston 50, 53, 54, 67
Lincoln, Thomas 50
Lincoln-Douglas Debates 51, 65
Lloyd, Edward 71
London University 182
Lord Dunmore 35

Madison, James 36, 101
Mandela, Maki 185
Mandela, Nelson 171–192; Lilliesleaf Farm 178; MK (Umkhonto We Sizwe) 177, 178; Pollsmoor prison 185; P. W. Botha, 185; Robben Island 172, 180, 181, 182
Massachusetts Anti-Slavery Society 74
McKinley, William 126, 127, 132

Milligan, George 41
Murray, Anna 73, 78, 86

National Council of Women 88
National Equal Rights Association 101
Natural Bridge 29
Nehru, Jawaharlal 177, 187
New Bedford, Massachusetts 73
New England Courant 11, 14
Nineteenth Amendment 94

Page, John 35
Paine, Thomas 101
Palmer's Printing House 6
Philadelphia Gazette 16, 24
Pitcher, John 54
Pitts, Helen 86, 88
Poor Richard's Almanac 16

Randolph, Cornelia 37
Randolph, Peyton 34
Read, Deborah 7
Riley, James 62
Rogers, Will 134
Romine, John 58
Roosevelt, Franklin 47, 177
Ruffner, Lewis 118
Ruffner, Viola 118, 119
Ruggles, David 73

Second Continental Congress 28, 35, 42
Sibley Expedition 151
South African Communist Party 175
Speed, James 60
Stalin, Joseph 177, 179
Stanton, Elizabeth Cady 94, 96, 100, 103, 106
Statute of Virginia for Religious Freedom 29, 43
Stuart, John T. 59
Stuart and Drummand Law Firm 59
Swaney, James 54

Tambo, Oliver 191
Taylor, James 55
Taylor, John 39
Truman, Harry S 179
Tse-tung, Mao 177

198

Index

Underground Railroad 83
University of Pennsylvania 18

Virginia House of Burgesses 28, 35, 42
Vorster, John 184
Voting Rights Act 102, 108

Walsh, Richard 134, 143, 144
Washington, Booker T. 111–129; Cotton States International Exposition 125; Miss Mackie 112, 113; National Negro Business League 126; Wayland Seminary 113, 120
Washington, George 5, 29, 35, 54, 59, 60, 61, 62, 65, 66, 184
Wayles, John 35
Weems, Mason Locke 60, 61
Wellesley College 133
Westward Mill Library Society 45
Whig Party 96
Wilson, Douglas, L. 35
Wythe, George 27, 31, 32, 33, 36, 42

www.ingramcontent.com/pod-product-compliance
Lightning Source LLC
Chambersburg PA
CBHW081558300426
44116CB00015B/2924